CECILIA RAZOVSKY AND THE AMERIC

RESCUE OPERATIONS IN THE SEC

Cecilia Razovsky

and the American-Jewish Women's Rescue Operations in the Second World War

BAT-AMI ZUCKER
Bar-Ilan University, Israel

VALLENTINE MITCHELL
LONDON • PORTLAND, OR

First published in 2008 by Vallentine Mitchell

Suite 314, Premier House,	920 NE 58th Avenue, Suite 300
112–114 Station Road,	Portland, Oregon,
Edgware, Middlesex HA8 7BJ	97213-3786

www.vmbooks.com

British Library Cataloguing in Publication Data
A Catalogue record has been applied for

ISBN 978 0 85303 764 4 (cloth)
ISBN 978 0 85303 765 1 (paper)

Library of Congress Cataloging-in-Publication Data
A catalog record has been applied for

Printed by Biddles Ltd, King's Lynn, Norfolk

In loving memory of my husband, Moshe,
who passed away
as this book went into print.

In memory of my beloved parents,
Hanna and Samuel Bershtel and my
parents-in-law, Shoshana and Daniel Zucker.

This book was written with the generous assistance
of Bar-Ilan University, Ramat-Gan, Israel.

Contents

Acknowledgments

This book has been as difficult to research as it was to write. The facts that emerge from the documents on which it is based are almost inconceivable and often hard to digest. Who would believe that the United States, the most sought-after haven for the oppressed, the homeless and desperate refugees, did not extend a helping hand to 'the tired [and] the poor', and abandoned thousands of European Jewish refugees to their miserable fate?

However, this research does have some positive sides, mainly by evolving within me a new trust in people, and a profound pride in being Jewish. The incredible efforts on behalf of Jewish refugees made by anonymous American Jewish women at a difficult time in German, as well as United States, history, raise hopes for a better world.

So many people have helped me with this research. First of all are the archivists, without whom no researcher can make much progress. My deepest appreciation goes to Mr Gunnar Berg at the YIVO Institute for Jewish Research, Lynn Slome at the American Jewish Historical Society, Dr Erik Nooter, Sherry Hyman and Shelley Helfand at the American Jewish Joint Distribution Committee, Jack Sutters at the American Friends Service Committee, and to my dear friend Kevin Proffitt, who introduced me to the relevant, well-organized collections of the American Jewish Archives in Cincinnati and to the staff, who made all visits to the archives not only rewarding but very pleasurable. They were always ready to share their knowledge and experience, offer a gentle and kind word and, often, open new channels for my research.

To them I will be eternally grateful.

I am enormously grateful to the survivors, however difficult it was for them, for their willingness to recall their memories of pain and loss, assisting me to better understand the full scope of the tragic circumstances in which they found themselves.

To my dear friends Iris Posner and Lenore Moskowitz, I owe more than I can ever repay. It was their unwavering belief in their mission that helped to raise – almost single-handedly – the interest of the

American public to the hereto unknown story behind the arrival in the United States of over one thousand unaccompanied children, aged between 18 months and 16 years. Iris stood by me throughout the research and writing process. She encouraged me in my darkest moments, providing her inner knowledge, connections and her strong desire for this book to succeed.

Special thanks to the American Jewish Archives for providing me with a research grant to work in their excellent archives, and to my University for their generous grant. Last but not least, my deepest appreciation to my editor Ora Commings, for her wise input and help in turning the manuscript into a readable book, and to Heather Marchant, editor at Vallentine Mitchell, for her kindness and compassion. Her warmth and solid support helped me survive the last tedious stages of completing the book.

But it is my family, foremost my husband Moshe, who deserve all the credit; for it is their infinite patience and understanding that have sustained me on this long and tiring journey.

Abbreviations

AJA	American Jewish Archives
AJC	American Jewish Committee
AJCA	American Jewish Committee Archives
AJ Congress	American Jewish Congress
AJH	*American Jewish History*
AJHQ	American Jewish Historical Quarterly
AJHS	American Jewish Historical Society Archives
AJYB	American Jewish Year Book
DORSA	Dominican Republic Settlement Association
FRUS	*Foreign Relations of the United States*
GJCA	German Jewish Children's Aid
HIAS	Hebrew Sheltering and Immigrant Aid Society
HUC	Hebrew Union College
IGCR	Inter-Governmental Committee on Refugees
INS	Immigration and Naturalization Service
JAMA	*Journal of American Medical Association*
JCA	Jewish Colonization Association
JDC (Joint)	American Jewish Joint Distribution Committee
JSS	*Jewish Social Studies*
LBIY	*Leo Baeck Institute Year Book*
NA	National Archives, Suitland Maryland
NCC	National Coordinating Committee for Aid to Refugees and Emigrants Coming from Germany
NCJW	National Council of Jewish Women
NRS	National Refuge Service
OSE	International Health Association
PAJHS	*Publications of the American Jewish Historical Society*
UNRRA	United Nations Relief and Rehabilitation Adminstration
YAJSS	*YIVO Annual of Jewish Social Science*
YIVO	Institute for Jewish Research, New York

Introduction

While working on my recent book, *In Search of Refuge: Jews and US Consuls in Nazi Germany,*[1] my attention was drawn by two great women, President Roosevelt's Secretary of Labor, Frances Perkins, and Cecilia Razovsky, a Jewish social worker. These two women joined forces to fulfill an important moral mission – to save as many Jewish refugees as possible from Nazi Germany and to bring them safely into the United States.[2]

Although they shared similar moral values and both were dedicated activists on behalf of the needy, the contrast between the two women was notable. Born in Boston in 1880 into a comfortable middle-class family, and descended from a long line of Maine farmers and craftsmen with deep religious convictions, Frances Perkins soon developed a strong desire to help those less fortunate than herself. After graduating from Mount Holyoke College in 1902 she volunteered to work in settlement houses, where she first encountered the dangerous conditions under which factory laborers were required to work and the sad plight of immigrants – especially children. It was this exposure to harsh realities of the 'real' world which later influenced her career.

As an aristocratic progressive, Perkins was imbued with a nineteenth-century Puritan social ethic. Her firm stand over what she considered 'just causes' was especially evident on the issue of Jewish refugees from Nazi Germany. No one could intimidate or deflect her from following 'the command of duty', even if it meant facing animosity and criticism from the anti-immigration Department of State. As she put it, 'Immigration problems usually have to be decided in a few days. They involve human lives. There can be no delaying.'[3] Although secondary to the Department of State in visa affairs, the Department of Labor was, until 1940, in charge of immigration and naturalization issues and it soon emerged as a prominent agency with respect to the German-Jewish refugee issue.[4]

The desperate conditions of German Jews under the Nazi regime moved Frances Perkins to help and, beginning in April 1933, she made it her cause. She stood alone in Roosevelt's cabinet as an advocate for the liberalization of immigration procedures, boldly confronting the secretary of state and his deputies when trying to find ways and means to enable the entry of as many Jewish refugees as possible into the United States. At a cabinet meeting on 18 April 1933, she pointed out that the right of asylum was based on American tradition, and it was up to her own department, not that of State, to decide whether or not the admission of Jewish refugees would affect economic conditions in the United States.[5] Perkins' concern for refugees and, especially, refugee children brought her into a close and mutually beneficial working relationship with Cecilia Razovsky.

Unlike Frances Perkins, Cecilia Razovsky was born into a family of Jewish immigrants in St Louis in 1886 and brought up in a poor neighborhood surrounded by Jewish immigrants from eastern Europe. Her parents instilled in her their Jewish morals, dedication to Jewish tradition and the need for Jewish solidarity. Very much like Perkins, Razovsky's vocation was also decided at an early age. For her, it was not necessary to volunteer in settlement houses in order to learn about the miserable conditions of the unfortunate, the poor, the immigrants and their children. She had only to walk down the street where she lived to realize that urgent help was needed. In order to fulfill her 'calling' in life she first attended several mid-western universities and, in 1917, after graduating from the Chicago School of Civics and Philanthropy, she moved to Washington DC to become an inspector in the child labor division of the United States Children's Bureau. According to her employers, 'Her work as inspector in the child Labor division was highly satisfactory in all particulars. She is an earnest worker and has ability to gain the cooperation of those who work with her.' Another letter suggests that 'She has shown ability, excellent practical reputation for personal and professional character.'[6] Her lengthy and impressive report, 'Of the Administration of the Child Labor Law of the District of Columbia', dated 19 May 1919, reveals her moral stand and human aspirations: 'it would seem meet and proper that the district of Columbia should stand out among the states of the Union as an especially well-equipped community with excellent child labor and compulsory school attendance laws, which are backed up by a good school plant.'[7] But notwithstanding her achievements in the enforcement of the federal Child Labor Law, Razovsky knew that there was plenty more that needed doing in order for immigrants to be satisfactorily integrated into American society.[8]

Her career began when she was appointed secretary of the National Council of Jewish Women's Immigrant Aid Department in 1921. In 1932, she became the Council's associate director. Her skills and dedication and her ability to communicate with immigrants in several of their own languages enabled her to make connections with the newcomers.[9] Over the years she often represented her institution at international conferences and published articles in Yiddish and English on behalf of the migrants. In this way she acquired valuable experience and built a reputation as an expert on immigration and child-related issues.

Moral values, deep concern for refugees and Jewish solidarity inspired Cecilia Razovsky to literally dedicate her life to the rescue of German Jewish refugees. Like Frances Perkins, she possessed integrity, assertiveness, strong will and the courage to face higher authority in what she believed was a just moral cause, even if it meant taking an unpopular stand.

Hitler's accession to power in January 1933, and the brutal persecution of German Jews that followed, called for an emergency solution. Because of its humanitarian traditions, its history of granting asylum to the needy, and its rhetoric of freedom and democracy – and because much of the rest of the world was closing its doors – America in the 1930s became the most sought-after haven for German Jews. However, America at that time had its own domestic crisis: the Great Depression, with millions of Americans out of work. The result was that the plight of German Jews was the least of America's concerns. On the contrary, the anti-alien, anti-immigration and antisemitic atmosphere that prevailed tragically affected the German Jewish refugees desperately seeking shelter.[10] These trends intensified toward the end of the 1930s and were followed by anti-war feelings and demands that the United States remain neutral while at the same time, Jewish leaders and the Roosevelt administration were criticized for pushing the United States toward war.

Throughout the 1930s American policy dictated minimal official involvement in Jewish matters. Not only did the US administration emphasize that Germany's mistreatment of Jews was clearly a domestic matter, it also justified its stand by repeatedly stating that any outside intercession would produce undesirable consequences for the Jews themselves and would surely aggravate the situation.[11] Such a view was emphatically shared by embassy officials in Berlin, including Ambassador William Dodd, who believed he was following advice the president gave him, prior to his departure for Germany.

The entry for 16 June 1933 in Dodd's diary describes his meeting with the president, who told him that the matter was not one that concerned the US government, notwithstanding the German authorities' shameful treatment of the Jews.[12] The Department of State maintained its non-intervention policy and, when inquiring about the situation in Germany, was interested only in how it might affect public opinion in the United States.[13]

In face of the unequivocal anti-immigration approach of the Roosevelt administration, American Jewish groups revealed a somewhat ambivalent attitude. There is no doubt that American Jews were deeply concerned over the grave situation in Germany; however, they did not feel secure enough to voice a demand that the administration intervene on behalf of their German co-religionists. Though religious solidarity has always been one of the Jews' strongest characteristics, the history of the Jews in the United States points to a variety of political and social positions as well as to different interests and aspirations. These factors tended to influence their response to crises which affected them as Jews. It was the American experience which was instrumental in dictating and shaping their response to Nazism. More than the developments in Europe or the immediate domestic adversities of antisemitism and the Depression, it was the Jews' desire to adapt themselves to the host culture's conditions for acceptance that shaped the Jewish response to this most catastrophic chapter in Jewish history. Nonetheless, it is important to emphasize that however restricted they may have been by objective circumstances, American Jews had choices to make and, like any other people, they acted upon a reality which in no small part was shaped by their own perceptions.

Only in retrospect is it possible to understand the notion that American Jews should have identified totally with the plight of their European co-religionists in the belief that unequivocal altruism, itself based on an idealized vision of kinship solidarity, could have overcome any objective obstacles to a determined will to help – especially in the early twenty-first century, when the status of Jews in the United States has been established. During the 1930s and 1940s, American Jewish leaders found themselves torn between identification with their German co-religionists and their wish to assert their loyalty to America.[14] Given public reluctance and the prevailing anti-alien climate, Jewish spokesmen feared that strong pressure on the administration to open the gates to Jewish refugees at that time would reinforce antisemitic propaganda in the United States, which was already rising, and endanger their still tenuous status. Thus Jewish leaders stressed the need for caution and to maintain a low profile, so as to avoid accusations of being un-American.[15]

> Rabbis and Jews in public life should express themselves in no uncertain terms along the lines of their beliefs, namely, that Americans must think of America first ... American Jews are Americans, and if in the present crisis they *show* that they are *acting* as such, they will do much to deflect the impact of the war-monger propaganda which is being released against them.[16] [emphasis in original]

The results of the American 'Jewish diplomacy' were null. Jacob Fishman, a member of the American Jewish Congress governing council and a columnist and managing editor of the *Jewish Morning Journal*, openly blamed the Jewish leaders:

> Jewish diplomacy has proven itself bankrupt in the most dangerous crisis in Jewish history and it does not mean that only one tendency, that of the *'shasha'* Jews and *shtadlonim* is bankrupt, but even the so-called democratic tendency in Jewish diplomacy is just as helpless and powerless ... What did the American Jewish Congress learn from its five years of its unsuccessful interventions with the New Deal Government with 'splendid isolation' every time when there is a need of a strong word against these anti-Semitic countries?[17]

Notwithstanding the deteriorating situation in Europe, Jewish leaders were not sure that pressure on the president would produce any results. In a letter to Judge Mack in November 1937, Rabbi Stephen Wise admitted that he was not sure 'what the President can do', but at the same time, he wondered if 'we have the right to omit to do anything which holds out the faintest promise of relief for our people'.[18] However, concern for their community dominated their behavior. Jewish leaders continued to screen Jewish private as well as public efforts to press for rescue operations. When Congressman Emanuel Celler of New York was joined by Representative Samuel Dickstein – both Jews – in announcing the intention to introduce a bill calling for unrestricted immigration for victims of religious or political persecution, Wise rejected the intention as 'very bad ... so bad that it seems the

work of an agent provocateur'.[19] The Executive Committee of the
American Jewish Committee was also troubled by the Celler proposal.
'The resolution [would] bring to the surface a great deal of ill-liberal-
ism and hostility to aliens.'[20] In private, Morris Waldman of
the American Jewish Committee warned that any statement by Jewish
representatives about the immigration problem 'might have an undesirable effect here by creating the impression that these Jewish organizations were trying to promote a larger immigration of refugees into
the United States'.[21] Indeed, the position of the American Jewish
Committee was that 'giving work to Jewish refugees while so many
Americans are out of work has naturally made bad feelings. As heartless
as it may seem, future efforts should be directed toward sending Jewish
refugees to other countries instead of bringing them here.'[22] And these
attitudes prevailed at the time when every other country was also
closing its doors against Jewish migrants.

Even news of *Kristallnacht* (the night of broken glass) in 1938,
however devastating, and which was covered fully by the American
press denouncing and condemning Germany, was not reflected in
Jewish public demonstrations.[23] According to a proposal by B'nai B'rith
President Henry Monsky at a meeting on 13 November 1938 of the
General Jewish Council, an umbrella group for coordinating policies
among the major Jewish organizations, 'there should be no parades,
public demonstrations, or protests by Jews'.[24] A few days later Wise
explained confidentially that 'the silence of the American Jewish
Congress must not be regarded either as lack of activity or vigor on our
part. Both are the result of well considered policy.'[25] There are further
indications that American Jews were in a state of existential conflict,
caught between American and Jewish loyalty. Given their fragile status,
their considerations were first of all to safeguard their well-being.
Though both Jewish and non-Jewish spokesmen expressed unprecedented shock at the pogroms and sincere sympathy for the German
Jewish victims, the basic attitude and policies of the Roosevelt administration and American Jewish leaders did not change. Mainstream
American Jewry, which was constantly clashing over any issue – trivial
as well as major – acted this time in uniformity, choosing the policy of
public silence. Analyzing American Jewry's reaction to the dreadful situation in Europe, Arad Ne'eman concludes that 'with anti-Semitism
spreading and charges of warmongering and disloyalty mounting,
retreat from the public sphere was envisioned as a sound means of
protection'.[26]

Cecilia Razovsky, a Jewish social worker involved in immigration and rescue operations, often without the backing of large Jewish organizations, proved an exception. But it is this kind of exception that is far more fascinating than the commonplace, since it demonstrates the independant moral conscience at work in human behavior and provides a point of reference in our moral discourse. In contrast to the widespread accusations that American Jewry did not do enough to help their co-religionists during those tragic years,[27] I wish to claim that Jewish women, from all kinds of background – from homemakers to professionals – were actively involved in organizing rescue operations and assisting refugees.

My focus is on one extraordinary woman – Cecilia Razovsky. Active in all major Jewish and non-Jewish American immigration and rescue organizations for almost half a century, she was an acknowledged authority on immigration, refugees, Jewish refugee children and displaced persons. As the Executive Director of the National Coordinating Committee for Aid to Refugees and Emigrants Coming from Germany (NCC), the German-Jewish Children's Aid (GJCA), and the Head of the Migration Department of the National Refugee Service (NRS) – among other organizations,[28] Razovsky was highly effective in helping refugees obtain the visas, affidavits and other information necessary for their entrance into the United States. After their arrival, she helped the refugees locate relatives in the country, and find jobs and permanent homes. Most important, she initiated and administered a successful program that brought over 1,000 Jewish refugee children to the US, and saw to their placement with Jewish foster-families. She created and administered a network in over 100 cities all around the country with the aid of professional and non-professional women that she recruited – all working long hours for what Razovsky considered 'a sacred mission' – for the purpose of rescuing Jewish refugees from Europe.

This book is dedicated to these rescuers – to Cecilia Razovsky and the anonymous thousands of American Jewish women who accomplished the impossible, under the most difficult conditions, proving that where there is a will there will always be a way.

NOTES

1. Bat-Ami Zucker, *In Search of Refuge. Jews and US Consuls in Nazi Germany 1933–1941* (London and Portland, OR: Vallentine Mitchell, 2001).
2. On 10 August 1933, the Bureau of Immigration and Naturalization were combined into the Immigration and Naturalization Service (INS) by executive order. The INS was in charge of matters relating to the status of aliens in the US and to the deportation of undesired aliens.

3. Cited in Lillian Holman Mohr, *Frances Perkins: That Woman in FD'S Cabinet* (Croton-on Hudson, NY: North River Press, 1979), p. 131.

4. Bat-Ami Zucker, 'Frances Perkins and the German-Jewish Refugees', *American Jewish History*, 89, 1 (March 2001), pp. 35–59. In 1940 the Immigration and Naturalization Service was transferred to the Justice Department.

5. Both Jay Pierrepont Moffat, chief of division of Western European Affairs, and Assistant Secretary of State Wilbur J. Carr commented on the matter in their diaries. See entry of 20 April 1933, Diary of Jay Moffat, Moffat Papers, Houghton Library, Harvard University, and Carr Diary, entry of 20 April 1933, Carr Papers, Manuscript Division, Library of Congress.

6. Caroline Fleming, Assistant Chief, Department of Labor, Children's Bureau, Washington DC, 17 September 1919. Julia C. Lathrop, Chief, Department of Labor, Children's Bureau, Washington DC, 1 October 1919. Razovsky Papers, Box 1: Folder: Early Years, 1912–1932. AJHS Archives, New York.

7. Razovsky, 'Of the Administration of the Child Labor Law of the District of Columbia,' 31 May 1919. Razovsky Papers, Box 1: Folder: Early Years, 1912–1932, p. 21. American Jewish Historical Society Archives, New York.

8. Razovsky to Miss Winkler, 23 May 1919: 'I should like to go back to immigration work. I should prefer to act in a directing or organizing capacity.' Razovsky Papers, Box 1: Folder: Early Years, 1912–1932. American Jewish Historical Society (hereafter AJHS) Archives, New York.

9. She spoke English, German, Yiddish, Spanish, French, Romanian and Hebrew.

10. Zucker, *In Search of Refuge*, pp. 18–27.

11. Cable from Secretary of State to the embassy in Berlin, 24 March 1933, 862.4016/80; Pierrepont Moffat, Chief, Division of Western European Affairs to Albert Kleemeyer, 13 June 1933, 862.4016/1141; Assistant-Secretary Carr to John McDuffie, House of Representatives, 1 July 1933, 862.4016/1141. United States Department of State, Central Decimal Files, Record Group 59. National Archives, Suitland, Maryland.

12. William E. Dodd, Jr. and Martha Dodd (eds), *Ambassador Dodd's Diary, 1933–1938* (New York: Harcourt, Brace and Company, 1941), pp. 5, 21.

13. Report by American Consulate-General 'A Summary of Recent Developments in the Political, Economic, Social and Industrial Situation in Germany', 10 July 1933. Dodd Papers, File 42, Folder: 1933 Library of Congress, Manuscript Division, Washington DC.

14. Waldman to Strook, 9 June 1938. Morris Waldman Files, Folder: Immigration File 1938–1939, Yivo Archives, New York. For the attitude of Jewish spokesmen, see the excellent review in Gulie Ne'eman Arad, *America, Its Jews, and the Rise of Nazism* (Bloomington, IN: Indiana University Press: 2000), esp. Chapter Eight: FDR 'The greatest friend we have.' pp. 187–208.

15. At the Wagner-Rogers Hearings, Wise openly stated that 'our country comes first ... we should not undertake to do anything that would be hurtful to the interests of our country'. Joint Hearings Before a Subcommittee of the Committee on Immigration and Naturalization. House of Representatives: 76th Congress, 1st Session, on SJ Res. 64 and HJ Res. 168. p. 155.

16. Richard C. Rothschild, 'Are American Jews Falling into the Nazi Trap?' *Contemporary Jewish Records* (January–February 1940), pp. 9–17 (emphasis original).

17. Quoted in Arad, *America, Its Jews, and the Rise of Nazism*, p. 195.

18. Rabbi Stephen Wise, American Jewish Congress, to Judge Julian Mack, 10 November 1937, in Carl Herman Voss, *Rabbi and Minister: The Friendship of Stephen S. Wise and John Haynes Holmes* (New York: Association Press, 1964), pp. 222–3.

19. Wise to Justice Frankfurter, 30 March 1938. Box 109, AJHS; Wise to Judge Mack, 29 March 1938. Box 115, ibid.

20. Account of Executive Committee Meeting, American Jewish Committee, 5 April 1938, Morris Waldman Files, Folder: 1938–1939, Yivo Archives, New York. Under massive pressure from Jewish spokesmen, both Celler and Dickstein withdrew their proposals. See Rafael Medoff, *The Deafening Silence* (New York: Shapolsky Publishers: 1987), pp. 42–3.

21. Waldman to Strook, 9 June 1938. Morris Waldman Files, Folder: Immigration File 1938–1939. Yivo Archives, New York. For the attitude of Jewish spokesmen, see the excellent review in Arad, *America, Its Jews, and the Rise of Nazism*, esp. Chapter Eight, 'FDR: 'The greatest friend we have', pp. 187–208.

22. Cited in Medoff, *The Deafening Silence*, p. 53.
23. Alfred Gottschalk, 'The German Pogrom of November 1938 and the Reaction of American Jewry', *The Leo Baeck Memorial Lecture* (Leo Baeck Institute, New York, 1988).
24. Cited in Haskel Lookstein, *Were We Our Brothers' Keepers? The Public Response of American Jews to the Holocaust, 1938–1944* (New York: Vintage, 1988), p. 59.
25. 'Report', 18 November 1938. Stephen Wise Papers, Box 109. AJHS Archives, New York.
26. Arad, *America, Its Jews, and the Rise of Nazism*, p. 206.
27. Medoff, *The Deafening Silence*. For a discussion on the writing of 'judgmental history,' see Arad, *America, Its Jews, and the Rise of Nazism*.
28. To mention only the most important organizations: National Council of Jewish Women (NCJW), American Jewish Joint Distribution Committee (JDC), United Nations Relief and Rehabilitation Administration (UNRRA), and her activities in non-Jewish Committees: National Council, US Committee for Refugees, American Council for Nationalities, General Committee of Immigrant Aid at Ellis Island.

1 American-Jewish Rescue Organizations

Several dozen national organizations were active in America between 1934 and 1945 in the rescue and resettlement of Jewish refugees from Europe. Although the groups cooperated with each other, as well as with the State Department and the Department of Labor, the fact that they were all involved in the same issues caused some confusion. Some agencies were ignorant of the basic procedures necessary for obtaining immigration visas, others wasted time and resources by duplicating their efforts, with the result that similar petitions were often submitted more than once to the same authorities. With a growing increase in the number of requests for immigrant visas during the summer of 1934, American Jewish leaders involved in rescue operations and officials in the administration began to realize that a central, umbrella organization would have to be established, where they could concentrate all their efforts and achieve the best results.

On 9 March 1934, a meeting was called by James McDonald, High Commissioner for Refugees Coming from Germany and Joseph Chamberlain, Professor of Public Law at Columbia University, US representative on the High Commission's governing body, in order to discuss possible coordination between various American Jewish and non-Jewish organizations that would serve as a clearing agency on behalf of émigrés to the United States.[1] The aim, explained McDonald at the meeting, was not to curtail the activities of the existing agencies, but rather 'to coordinate the activities and to advise agencies abroad, as well as agencies and individuals in [the United States]'.[2] This would enable officials to refer the many persons and agencies coming to Washington with plans and suggestions to a single committee, which could investigate the merits of such plans. Moreover, such a committee would supply services not provided by

other organizations.[3] Citing several cases of overlapping and duplication in her own organization, Cecilia Razovsky described how officers of a Milwaukee orphanage had made a public announcement of
their willingness to adopt fifty German children for placement in
their institution and detailed their communication with Washington
to make final arrangements.[4] The publicity and criticism that followed was negative although no one knew whether the orphanage
had already selected a group of children to bring to the United States
or whether the state of Wisconsin and the government had secured
permission to bring them, nor even if any plans had been made for
keeping the children under observation, once they were brought to
the US. Razovsky cited other instances where coordination would
have solved many problems and stressed that State Department and
Labor Department officials had urged her to explain to other organizations the need for having one central agency through which all
such matters could be cleared.[5] The debate that followed revealed the
readiness of most representatives to fully cooperate. Mrs Maurice
Goldman of the National Council of Jewish Women (NCJW) stated
that her organization had for many years carried out the immigrant
aid service for European (particularly east European) immigrants.
When 'the German situation' arose, the Council was already in possession of the necessary mechanism and equipment which would
enable it to include the extra work in its routine, without the need to
reorganize.[6] Mrs Goldman added that Miss Razovsky, a recognized
authority in this field, had received her training and experience during fourteen years' work with the Council and could vouch for its
efficiency, and that the Council had 200 branches throughout the
country doing follow-up work for new immigrants. She stated that
the NCJW was ready to cooperate in every way in the formation of
this central committee and went on to explain that the personal connections NCJW officers had with various national organizations
could enable the most efficient working relations. As a member of the
Joint Consultative Council of Nine, which consisted of the American
Jewish Committee, the American Jewish Congress, and the B'nai
B'rith, Cecilia Razovsky was secretary of the Committee on German
Jewish Immigration Policy, of which Max Kohler was chairman, and
secretary of the Committee on Aid to German Jewish Children.

At the same meeting, Max Kohler stated that the purpose of the
Committee on German-Jewish Immigration Policy was to secure a
more sympathetic application of the immigration law vis-à-vis the
admission of German refugees. He added that his committee had also

consulted with representatives of non-Jewish organizations, that at the request of the Department of State, Judge Mack had been asked to act as liaison officer between the Jewish agencies and the State Department, and that Dr Henry Moskowitz had been asked to act in that capacity for the Department of Labor.[7] Mr George Warren of the International Migration Service was in favor of creating such a coordinating committee and recommended that it should be responsible for:

1. Concentrating all efforts directed at the government towards a single Washington source.
2. Acquiring complete knowledge of each other's functions in order to get a clear picture of the functions of all agencies represented.
3. Clearing all names and addresses of clients of the different agencies and storing them under one authority.

In other words, the three functions of a central committee would be to concentrate efforts in Washington, define and exploit the functions of each agency and clear cases.[8]

Cecilia Razovsky suggested adding a fourth function, which would explore the various employment fields, and seek out possible positions for refugee professionals. This, she emphasized, might be done by enlisting the aid of existing professional agencies throughout the country.[9] It was agreed by all to set up a national coordinating bureau along the lines indicated by High Commissioner McDonald and Professor Chamberlain.[10]

Thus the National Coordinating Committee for Aid to Refugees and Emigrants coming from Germany (NCC) was established in New York City on 7 June 1934 by the major Jewish and nonsectarian social agencies involved in assisting refugees from Germany.[11] Local coordinating committees were created to handle pre- and post-emigration problems, which ranged from obtaining affidavits to providing the needy with housing, jobs and financial assistance. According to the first report of its Executive Committee, dated 13 November 1934, the NCC would undertake:

1. To act as a central registry and clearing bureau for all organizations interested in the refugee problem.
2. To explore possibilities for employment throughout the US.
3. To organize local committees to co-operate with the National Committee.
4. To exchange information with the High Commissioner.
5. To collaborate with other national social agencies working with the German refugees.

6. To stimulate non-Jewish interest.[12]
7. To analyze projects submitted for social workers, musicians, physicians, etc.
8. To cooperate with the Federal, State and Labor Departments.
9. To organize an information service for local and international groups.
10. To energize the work of existing agencies.[13]

As for relations between the national and local committees, the decision was that the former would not interview or take care of any refugees residing in greater New York. Cases in which the local committee felt the need for contacts in other parts of the country were referred to the national bureau, which then approached different institutions and committees in order to find employment and/or housing solutions. In certain cases – usually where changes were required in status – immigrants were sent by local committees to the national committee, which was better equipped to deal with government officials.

As Executive Director, Cecilia Razovsky was in charge of all contact with government officials and held several successful conferences with representatives of the State and Labor Departments to discuss individual refugees whom she felt were especially meritorious and deserving. High commissioners and refugee committees in other countries – including individual cases requiring connections in America – occasionally contacted Razovsky on matters relating to immigration policy and conditions of admission. In such cases, the NCC cooperated with the International Migration Service, NCJW and the Hebrew Sheltering and Immigrant Aid Society (HIAS) in the United States, as well as the *Comité International pour le Placement des Réfugiés Intellectuels* in Geneva, which kept a comprehensive file of all refugees from Germany.[14]

The Executive Committee also held several meetings with representatives of the various existing professional committees (physicians, scholars, students and lawyers) in order to clarify and coordinate their activities and to prevent duplication.[15] For example, it was understood that the existing Emergency Committee in Aid of Displaced Foreign Physicians and the NCC would keep a complete register of all German-born physicians in the United States while the national committee would also keep a central file for clearing purposes.[16]

The NCC was originally organized as an emergency committee in the hope that it would be disbanded within six to twelve months. But the developments in Europe forced the Committee to reorganize on a sounder, more permanent basis. Although the NCC did not intend to supplant existing organizations, it slowly became a parent body to other groups and took the form of a data-pooling center. In its efforts to insure prompt service and maintain contacts with other communities in the United States, Canada, Central and South America, and with Germany and other refugee countries, the NCC served as the central body in dealing with the federal authorities on all matters pertaining to immigration from Germany. It issued leaflets and bulletins, and arranged for repatriation and settlement in other countries-of-final destination for refugees to the US in transit to those destinations, and who were stranded because of lack of funds or incomplete documents. It provided a central body in clearing all cases of émigrés and refugees known to other national and local agencies. A special clearing service was made open to all interested agencies, and close and effective relations were maintained with organizations dealing with miscellaneous or specialized groups.

Gradually the objectives were met. A central card index was established in the NCC offices listing all refugees, including those already in the United States and/or applicants who had registered in American councils in Germany. The NCC sent out circulars to all its affiliated organizations with the latest information on immigration and integration in the United States.[17] While the NCC's main objective was coordination and liaison, the deteriorating situation in Germany forced it to expand and increase its ventures. The ever-increasing flow of migrants from Europe, their tendency to concentrate in the New York area and their competition for jobs at a time of economic recession, made integration difficult. Already in October 1934, Razovsky insisted that refugees be distributed outside of New York and pointed out to volunteers in charge of resettlement that '[t]his desire on the part of people inland to come to New York is one which must be immediately discouraged'.[18] Inasmuch as over 60 per cent of the new arrivals settled in greater New York, a special committee, known as the Greater NY Coordinating Committee for German Refugees, was organized under the chairmanship of Mr David Sulzberger.[19] That committee dispensed financial aid to refugee individuals and families and, through its employment bureau, was able to find satisfactory employment in New York City for a significant number of people. It was agreed that the Greater NY Committee had done a very good job since very few, if any, complaints had been received from lay people, unlike the previous year. It was most important for the committee to function satisfactorily so as to avoid any additional pressure from Washington, since it only took a few complaints to create a disproportionate reaction to the issue at hand. Not only did New York carry the greatest financial burden but even from the point of view of job placements, the city was doing more than its fair share.[20] The main problem remained money: it was quite obvious that with the growing number of people turning to the committee for service and assistance, the amount of money expended was also greater. Yet the committee's increased scope of activities was accompanied neither by any expansion of its administrative machinery nor funding resources.

The growing burden of work and expenses and the consequent personnel shortage caused delays, which were followed by constant and repeated criticism of the NCC's working methods.[21] In spite of the administrative difficulties, the NCC succeeded in the year 1935/6 in handling 1,251 new files, 92 welfare cases and 1,159 cases of counseling and service, and its expenses amounted to $337,000.[22] However, in face of increased demands for aid from German Jews, it was agreed in 1936 that immediate reorganization was imperative.[23] William Rosenwald was appointed vice-chairman, soon to rise to co-chairman, and the committee was ready to enter the second stage of its work. The reorganization of the NCC structure in mid-1936 enabled the committee to be more efficient and professional. The body's Executive Committee and working procedures were reorganized, with Razovsky assuming more responsibilities, supervising, among other functions, the activities of the affiliated agencies. In her capacity as Executive Director, Razovsky was in charge of enormous projects, dealing not only with assisting immigrants already in the United States but also with applicants for immigration from Europe. She was in constant touch with officials in the Labor Department and the Department of State. Her work was highly appreciated in Washington.[24]

The twenty agencies connected with the NCC were divided into four groups: service agencies – to provide welfare, placement and rehabilitation;[25] immigration organizations – to deal with the admission and social integration of refugees;[26] committees concerned with more general questions of immigration policy and the creation of public opinion sympathetic to the refugees,[27] and Christian committees.[28]

By October 1936 the committee expanded its central office to create an official and active Resettlement Division, and Jacob Billikopf toured the country, visiting smaller communities in search of locations in which migrants could be integrated. The Resettlement Division undertook to effect a better distribution of émigrés throughout the US. In order to do this the Resettlement Division organized a program in New York City to prepare émigrés for resettlement. This was achieved on both an individual casework basis and through a program of frequent lectures and widely distributed publications in German and English. The committee also undertook to organize and stimulate local Coordinating Committees throughout the country, which would assume responsibility for the integration of refugees referred from New York. Funding for this endeavor was supplied by the American Jewish Joint Distribution Committee (JDC) and by two additional affiliated organizations: the NCC Fund, Inc. and the Greater New York Coordinating Committee.[29]

While not engaged in direct casework, the JDC was the largest financial contributor to the NCC. Between 1934 and 1937, about 60 per cent of the entire budget came from the JDC; in 1938 the JDC contributed $523,000 in a yearly budget of $812,300.[30] The JDC was entitled to supervise the use of the funds it contributed, so that it was only natural that the JDC occasionally found it necessary to intervene in NCC decisions.[31] The JDC was also permanently in touch with the work and problems of the NCC. A number of the officers and members of the Board of Directors of the JDC served on the NCC's Board of Directors, thus making for close interaction between the two organizations.

Ever since World War I the JDC had worked with local populations in eastern and central Europe to establish and promote various types of self-help activity, including childcare, medical sanitary activities, economic aid, vocational retraining and cultural-religious work. It had built up local and national self-help units, especially in Poland and Romania, which constituted the backbone of Jewish activity in those countries. The JDC had also engaged in emergency relief programs when these were made necessary by pogroms or other disasters. Since the German emergency, in addition to continuing its programs of relief and rehabilitation in eastern and central European countries, the JDC had granted substantial sums for refugee aid in many countries throughout the world – in Europe and in North, South and Central America – working through established local refugee aid committees, or committees which it helped to establish, as well as through emigration bureaux and agencies such as the HICEM.[32] The refugee aid programs consisted not only of emigration services and funding transportation to many countries of the world (including Palestine), but an important aspect of the JDC's activity had been the training and retraining of young people in agriculture and manual labor.

In Germany and Austria the JDC expended very large sums of money for emigration aid, vocational retraining, financial assistance, education and for kindred services and, after 1938, for feeding hungry Jews in Austria. In the US the JDC was instrumental in establishing the NCC by granting large subventions and, by doing so, assisting a number of the service organizations dealing with special phases of refugee requirements in the US. Thus, each of the beneficiary organizations affiliated with the NCC Fund, Inc. was supported, directly or indirectly, by the JDC.

Good working relations were established between the NCC and the JDC. See, for example, Chamberlain's letter to Paul Baerwald, chairman of the JDC, 9 November 1938: 'Our Executive Committee is deeply appreciative of the splendid cooperation which we received so promptly from the JDC committee – and at our meeting a motion of thanks and appreciation to the JDC was unanimously voted by the members of the Executive Committee.'[33] The NCC Fund was an entirely Jewish organization looking for national support for its work.[34] Its aim was to provide for central financing and also to secure more widespread support and to enable the NCC to organize campaigns and collect contributions from the Federation and Welfare Funds. The management of the Coordinating Fund, which supervised the expenditures of the NCC, was placed entirely in Jewish hands.[35]

Thus the two organizations whose purpose was to coordinate the work for refugees on a national basis were the NCC Fund and the National Coordinating Committee for Aid to Refugees and Emigrants Coming from Germany (NCC). The former was the money-raising organization and took care of the finance of NCC's affiliated agencies. The latter was the functional organization, which was responsible for national planning and coordination, including resettlement.[36] Each local community was requested to assist in financing the national program by contributions to the NCC Fund, Inc. and to organize a committee to be responsible for the conduct and financing of a program in the local community for refugees who had come there directly or via the national offices.[37] The Fund was organized in April 1937 for the purpose of raising money to finance five organizations which served refugees in the US. The Budget of Allocations Committee reviewed the proposed budget of its affiliated organizations and determined the total campaign objective and amounts appropriate to allocate.

The annexation of Austria to the Reich in March 1938 and the terror subsequent to *Kristallnacht* in Germany increased the NCC's clientele and, again, there arose the need to reevaluate its structure.[38] By the late 1930s, the NCC was non-sectarian in name only; the majority of its clients and activists were Jewish. The NCC staff was almost entirely Jewish: heads of departments,[39] the treasurer, the secretary and other senior officers were Jewish, and financial support was drawn exclusively from Jewish sources. However, it kept its reputation as a non-sectarian organization due to the need to present the rescue operation as an all-American humanitarian effort and not an exclusively Jewish issue.

In the past, the NCC had assumed responsibility primarily for German Jewish refugees. No uniform policy in this respect was maintained regarding the agencies that claimed to engage in all phases of refugee aid. While it was quite true that a substantial proportion of the refugees were Jewish by religious or 'race', there was an increasing number who were not Jewish. The problem, therefore, was an American problem in so far as all American citizens had undertaken to control it and direct it into proper fields of activity. It was, therefore, important that the proposed new organization should be concerned with the broad aspects of the refugee problem in the US. With this in mind, the Board of Directors recommended that a Refugee Consultative Council be set up consisting of representatives from Jewish, Protestant, Catholic and non-sectarian national agencies. In fact there were many instances of collaboration between the various groups in the field of refugee aid,[40] and it was essential for the new body to provide some elastic formula whereby matters of common interest and common purpose might become the concern of Jews and Christians alike.[41]

In early 1939 Harry Greenstein, Executive Director of the Jewish Welfare Funds in Baltimore, was asked to prepare a survey of the structure and operational procedures of the NCC. His report, presented in May 1939, recommended reorganizing the NCC and establishing a new agency: the National Refugee Service (NRS).[42] Giving the reasons why a new body was required, Mr Rosenwald – the new president of the NRS - explained that the NCC had been organized at a period when the refugee problem was less serious and the need less urgent. The committee had developed without a plan and adopted such procedures as were required to meet each emergency as it arose. The refugee problem had grown at a tremendous pace in wake of the critical events in Europe in the summer and fall of 1938. To meet the increased responsibilities and demands, the NRS was organized as a functioning body to replace what had originally been a coordinating committee. The problem was national in character and therefore the NRS was organized on a national basis, designed to draw from and contribute to the local communities the fullest measure of aid and guidance.[43]

Rosenwald recommended setting up departments, each of which was to be administered by a departmental head answering to the Executive Director: (a) Immigration; (b) Resettlement; (c) Employment; (d) Special Categories; (e) Relief and Case Work; (f) Information and Research; (g) Comptroller; (h) Central Office Management. The proposed NRS program included a migration service which would deal with affidavits, sponsorship, visas and other legal aspects of the immigration process; financial aid; a placement service; vocational and retraining programs; a capital loan service; resettlement to smaller communities, and an Americanization program. The NRS also communicated with the US government on matters relating to immigration legislation and special cases.[44] It was agreed from the start that the NRS would extend its services to all refugees who came within the scope and jurisdiction of the organization, regardless of country of origin.

The initiators of the reorganization of the NCC hoped the operation would provide a much more effective administration of the refugee program within and beyond New York City. The new agency's centralization of intake, reduced waiting period and closer integration of the Resettlement Division with central relief and employment departments would help tremendously in intensifying the flow of refugees out of New York. In addition, local coordinating committees were now able to look forward to more effective service from the national office in the city.

At its first regular Board of Directors' meeting on 21 July 1939, the NRS was authorized to take over the activities of the NCC and certain of its affiliates directly concerned with granting aid and assistance to refugees.[45] The following departments and committees were established: Social and Cultural; Publicity; Division for Social Adjustment; Steering Committee – Joint Supervisory Group; Community Relations Department; Employment Department; Department of Research and Information; Migration and Alien Status; Retraining Committee; Technical Advisory, Employment and Retraining Division; Migration Department; Resettlement Division, Relief and Case Work Department; Family Service, Central Reception and Information Service; Department of Economic Adjustment; subcommittee on Reclassification, and a Speaker Bureau.

After careful consideration, authorization was granted for the release of a statement on affidavit policies and procedures. In view of the increasing number of refugees coming to the US from countries other than central Germany, the Executive Committee authorized a statement to the effect that the NRS should provide assistance to refugees coming to the US not only from Germany but also from former Austria, Czechoslovakia, Italy, Hungary and such other countries where definite, official, anti-racial legislation was responsible for migration to the US.

In a series of weekly meetings the Executive Committee dealt with various problems needing immediate attention, for example, the question of the proper relations and cooperation with the Christian organizations. Despite the decision to focus the new organization's operations on Jewish refugees, the NRS favored 'the closest possible cooperation and understanding with the Christian rescue organizations'.[46] In order to provide for effective cooperation among the various bodies engaged in Jewish and non-Jewish refugee work, the Executive Committee recommended establishing a National Consultative Refugee Council. With regard to cases brought to the Executive Committee concerning refugees whose mental or physical disabilities were likely to cause them to be permanently dependent, the Committee decided that even if deportation could be arranged, the NRS should not, under any circumstances, encourage such a procedure.[47]

The Executive Committee also considered the request of the German-Jewish Aid Committee in London for the NRS to guarantee payments by Americans who desired to transfer relatives from Germany to England for a temporary stay.[48] The Executive Committee voted to assist such American relatives by holding their cash deposits, although the NRS could not guarantee to the British committee any payments beyond amounts deposited with the NRS, Inc.

Faced with rapidly increasing requests from Europe, particularly as a result of the racial laws in Italy, Hungary and other countries under the influence of the Axis powers, there was need for a strong organization. The majority of those immigrants lucky enough to reach the United States were without resources. The immigrants' psychological problems, their need for rapid adjustment and the elementary requirements for immediate financial assistance strained the organization's financial and personnel resources.[49] The problems facing the agency were enormous. The Migration Department was concerned with complex technical questions and was working under terrific pressure to respond to the many demands from Americans wishing to assist relatives and friends to escape from central Europe. The Employment Department had difficulties finding suitable work opportunities for refugees which did not displace American employees. The Resettlement Department, which had by 1939 succeeded in resettling nearly 3,000 families in various parts of the country, was examining its procedures with a view to increasing the number of refugee families for resettlement.[50] Compared with the 1,256 refugees settled in 150 locations in 1938, the number of refugees settled in 300 communities was almost tripled, to 3,546 in 1939.[51] The Relief and Service Department, which was already providing for the elementary needs of nearly 2,000 families, was facing increasing demands for assistance from refugees who were unable to support themselves.[52]

Another problem that called for an immediate solution concerned the relationship between the Council of Service to the Foreign Born of the NCJW and the NRS.[53] At a preliminary meeting with NCJW representatives, it was agreed that the following activities would continue to be the responsibility of the NCJW: port and dock work; international case work; adult immigrant education (Americanization and naturalization), and immigration adjustment.[54]

As for port and dock work, it was agreed that all transit cases detained at Ellis Island and all cases requiring bonds from the NRS would be turned over to the NRS for attention.[55] All contacts with consular offices regarding passports, visas, and other papers. in connection with detained persons would be handled by the NRS, Inc. The NRS would receive from the NCJW lists of names of all visitors settled outside New York. Where the NRS had been asked to handle the case at Ellis Island, it would continue to assume complete responsibility once the person was released. This also applied to other ports of entry outside the city.

With regard to international case work, it was decided that where requests for affidavits or advice came from persons abroad and where the letters did not give addresses of any relatives or friends, the organization which received such letters would make the necessary acknowledgments. It was also agreed that the NCJW would be responsible for all requests to trace lost relatives in the US. The NRS would refer to the NCJW all such inquiries, except when a specific request was made for the services of the NRS, in which case the NCJW would be asked for a report. Requests for communication with relatives whose addresses were given for the purpose of securing affidavits, collection of legacies, and related matters, would be handled by the relevant organization.

All requests for settlement in third countries, for temporary asylum or for permanent residence were to be referred to the NRS, especially those requiring transportation or deposits of funds for visas and other papers. In principle, the NRS would handle all third-country cases.[56] However, in cases of international migration where the refugees from central Europe were to be settled permanently in a country other than the US, the case would remain with the NCJW up to the point at which the services of the NRS were required, at which time it would be turned over with a full summary of necessary data.

It was understood that the NCJW would not send field workers to handle individual cases in local communities, even where no professional social workers were available. For that function the NRS had established a National Field Service to organize State Committees responsible for the individual cases requiring service in that state. At the same time it was agreed that the NCJW would send its field workers to advise and train local organization sections in the conduct of their local activities.

Among the many problems that needed immediate attention by the new organization was also the matter of changed status, especially for those persons who stayed in the United States on visitor visas and who could not or would not return to Germany. Those cases, and even others originating with the NCJW, were the responsibility of the NRS.[57] It had also been agreed between the NRS, NCJW and other Jewish agencies that it was best to clear all cases through one person who had established relationships with federal government representatives in matters of immigration and naturalization. It was thus unanimously agreed that Miss Razovsky, who had been doing this effectively for years, should continue to carry responsibility for all Jewish agencies in this area.[58] Though many former functions were turned over to the new organization, the NCJW kept the important task of adult immigration education, aiding newcomers in the naturalization process toward Americanization. This was done mainly through the local sections of the NCJW, with the supervision and advice of the NCJW.

The Social Adjustment Department, formerly known as Immigrant Aid, included naturalization aids, education for citizenship, recreation, and other community activities which assisted with the integration of foreigners born into the community, enabling them to become Americanized as rapidly as possible. In a detailed letter, Mrs Goldman, president of the NCJW, assured William Haber that her organization had no desire to supplement the work of the NRS nor to duplicate or act in conflict with it. She described in detail the work done by her volunteer women:

> Our only desire is to set up a program of social adjustment ... and that the only professional aspect of it would be to train our women and to raise the standard of social work in our Sections ... our goal being to train Council women to help the immigrant family adjust more quickly by familiarizing the woman with her economic and social life, acquainting her with educational facilities for herself and her children, adjusting the family psychologically to democracy and American ideals, strengthening the family's community relations, and seeing them through all the steps which ultimately mean naturalization and good citizenship.[59]

It was understood that at regular intervals, possibly once a month, conferences would be held to exchange experiences and for mutual discussion and benefit. Where cases originated simultaneously in both the NRS and the NCJW, the decision as to which organization would handle the case would be made after discussion between the supervisors designated for this purpose by the two organizations. It was also agreed that Cecilia Razovsky, operating as the head of the Migration Department, NRS, would be given responsibility for all relations with government officials in Washington for general procedures and for appeal cases.

To sum up, in accordance with the agreed division of categories between the NCJW and the NRS, the NRS was entrusted with responsibility for cases requiring connections with governmental authorities, concentration-camp cases, requests for stipends and contracts, property and estate cases involving greater Germany, transit cases, temporary asylum in third countries, visitors' and transit visas, and change of status which included relief.[60]

Although it seemed that the agreement covered all important issues, a few issues remained between Razovsky and the NCJW with regard to policies and technical procedures, and these led to hard feelings among NCJW activists. Emma Schreiber, Director, Council of Service for Foreign Born, NCJW, openly accused Razovsky of 'continuous attacks against their [NCJW] existence'. She blamed the NRS for opening cases without first clearing them with their workers, thus causing delays and duplications.[61] In a letter to the Executive Director, NRS, Mrs Goldman, President, NCJW, stated that she was under the impression that the difficulty was more to do with the personalities involved (Razovsky and Emma Schreiber), than the program itself.[62] Eventually, Mrs Schreiber suggested a meeting with Razovsky to iron out their differences 'regarding policies and mechanics on a number of points'.[63] On the surface, things were back to normal but hard feelings remained to hound the relations between the two women and this reflected on the work of the agencies.

By winter 1939 about 200 Coordinating Committees were already organized to include representatives of smaller towns where there were no established Jewish community organizations.[64] Also, the Resettlement Division, which undertook to effect a better distribution of immigrants throughout the United States, launched a program in New York to prepare immigrants for resettlement. This was done both on an individual casework basis and through a program of frequent lectures and widely distribubed pamphlets in German and English.[65] For example, the Emergency Committee in Aid of Displaced Foreign Physicians, formerly under the chairmanship of Dr Bernard Sachs and later under the chairmanship of Dr Emanuel Libman, made its objective to place outstanding physicians in hospitals and universities to pursue research. In addition to university and hospital placements, paid positions were found for many physicians in laboratories, institutions and Departments of Health. A number of physicians were also employed in Outpatients Departments in various hospitals in order to acquire American training and experience.[66] Another committee, the Emergency Committee in Aid of Displaced German Scholars, which was organized by President Livingston Farrand of Cornell University with the cooperation of Dr Alfred E. Cohn, Mr Fred M. Stein and Mr Bernard Flexner, had since its inception granted aid to a number of scholars for a period of one or more years, through American universities. According to a Rockefeller Foundation report, the anti-Jewish laws and difficult situation had forced at least 1,500 scholars to leave Germany since 1933; the foundation recommended creating new positions for these émigrés.[67]

The issue of Jewish refugees in America was of great concern to American Jews, due both to their humanitarian urge to aid the persecuted and because of the effect it had on the 4,500,000 Jews residing in the United States. The entire issue had been obscured by misinformation and lent itself to misinterpretation, and a prime function of the new organization was to make the truth about refugee life in America available to the public at large. A 1939 memorandum refuted claims made by people who opposed immigration that migrants were flooding into the United States. Figures provided by the American Jewish Committee in March 1939, together with the American Friends Society Committee (AFSC), reflected a different story. According to the memorandum, 'to be released to the chief editorial writers of all newspapers throughout the country', the net increase in German immigrants from 1 July 1932 to 30 December 1938 was 44,886 – an annual average of 6,906. Moreover, 'from 1932 to 1938 more people emigrated from the United States than came in as immigrants – the first time in all of American history that this had happened'.[68] Thus, both absolutely and relatively, the United States was far from being flooded with Jewish or any other immigrants during that period. Hundreds of thousands were forced to remain in Germany and Nazi-dominated countries as refugees deprived of legal protection and exposed to persecution. Notwithstanding the true facts, public opinion, Congress and the State Department continued to oppose increasing the number of Jewish immigrants.[69]

The refugee problem was not one that could be settled merely by money or sympathetic enthusiasm. Placing refugees in such a way as to allow them to be self-supporting, without disrupting existing community life, was a challenge to the skill and resources of the NRS, and to Jewish groups in communities throughout the US.[70] According to a confidential memorandum comparing the activities of the NRS in November 1939 to those in November 1940 and 1941, and contrary to public opinion, refugee immigration to the US had not ceased. According to US government figures more than 28,000 Jewish refugees entered the US – 'the largest Jewish immigration received by any country in the world during this period'.[71] The NRS, therefore, had to provide increased services in all its departments, and did so.

Changes in regulations affecting the entry of refugees to the US had markedly increased the need in the Immigration Department for expert services to refugees and Americans acting on their behalf. Nearly 9,000 requests a month for migration services were given full and expert attention. In the Relief Department more than 6,000 individuals were receiving NRS aid each month. Data indicated that the relief problem could not be considered a temporary matter. Sixty per cent of the cases were on relief for a year or more; aged 50 years or over, two-thirds of the family heads were past the employment borderline. War refugees were older, completely without resources and less capable of assisting themselves. These facts affected the Capital Loan Service. The Loan Committee provided more than 165 loans a month to help refugees with business skills establish themselves in small private undertakings. Such loans helped other refugees secure vocational retraining and enabled physicians and dentists to establish their own practices. As for its retraining program, the NRS enlarged its activities to provide refugees with new skills. Over 800 refugees had entered or completed retraining courses, and an additional 700 were retrained by the end of 1941. A notable increase had taken place in the assistance provided to refugee professionals whose skills could still be utilized in the US, such as physicians, scientists, scholars, musicians and others. Over 1,800 refugees each month obtained English instruction and other educational and cultural opportunities. Approximately 1,000 refugee children were placed by the NRS in free camps for the summer. In all, 20,000 refugees were aided in 1940, a number exceeded by the end of 1941.[72]

To conclude, there could be no doubt that the NCC and NRS worked miracles in assisting and absorbing Jewish refugees from Europe by helping them adapt to American society, and turning them into American citizens who eventually contributed to their adopted country. Moreover, it is worth remembering that Hitler's accession to power in January 1933 and the ensuing brutal persecution of German Jews coincided in the United States with the Great Depression. This breakdown of the economy resulting in millions of the unemployed gave way to widespread anti-immigration, anti-alien and overt antisemitic sentiments. It certainly was not the best time to seek refuge in America, particularly for Jewish refugees. The misfortune of these migrants was that the tragic events in Germany occurred when public opinion was, at best, largely indifferent to international problems – including the plight of German Jewry.

Under such devastating conditions, it was Cecilia Razovsky who established an efficient nationwide network of dedicated Jewish women who spared no effort to save Jewish refugees from Nazi persecutions. Their diverse operations included having to deal with delicate legal problems involving refugees who were still in Europe, by locating American relatives and friends capable of supplying affidavits which facilitated their entrance into the United States. In addition, after the migrants' arrival, Razovsky launched a comprehensive operation which included locating available housing, employment, loans and, no less important – sympathy, compassion and solidarity. Razovsky's team was there for the refugee, solving both small and major problems in the best way they could. Razovsky was fully aware of the seriousness of the migrants' situation and she constantly reminded her team that it was a matter of life or death, letting no administrative, financial and/or political difficulties prevent her from what she considered to be her 'mission'.

Given the severe economic conditions, the anti-immigration atmosphere in Congress and the resentment and fear on the part of the general public of 'a Jewish flood', the tireless efforts of the Jewish rescue organizations and those of thousands of American Jewish women volunteers throughout the United States, which we shall explore in the follow chapters, ought to be singled out for praise and all due credit.

NOTES

1. Attended by representatives of sixteen Jewish, Christian and non-sectarian organizations: Hon. James G. McDonald; Professor Joseph Chamberlain; Dr Ashworth – American Christian Committee on Refugees; Dr Cabert – American Christian Committee on Refugees; William Eves III, American Friends Service Committee; Morris Waldman – American Jewish Committee; Max Kohler – American Jewish Committee, B'nai B'rith, Committee on German Jewish Immigration Policy; Oscar Leonard – American Jewish Congress; Lewis Strurs – American Jewish Congress; Joseph Hyman – American Jewish Joint Distribution Committee; Mrs Stephen S. Wise – Child Adoption Bureau; Harold Fields – Child Adoption Bureau; Miss Moriarta – Emergency Committee for Musicians; Dr Bernard Sachs – Emergency Committee in Aid of Displaced Foreign Physicians; Dr Emanuel Libman – Emergency Committee in Aid of Displaced Foreign Physicians and the OSE; John L. Bernstein – HIAS; Isaac L. Arofsky – HIAS; George Warren – Hospites and International Migration Service; Miss Mary Hurlburt – Hospites and International Migration Service; Jonah Goldstein – Joint Clearing Bureau; Maurice Goldman – NCJW; Cecilia Razovsky – NCJW; Dr J. J. Gelub – OSE – International Health Association; Morris Rothenberg – Zionist Organization of America; Dr Bernstein – Zionist Organization of America.
2. Minutes of a meeting called by James McDonald and Joseph Chamberlain, 9 March, 1934. NCC Records, Yivo Archives, pp. 1607–10.
3. Statement Issued to Press Representatives on 2 September 1938, by Chamberlain, chairman, NCC. Chamberlain Records, Folder 28: NCC Minutes 1937–1938. Yivo Archives, New York.
4. At that time Razovsky was Executive Director of German-Jewish Children's Aid, Inc. See Chapter 2.
5. Razovsky at the meeting called by James McDonald and Joseph Chamberlain, 9 March 1934. NCC Records, p. 1608.
6. Mrs Goldman, ibid., pp. 1608–9.
7. Max Kohler, ibid. p. 1610.
8. Warren, ibid., p. 1610.
9. Razovsky, ibid., p. 1610.
10. Max Kohler, chairman of the Committee on German-Jewish Immigration Policy and John L. Bernstein, the representative of HIAS were against a new organization. They reluctantly agreed, eventually.
11. The officers for NCC were: Hon. James G. McDonald – Honorary Chairman; Professor Joseph P. Chamberlain – Chairman; William Rosenwald – Vice-Chairman; Paul Felix Warburg – Treasurer; Dr Jacob Billikopf – Honorary Consultant, Resettlement Division; Dr S.C. Kohs – Director of Resettlement Division; and Cecilia Razovsky – Secretary and Executive Director.
12. Given the antisemitic atmosphere in the country, it was important to portray the rescue efforts as a non-sectarian organization.
13. Report of the Executive Director of the NCC (Razovsky) 13 November 1934. NCC Records, pp. 1639–41.
14. Minutes of Meeting of Board of Directors, NCC, 31 December 1934. NCC Records, pp. 1642–5.

15. See Chapter 4.
16. For a detailed analysis of the work with the professional committees, see Chapter 4.
17. See William Rosenwald, 'Report of the Activities of NCC', 14 May 1937; 'Manual on Immigration', *Bulletin of the Coordinating Committee,* No. 1, February 1939. NCC Records, Folder 89. Yivo Archives, New York.
18. Razovsky to all NCJW Branches, 17 October 1934. NCC Records, Folder 3: Correspondence of Cecilia Razovsky when she was Associate Director of the NCJW. Yivo Archives, New York.
19. It consisted of four organizations: Jewish Social Service Association, German Department; Brooklyn Jewish Family Welfare Society; New York Section, NCJW; Brooklyn Section, NCJW. See Dr Sulzberger's report, Minutes, Meeting Board of Directors, 12 November 1934. NCC, Folder 3, pp. 1637–8. Yivo Archives, New York.
20. New York took over 2,000 job placements in 1938, whereas the rest of the country arranged for three or four hundred resettled cases.
21. See Hyman to Razovsky, 10 July 1936; Razovsky to Chamberlain, 3 November 1938. NCC Records, Folder 6: Correspondence between Razovsky and Chamberlain. Yivo Archives, New York.
22. 'NCC Activities, 1936–1938', NCC Records, Folder 6. Yivo Archives, New York.
23. Memorandum, 'Re-Meeting to consider Program for German Refugees in this Country', 25 June 1936; Memorandum from Joseph Hyman to Paul Baerwald, 1 October 1935. NCC Records, Folder 7.
24. James L. Houghteling, Commissioner–General of the Immigration and Naturalization Service, to Cecilia Razovsky, 28 December 1938, praising the 'splendid work being done by the NCC'. Razovsky Papers, Box 6, Folder: Published Works about Immigration, 1929–1939. AJHS Archives, New York.
25. This division included the Greater New York Committee for Aid of German Jewish Refugees; Emergency Committee in Aid of Displaced Foreign Physicians; Emergency Committee for Musicians, and German-Jewish Children's Aid. See Chapters 2, 4.
26. This group included the NCJW and HIAS.
27. This group included the three major Jewish organizations: American Jewish Committee, American Jewish Congress and B'nai B'rith.
28. Among the nine Christian and 'non-sectarian' organizations affiliated with the NCC, the American Friends Service Committee (AFSC) was the most active.
29. See below, notes 34, 35.
30. Louis Rosner to Edwin Goldwasser, n.d.; 'NCC Activities, 1938–1939', NCC Records, Folder 6. Yivo Archives, New York.
31. Yehuda Bauer, *My Brother's Keeper: A History of the American Jewish Joint Distribution Committee, 1929–1939* (Philadelphia: Jewish Publication Society of America 1974), p. 26.
32. HICEM was created in 1927 when three Jewish agencies involved with Jewish immigration were combined: The New York-based Hebrew Sheltering and Immigrant Aid Society (HIAS), the Paris-based Jewish Colonization Association (ICA) founded by Baron Maurice de Hirsh, and the Berlin-based Emigdirect – an association founded in 1921 to centralize the work of the organizations and local communities involved with Jewish immigration. The name HICEM is an acronym of HIAS, ICA and Emigdirect. Its headquarters were in Lisbon and its activities focused on helping refugees with information, visa applications and transportation. It enabled approximately ninety thousand Jews to escape from Nazi Europe by way of Lisbon.
33. Quoted in Chamberlain to Razovsky, 17 November 1938. NCC Records, Folder 6: Correspondence between Razovsky and Chamberlain. Yivo Archives, New York.
34. Two dates are given for the creation of the NCC Fund, Inc. One is 1938, the other is April 1937.
35. The officers were: William Rosenwald – President; David H. Sulzberger – Vice-President; S. Marshall Kempner –Treasurer; Paul F. Warburg – Secretary; Eustace Seligman – chairman of the Board of Directors. NCC Records, Folder 2. Yivo Archives, New York.
36. On 1 January 1938 the NCJW took over responsibility for the national program and financing of the GJCA, Inc.; details in Chapter 2.
37. 'NCC Fund, Inc.', (n.d. but probably between January 1938 and December 1939). NCC Records, Folder 21: Correspondence and Bulletins. Yivo Archives, New York.
38. There were again complains about inefficiency and a rigid attitude towards the refugees.

See Summary of the Proceedings of the First Regular Meeting of the Board of Directors of the NRS, 21 July 1939. Chamberlain Records, Folder 34. Yivo Archives, New York

39. Apart from Professor Joseph Chamberlain, who was a Protestant.
40. Close collaboration was established especially with the Quakers' American Friends Service Committee. See, Bat-Ami Zucker, *In Search of Refuge, Jews and US Consuls in Nazi Germany* (London and Portland, OR: Vallentine Mitchell, 2001).
41. Harry Greenstein, *Reorganization Study of the NCC and Its Affiliated Agencies* (New York: NRS, May 1939).
42. Greenstein, *Reorganization Study*; Greenstein to Joseph Hyman, 17 April 1939. NRS Records, Folder 120. Yivo Archives, New York.
43. Proceedings of the First Regular Meeting of the Board of Directors, 21 July 1939. NRS Records, Folder 34, Yivo Archives, New York. In 1946 the NRS became the US Service for New Americans.
44. Officers of the NRS: Professor Joseph Chamberlain – Chairman; William Rosenwald – President; Paul Felix Warburg – Secretary, and Albert Abrams and Arthur Greenleigh. The Executive Committee included Harry Greenstein, William Haber and Joseph C. Hyman. In 1946 the NRS became the US Service for New Americans. Executive Officers: William Haber, Ann S. Petluck, Cecilia Razovsky, Albert Abramson, Stella Baruch, Milton Feinberg, Arthur Greenleigh, Augusta Mayerson, Ephraim Gomberg.
45. Summary of the Proceedings of the first Regular Meeting of the Board of Directors, New York, 21 July 1939. NRS Records, Folder 34. Yivo Archives, New York.
46. Harry Greenstein to Joseph Hyman, 17 April 1939. NCC Records, Folder 34.
47. Statement of Division of Responsibility between NRS, Inc., and Council of Service for Foreign Born, Inc., of the NCJW, 11 October 1939 (for NCJW, Council of Service for Foreign Born Inc., Emma S. Schreiber, Director and for NRS, William Haber, Executive Director). NSR Records, Folder 122. Yivo Archives, New York.
48. Ibid. See also NRS Records, Folder 116.
49. Report of William Haber, Executive Director, NRS, 21 July 1939: 'from five to six thousand persons come to the office of NRS each week seeking information, guidance or financial assistance'. NRS Records, pp. 1707–10.
50. NCC, William Rosenwald, 'Summary of NCC Fund Activities, 26 January 1938. NCC Records, Folder 7. Yivo Archives, New York; Lyman C. White, *300,000 New Immigrants*, Appendix A. p. 397; NCC Information: 'What We Have Achieved', 28 March 1939. NCC Records, Folder 7. Yivo Archives, New York.
51. NCC Information: 'What We Have Achieved', 28 March 1939. NCC Records, Folder 7. Yivo Archives, New York. See also, Henry Greenstein, Executive Director, Associate Jewish Charities, Baltimore, 'National Coordinating Committee Recast', reprinted from *Notes and News*, 5 June 1939. Published by Council of Jewish Federations and Welfare Funds.
52. Executive Committee Meeting, 21 July 1939. NRS Records, Folder 34.
53. For the agreement between the NRS and the NCJW, 31 August 1939, and Schreiber to Razovsky, 6 September 1939, see NRS Records, File 122. Yivo Archives, New York.
54. The NCJW representatives were: Mrs Maurice Goldman – President; Mrs Beatrice Spitzer – Chairman, Executive Committee; Mrs Emma Schreiber – Director, Council of Service to Foreign Born. The NRS Inc. representatives present at the meeting were: Professor Chamberlain – Chairman of the Board; Miss Razovsky – Director of Migration Division.
55. Razovsky to Haber, 26 July 1939. NRS Records, Folder 121: NCJW. Yivo Archives, New York.
56. Meeting, NRS Board of Directors, 21 July 1939. NRS Records, Folder 34. Yivo Archives, New York.
57. Ibid.
58. Acting Director, Migration Department NRS to Haber, 17 August 1939. Subject: 'Clarifying Relative Functions of the NRS and the Committee for Foreign Born of the NCJW', pp. 4–5. NRS Records, File 123. Yivo Archives, New York.
59. Goldman to Haber, 29 July 1939. NRS Records, Folder 121, Yivo Archives, New York.
60. Cecilia Razovsky, 25 July 1939. NRS Records, Folder 534. For cases of the different functions, see NRS Records, Folders 522, 523, 524, 535, 537, 538, 541, 542, 543, 544. Yivo Archives, New York.
61. Schreiber to Haber, 3 August 1939. NRS Records, File 122. Yivo Archives, New York.

62. Goldman to Haber, undated. NRS Records, File 123. Yivo Archives, New York.
63. Schreiber to Razovsky, 13 September 1939 with a copy to Haber. NRS Records, File 123. Yivo Archives, New York.
64. See NCC Board of Directors Meeting 21 January 1939, Chamberlain Records, Box 4, Folder 97: NCC, January 1939. Yivo Archives, New York.
65. Dr Billikopf, in charge of the division, was highly commended by the NCC Board of Directors for his successful efforts. During 1937 the Resettlement Division transferred to other communities about 460 individuals, men, women and children. Billikopf reported in March 1938 that they had 'established contacts with about forty communities'. For his work with the Resettlement Division, Billikopf was granted a motion of appreciation to be included in the minutes and a position of Honorary Consultant to the Resettlement Division. He was also nominated to the Board of Directors. See, Meeting of the Board of Directors of the NCC, 15 March 1938. NCC Records, Folder 18. Yivo Archives, New York.
66. See Chapter 4.
67. Ibid.
68. Henry W. Levy, American Jewish Committee, to Razovsky, 29 March 1939. Waldman Papers, Box 18: Immigration, Folder 8: Immigration 1936–1939. Yivo Archives. New York. See also Memorandum, 'Refugee Immigration Problem, Facts & figures' – Meeting with Clarence Pickett (AFSC), 29 December 1938. Waldman Papers, Box 19, Folder 8: Immigration–Refugees, 1939–1940. Yivo Archives, New York; pamphlet published by AFSC, 'Quaker Refutes Propaganda against Refugees', for release on 8 June 1939, Cyrus Adler Papers, Subject File 1929-1939, Folder 4: AFSC, American Jewish Committee Archives, New York. See *The Immigration Problem*, compiled by Clarence A. Peters (New York: H.W. Wilson Company, 1948), p.23.
69. For the atmosphere in Congress, see David L. Porter, *The Seventy-Sixth Congress and World War II* (Columbia and London: University of Missouri Press, 1979). See, also the *Fortune* poll published in July 1938 stating that two-thirds of the respondents, about 67.4 per cent, opposed increasing the number of immigrants into the United States. Cited in Charles Herbert Stemberg *et al.*, *Jews in the Mind of Americans* (New York: Basic Books, 1966), p. 145.
70. Harry Greenstein, 'NCC Recast', reprinted from *Notes and News*, 5 June 1939, published by the Council of Jewish Federations and Welfare Funds. NRS Records, File 120. Yivo Archives, New York.
71. Cited in 'Activities of the NRS Fall, 1941', NRS Records, pp. 1772–3.
72. Ibid.

2 The German-Jewish Children's Aid Project

It all began on 20 August 1933, when the Executive Committee of the American Jewish Congress voted in a resolution to organize a movement to bring Jewish children from Germany for adoption by American Jewish families.[1] The idea was to arrange for affluent American Jewish families to willingly agree to adopt German Jewish children, who were suffering from the mental, physical and moral terrors to which they were being subjected in Nazi Germany. The American Jewish Congress and the Joint Council on Immigration, together with representatives of other Jewish groups, believed that such an arrangement should be in full compliance with immigration laws and, therefore, have a better chance of being approved by the administration and accepted by the American public. Moreover, sufficient evidence would be produced by the Jewish organizations to show that these children would not become public charges and that the adoptions would be carried through in good faith. Mr Hyman Bloomfield[2] was asked by the Executive Committee to meet with the Secretary of State to obtain the State Department's consent to instruct its consuls in Germany to exercise leniency in expediting the humanitarian migration of these minors.[3] Instead of a meeting and in the absence of Acting Secretary of State Phillips, Assistant Secretary of State William Carr informed Bloomfield that since the quota for Germany was under-issued, there would be no problem with regard to children 'as well as to adult visa applicants'.[4] In other words, no special preference was approved for German Jewish children.

Similar initiatives were made by other American Jewish and gentile organizations. On 31 August 1933, the American Committee for the Relief of Victimized German Children notified Max Kohler, an attorney and immigration expert, affiliated with the American Jewish Committee and chairman of the Committee on German-Jewish Immigration Policy, that a committee had been convened for the purpose of aiding all German victims without distinction of race and creed. Their task was to secure funds for maintaining children's homes in Europe as well as for the relief of children still in Germany.[5] The Jewish organizations, however, focused their main efforts on German Jewish children. Indeed, the newly organized committee, the German-Jewish Children's Aid (GJCA), decided on 3 January 1934, at a meeting chaired by Dr Solomon Lowenstein,[6] to consolidate the existing National Conference of Social Work and the Committee on German-Jewish Immigration Policy in order to maximize efforts on behalf of these children.[7] Against the original offer by the American Jewish Congress with regard to adoption of children, it was unanimously agreed that the adoption plan was both unwise and inhuman. The B'nai B'rith representative argued that only a 'very few families … would be willing to take the responsibility for adoption and on the other side you might expect that any self-respecting family will refuse to surrender their children for adoption simply because of the present emergency… I cannot imagine Jewish parents exercising pressure for children' to be adopted. 'Furthermore, the word "adoption" … carries with it a great many implications and might frighten most families away',[8] Also, according to the US Adoption Laws, no child may be legally adopted unless he/she is present in court at the time the adoption takes place. It was only possible, therefore, to adopt children who were already in the United States. Since the children in question were still in Germany, any potential adoption was irrelevant.[9] It was therefore suggested that it would be preferable to consider bringing to the US children whose parents agreed to send them to America until the situation in Germany improved.[10] Dr B. Kahn, European representative of the Joint Distribution Committee, reported that a questionnaire asking for comprehensive data on the children's health, social background and other details., had already been sent to Germany.[11] He suggested preparing a provisional list of only 250 children, since it would be well advised to use them as a test case. The question of expenses was considered and it was decided that there might be a need for a bond, not exceeding $500 per child.[12]

The idea soon gathered momentum and various committees and subcommittees were created for what was regarded by the Jewish organizations as 'emergency measures' – to remove Jewish children from Nazi Germany and bring them into the United States as soon as possible.[13] Confusion among the several organizations and consequent duplication of efforts required that a single umbrella organization be created to coordinate the work of the various groups connected with aid to German refugees. On 9 March 1934, the Honorable James G. McDonald, High Commissioner for Refugees Coming from Germany and Professor Joseph Chamberlain, representing the US on the governing body of the High Commission, met in New York with representatives from Jewish and non-Jewish organizations to discuss the possibility of creating such a coordinating agency.[14]

One of the various possible plans under consideration for helping German Jews consisted of extending aid to Jewish children whose parents wished to smuggle them out of Germany in order to escape the persecutions and discriminations to which they were subject under the Nazis. A plan for bringing a group of such children to the United States was outlined and a subcommittee chaired by Dr Solomon Lowenstein was established to consider the problem. The members were Dr Maurice J. Karpf of the Graduate School for Social Work, Mr Harry Lurie of the Jewish Social Service Bureau, Mr Isaac L. Asofsky of the Hebrew Sheltering and Immigrant Aid Society, Mr Joseph C. Hyman of the American Jewish Joint Distribution Committee, Dr Henry Moskowitz, Mrs Cheryl Wise of the Women's Division for the American Jewish Congress, Judge Nathan D. Perlman, then Congressman, for the American Jewish Congress, and Cecilia Razovsky for the National Council of Jewish Women. Miss Razovsky was elected Secretary and later Executive Director of this special subcommittee. In consultation, both in person and by correspondence, with Dr Bernhard Kahn, then the JDC European representative, arrangements were made for an attempt to remove 250 children from German Jewish homes and bring them to the United States. At the same time negotiations commenced with the Department of Labor in Washington and many conferences were held with Colonel Daniel MacCormack, Commissioner of Immigration, and Labor Secretary, Miss Frances Perkins.

The subcommittee[15] appealed first to Francis Perkins with the plan for 250 Jewish children from Germany.[16] In fact, this followed earlier informal discussions with the State and Labor Secretaries and with the Commissioner General, Col. Daniel MacCormack. Jewish leaders believed that children-at-risk would arouse less antagonism, perhaps even some sympathy. Since they would not compete with other Americans for jobs, children might gain admission more readily.

Moreover, the Secretary of Labor, who had the legal authority to accept bonds for unaccompanied children without invoking the public charge clause, was 'sympathetic to the idea'.[17]

The executive board of the American Jewish Committee discussed the plan at its meeting on 1 September 1933 and the Joint Council on German Jewish Persecutions, consisting of representatives of the American Jewish Committee, the American Jewish Congress and B'nai B'rith, appointed a subcommittee to deal specifically with German Jewish children. At its 26 October 1933 meeting, the Council decided to inquire about the possibilities, both in government and among Jewish families in the United States and Germany. Noting the antisemitic climate in the United States, the consensus was to pursue the matter with discretion.[18] The discussions dragged on; it was only a year later that a substantive plan began to take shape.[19]

After careful investigations in Germany, the leaders of American Jewry and American social workers formulated a plan for formal presentation to the Secretary of Labor for her approval.[20] Meanwhile, 250 children, whose parents wished for them to be sent to the United States, were selected in Germany and approved by the GJCA. It was decided that none of the children should be from orphanages, asylums or other charitable or public institutions, for fear of their being classified paupers and refused admittance.[21] The plan was to place the children in suitable private homes where they could be schooled and taken care of. The children would all be aged under 16 and unaccompanied, thus giving the Labor Secretary the authority to grant permission in advance of their embarkation abroad, pursuant to Section 3 of the Immigration Act of 1917. Bonds against their becoming public charges were tendered to the Secretary for approval, pursuant to Section 21 of the same Act.[22] This provision had nothing to do with the advance posting of bonds for adults since the Secretary of Labor had a statutory right to accept such security only for unaccompanied children.[23] The plan also assured the Secretary of Labor that in compliance with the law (Section 136(k)) individual Americans would provide passage money for the children.

The Secretary's sympathetic attitude resulted in a conference with Col. Daniel MacCormack, Commissioner of the Immigration and Naturalization Service (INS) of the Department of Labor, where both Professor Chamberlain and Miss Razovsky stressed that the plan was unanimously accepted by all the relevant Jewish agencies, and that professionally trained childcare workers would follow up the children's education and behavior at all times, to ensure they did not become public charges. The Commissioner stated that this was a 'sensible reasonable plan', and that it would make for a good deal of friendly opinion as a gesture of goodwill from the American people. The meeting, no doubt, aired a positive response and gave the green light for a rapid implementation of the plan.[24]

It was agreed by MacCormack and Mr Simmons of the State Department, also present at the meeting, that the Department of Labor would be advised as soon as the corporation had been organized and named. It was also agreed that a list of names and addresses of German children would be furnished to the Department of Labor as soon as such was secured. Once the Department of Labor accepted the bonds and understood that the children were otherwise admissible and, subject to finding that the new organization had been established, the State Department would be advised and subsequently communicate with the consuls in Germany.[25] The Committee on German-Jewish Policy and the Committee on Aid to German Jewish Children then met to agree that the new organization would be named 'German-Jewish Children's Aid, Inc.', (GJCA).[26] The first requirement was thus completed.

Razovsky, Executive Director and Dr Solomon Lowenstein, GJCA Chairman, sent urgent letters to all branches of the NCJW, to B'nai B'rith and other Jewish organizations asking them to canvass their communities for possible homes for the children and to try raising a subscription fee of $100 transportation per child.[27] Chairman Lowenstein wrote to Mrs Brin, National President of the NCJW, notifying her of the new organization and asking her to contact the various local branches of her national body with request for cooperation in forming an Advisory Committee in each important city.[28] Each letter included a reminder to keep the project secret, '... *without any form of publicity in the newspapers or any other public method of advertising*' [in original].[29] The organizations' response was overwhelming. The gravity of the situation was evident and Jewish women all around the country were eager to take part in the rescue project.[30]

Although MacCormack's first reactions were positive and the final points were cleared in principle in July 1934, he reversed himself on one of the key points of his informal agreement with the Jewish leadership. When Cecilia Razovsky, Executive Director of the GJCA, came to meet him in Washington to work out details, she was told the Commissioner was too busy to see her and had instead sent his deputy, I. F. Wixon, who had been against the plan from the start. Much to

Razovsky's dismay, MacCormack proposed a temporary visitor status for the children instead of the permanent immigration visa previously agreed upon.[31] Max Kohler of the American Jewish Committee was furious: 'I consider McCormack's modification absolutely unsuitable, a grave violation of our understanding with him and likely to do more harm than good.'[32] Professor Chamberlain stated openly that it was 'quite contrary to the original attitude of the Department of Labor', and advised calling on them again to re-consider.[33]

The Board of Directors of the GJCA raised the following objections to the Commissioner's new attitude:

- All arrangements had already been made with the German agencies, with the parents in Germany and with all the relevant social agencies in the United States on the basis of the former decision to grant the children permanent status.
- Alternative arrangements would have to be made. It would create a great deal of resentment and, ultimately, cause more damage than the admission of 250 children on permanent visas.
- Children had been waiting in Germany for several months and any indefinite delay would prevent the parents from making alternative rescue plans.
- Refusal on the part of Germany to renew the children's German passports after they left the country on temporary visas would prevent their future return to Germany and render them stateless.
- American foster-families had been promised that the children would return to Germany once they had completed their education. Under the new plan, such families would be obliged to support the children indefinitely and might cause them to change their mind.
- Under the new plan the GJCA would have to ask agencies in Germany to select an entirely different group of 250 children; this would cause confusion and disappointment among the German families.
- The original plan had been accepted by American Jewish agencies. The new plan would cause further delays, require further meetings with the various representatives and would disrupt the coordination and centralization which had been so carefully achieved.
- A great deal of money has been gathered from individuals on the basis of the original plan. Under the new plan renewed communications would be required, asking them to re-subscribe – or to return their funds.[34]

Nonetheless, the GJCA together with the German Jewish organization in Germany continued with the necessary preparations, choosing the children, raising funds and completing the arrangements abroad and in the United States to assure the children's swiftest departure as soon as confirmation for the plan arrived. The Department of Labor's change of policy also created confusion in the State Department, notwithstanding the fact that officials there had been unenthusiastic about the plan from the start. Now they were aggravated because MacCormack had not consulted them, which they considered another attempt to bypass their department.

Legally the children could not be classified as visitors nor even students since they hoped to stay a few years in the United States. Visa Division officials feared that in such a case the responsibility would be shifted to the consuls abroad, who would have to confirm the children's statements about a brief stay, knowing them to be untrue.[35] Moreover, it should be stressed that beyond the Department of State's legal objections, there were also fears of 'possible future criticism of this action on the part of patriotic and restrictions groups should knowledge of the matter come to their attention'. The Department of State, therefore, made sure to act only as a transmitter of information from the Department of Labor to the consuls in Germany.[36] In other words, responsibility should fall entirely on the Department of Labor. If the matter were handled in this way, Simmons concluded, there would 'be very little justified criticism on the Department of State'.[37]

A 16 August meeting of the Secretary of Labor, the Commissioner, Judge Mack, Professor Chamberlain and Dr Moskowitz cleared the air. The Commissioner was convinced by Judge Mack's argument that it was necessary to issue the children with permanent visas because, although the organization expected to educate them in the US, there was no assurance that they would ever be able to return to Germany. It was agreed that Professor Chamberlain should draft a letter to Col. MacCormack asking for permanent visas and the latter would proceed to take the matter up with the State Department.[38] While there was nothing in writing, the impression was, according to Razovsky, 'that the children [would] get permanent visas'. MacCormack agreed to alter the requirement from placing bonds in advance to requesting them only upon arrival, if necessary. It was understood that the Department of Labor would recommend granting permanent visas to the children.[39]

That assumption proved right. After revisions compatible with the

State Department's terms, the final form was presented to Chamberlain in August 1934.[40] Its main paragraphs included a confirmation of the children's permanent immigrant status, a written guarantee by GJCA to place the children in proper homes, undertaking that they would not become public charges and would attend school until at least the age of 16. The organization was also responsible for the administrative arrangements in the US and undertook that the children's travel expenses from Germany to the United States would be defrayed from a fund formed by subscriptions from individuals and distributed by a person acting as their agent.[41] It was also agreed that all individual applicants qualifying under the immigration law for admission to the United States according to the examining consular officer, with due consideration to the information and findings received by him from the Department of Labor, would be issued an immigrant visa.[42]

On 4 September 1934, the Commissioner formally notified Professor Chamberlain that all the cases presented had been approved and that the State Department had been informed 'in accordance with the agreement between the two Departments'. MacCormack also requested to be informed in advance as to the name of the vessel, date of arrival and the port at which the children would arrive.[43] This was important in order to avoid taking them first to Ellis Island. These children were to be handed on to GJCA without further examination.[44]

GJCA pledged that:

> GJCA Inc., herewith submits a written agreement undertaking as its moral obligation, its responsibility for placing each child in a private home which has been carefully investigated and found satisfactory, that the children thus placed would not be permitted to become public charges and that each child will attend school until it is at least 16 years of age.[45]

There was no written agreement outlining the form in which the agency was expected to discharge its responsibility, but the Board minutes contain sufficient documentary evidence of discussions with government officials laying down the three fundamental principles:

1. That the children would be distributed over as wide a geographic area as feasible.
2. That a system of cooperation would be worked out between the national office of GJCA, Inc. and recognized local welfare services.
3. That the local agencies would be permitted to use funds donated by individuals for the specific purpose of maintaining a GJCA child wherever necessary.

Relevant government agencies had been kept informed of the agency's operations and repeatedly approved the manner in which it was discharging its responsibility.[46] Among other Jewish and non-Jewish refugee organizations, the GJCA was the first Jewish refugee organization in the United States created exclusively for the purpose of transferring Jewish refugee children from Germany to the United States and caring for them after arrival.[47]

GJCA's administrative structure consisted of a board of directors – no less than seven and no more than thirteen permanent members at any time – with an elected chair assisted by three supporting officers.[48] The national office had several distinct functions, which represented the professional activity of its staff. The first was acceptance of applications for individual children filed by the organization in Germany. These applications needed critical study, analysis, translation and interpretation. The second involved making individual placement plans for children by using opportunities offered by local social agencies throughout the United States. It was only after an individual plan for an individual child was made that the necessary affidavits were sent abroad. The third function consisted of placing the children in temporary homes on their arrival in New York, before transporting them to their final destination in the United States. The fourth function consisted of maintaining statistical records and regular reports on the children from the local agencies under whose auspices the children were placed. Finally, there was a consultation service on request, provided by local agencies, either by correspondence or through field visits.

Three committees were active in the national office: the finance committee which was responsible both for handling the internal budget and for allocations to regional offices, the placement committee and field services.[49] The placement committee, responsible for finding homes for the children, was originally directed by child expert, Mary Boretz, and Lotte Marcuse, a social work expert.[50]

Follow-up placement was carried out by the field services division. Apart from maintaining a comprehensive picture of the participating local agencies, the division workers also became acquainted with the local caseworkers responsible for the children's supervision. Together, the welfare professionals evaluated and analyzed individual problems of adjustment in foster-homes. In addition to visits to the local agencies, conferences were held in the New York office on request of these agencies, or participating organizations. Prior to the development of field services the director of placement was responsible for these tasks. Since actual care for the children was supervised by local agencies, GJCA went to great lengths to ensure that these bureaux followed the federal requirements for childcare such as recognition by the department of social welfare that the agency be part of a recognized Jewish federation unit with a budget sufficiently flexible to allow subsidized placement when free placement failed.[51]

The agreement between the national office and the cooperating agencies included the understanding that the staff of the national office would provide local agency staff with consultation services and make up-to-date information available to them on development of the project and on matters concerning legislation affecting the foreign children. Professionals from the national office would pay periodic visits to the local agency. In addition there was frequent contact between Board members and the national office and professional staffs of affiliated national agencies, who met with local community leaders and professionals.

Field services are summarized as follows:

a. Adequate information service to local agencies on the general and specific aspects of the program;
b. Consultation service for local agencies on the general or specific problems of children within the project;
c. Evaluation of the local agency's general function, its administrative set-up and its community interrelationship with a view to determine how best it can serve on the project;
d. Evaluation of the individual adjustment problems of children and agency's professional approach and treatment;
e. Evaluation of foster homes and their development through the local agency with the view to possible increased participation of the agency;
f. Acquaintance with and evaluation of the staff bearing the specific case load.

The methods consisted of current correspondence and news service to the cooperation agencies, field visits by GJCA staff to local agencies and conferences in the New York office with local agency representatives.[52]

The first group of ten children arrived in New York from Cherbourg on Friday, 9 November 1934, accompanied by Dr Gabrielle Kaufman, a Jewish professor of philosophy and subsequent director of the Clara de Hirsh Home in New York.[53] The first groups consisted of boys from wealthy Berlin families, who were to be sent to foster-families in and around New York City. But this was not the last bridge to be crossed. Although everyone involved tried to work discreetly, news of the children's arrival became public and soon the American Coalition of Patriotic, Civil and Fraternal Societies was attacking the Department of Labor for its cooperation in the 'systematic importation of indigent alien children'.[54] Its spokesman, Captain John B. Trevor, called for a congressional investigation to examine a possible violation of the immigration laws. The State Department was bombarded with phone calls complaining that 'international sentimentality runs riot and governs ... the immigration laws of the United States'.[55] Trevor even spread rumors that the children came from Communist families.[56]

Another unexpected difficulty arose when it proved impossible to find enough homes. Evidently no one had contemplated the possibility that finding 250 Jewish homes in the United States would constitute a problem. When it was found that there was difficulty in securing a sufficient number of free homes, it was agreed that subsidized private homes would be utilized for placing the children. As a result, from November 1934 to the end of April 1935 only about 100 children were admitted, and even for them the German-Jewish Children's Aid had to provide every family with $500 annually for each child they housed.[57] Although GJCA was a welfare organization recognized by government it received no official grant aid and suffered, throughout its existence, from lack of funds.[58] By 1938 over $60,000 were required annually to cover expenses.[59] Money was received for the payment of administrative expenses and for the care of children in private homes from many private individuals and from various welfare organizations, such as the NCC, NCJW and the JDC, and by initiating special drives, garden parties, lectures and benefits. However, it was the constant lack of resources during the whole period and the insufficient number of Jewish families willing to take in the children that crippled the plan in the first years of operation. In June 1935 the GJCA asked the *Reichsvereinigung der Juden in Deutschland* (Reich Association of Jews in Germany) to temporarily suspend sending children.[60] Reporting the GJCA activities for 1935, Razovsky stated, 'It is definitely decided now not to accept any more children from Germany.' She expressed heartache and shock at her inability to go on with the work, receiving letters from so many desperate German parents begging for help, and, on the other hand, letters from children already in the United States full of happiness and joy, describing their experiences in their new homes.[61]

Razovsky and 'her women'[62] doubled and tripled their efforts. Women in all local branches were asked to screen for suitable homes. Arrangements were made with the German-Jewish social agencies abroad, according to which children selected for placement in the United States were examined and questionnaires completed and returned to the US. In the meantime, German-Jewish Children's Aid attempted – via cooperation with local communities – to secure free homes, the actual selection of the homes to be endorsed by local childcare agencies and periodic supervision. At first it was felt that the children should be placed only north of the Mason-Dixon Line and east of the Mississippi. It was thought that there would be many more free homes available than there were children to fill them.

To assure the government that the children would not become public charges, a special guarantee fund was established and an arrangement made with the corporations or foundations that advanced these funds to have this money on deposit as long as it was required by the government. It was understood that if any of the children were likely to become public charges the GJCA would be responsible for the cost of their return to their native land. Transportation costs were met by contributions from individuals. Since the Immigration Act prohibited payment for transportation by organizations, the money collected was transferred to an agent, Stephen Koshland, who volunteered his services.[63]

Following the agreement with the Labor and State Departments, Razovsky tirelessly undertook the task of building up an apparatus that would successfully accomplish the project. It required work on both sides of the Atlantic. In Germany, this involved the participation of existing Jewish welfare agencies such as the Central Office – *Hilfsverein der Juden in Deutschland*, the *Kinderauswanderungs Abteilung* of the *Reichsvertretung der Juden in Deutschland* (the Children's Emigration Department of the National Representation of the Jews in Germany), under Dr Kaethe Rosenheim, in Berlin, Stuttgart, Hamburg and Frankfurt.[64] After 1938, the *Juedische Kultusgemeinde* (the Jewish Cultural Community) in Vienna were also involved.[65] They had to select children who answered the requirements, complete questionnaires giving full histories of the children, including medical histories, and they had to receive the parents' permission to take the children out of Germany and to ensure the children would adjust to American ways. It should be stressed that knowledge of English was not mandatory since most of the children did not speak the language, so workers had to communicate in

German or Yiddish until the children managed to – slowly – pick up English. If possible, it was preferable to choose German- or Yiddish-speaking families. Naturally, not all the foster-families spoke German, a fact that often presented another obstacle to overcoming the children's feelings of loneliness and loss. Not only did they miss their families, they also had to cope with the mockery of their school mates for their strange manners and behavior.[66]

Ostensibly, it looked an easy enough, though time-consuming task; but it was not so. In 1934 few German-Jewish parents were ready to part from their young children. In the early days of Hitler, when the plan was first broached, *Frauenverein*, the German equivalent of the American Council of Jewish Women in the United States, actually opposed the idea because they thought it was outrageous to separate children from their parents.[67] German Jews either hoped that the situation would improve, or made plans to leave together. It was only after 1935, with the imposition of the Nuremberg Laws, that more parents showed interest in the project.[68] But by then it had become harder to obtain proper documentation. It was difficult to obtain or to renew passports for the children and, when the complicated bureaucracy was completed, the visas proved to be outdated and it was necessary to start the process all over again.

After completing the necessary bureaucratic arrangements in Germany, the German organization cabled the GJCA with names of children sent, the name of the ship and the date of its departure. On arrival at the port of entry, the children were met by women volunteers and transferred as soon as possible to the city of permanent residence; the local community accepted the child and the community assumed financial responsibility where homes had been prepared. It was found advisable, after administrative procedures were set up, to take on a supervisor of national placements to deal with the local welfare agencies, childcare agencies or Councils of Jewish Women, to insure continuity of service and to be certain that suitable homes were found and supervised. Miss Lotte Marcuse was engaged, part-time, for this work. At the reception centers, volunteers worked with the children, along with GJCA members and special staff.[69]

Methods for financing the cost of maintaining children varied from one locality to another. At first it was agreed that whenever a local community accepted a child, that community would assume responsibility for its care. Once the first transport of children had arrived and been placed all around the country, some local sections of the NCJW assumed responsibility for financing the cost of maintaining children located in their community. In each instance this was to be regarded as an independent local project, unless other special arrangements were made.

In her capacity as Executive Director, Miss Razovsky controlled all activities in the United States and abroad. Professional workers, recruited and trained by her, were put in charge of the various departments. Miss Lotte Marcuse, who started as a part-time consultant in the Department of Placement, was soon promoted to head the department and, because of her fluent German, to liaise between the agencies in Germany and the New York headquarters.

Cooperation between the GJCA in New York and the *Hilfsverein der Juden in Deutschland* in Berlin did not always operate as smoothly as expected. Many misunderstandings during the first years were due to the language barrier and the discrepancies between the German parents' high expectations – these viewed their children's future in America with Hollywood colors – and the more prosaic realities, which caused frequent complaints from families, as well as aggravation in the New York offices. Razovsky was upset that 'these boys that find our food very disagreeable nevertheless eat with hearty appetites and gain considerable weight'.[70] There was also the question of who bore ultimate responsibility for the children's welfare.[71] The head office in New York, and especially Razovsky, kept asking the German organization to prepare the children and their parents and to explain to them that they might find themselves in homes where they would be required to help and adjust to unfamiliar surroundings.[72] In a report to the Board of Directors, GJCA, in May 1935, Razovsky stated that '[H]ad America not had the reputation that every American is a millionaire we would have escaped many of the worries in placing the children. It is very difficult for Europeans to understand that "Uncle Sam" is no longer the rich uncle and therefore cannot be as generous now as he has been in the past.'[73]

German children from orthodox families presented another problem. There were difficulties finding strictly orthodox American Jewish homes or homes where religion was practiced as the children had been used to in Germany. For example, a few children who arrived on a Saturday refused to continue to their destination by violating the Sabbath. Rosenheim asked that these children's feelings be considered and that everything possible should be done to leave them in New York until they could move on.[74] On the other hand, Razovsky explained that conditions sometimes prevented leaving the children in New York, and necessity dictated sending them immediately to their homes outside the city. She asked the German organization to explain to the parents and to the children before they left that circumstances sometimes dictated traveling on the Sabbath.[75] It should be stressed that religious Jewish families were eager to accept refugee children, but objective conditions were against it. By American law, children could only be placed in foster homes of their own religion, and those homes had to be able to offer a certain minimum standard that included a separate bed for each child and no more than two children in a room. The 1930s were the years of the Great Depression, when the average American family was under great financial strain. Orthodox Jewish families, though often attuned to the need for benevolent activities such as fostering, usually had a smaller income than the average Jewish family. They often had large families, lived in crowded quarters and thus were not eligible for the foster-family scheme. Thus, although they could offer a warm family atmosphere, they were unable to provide a refugee child the minimum conditions required by the government.[76] Razovsky was aware of the problem and discussed it with Rabbis Jung, de Sola Pool and Drachman. She also called for a meeting of orthodox rabbis of the American Jewish community and sent letters to all the orthodox rabbis in the eastern region, asking them to locate suitable foster homes.[77] An emotional plea was addressed to Rabbi Joseph H. Lookstein in New York on 28 February 1935, asking him to find homes for fifteen orthodox children who were already in the United States 'and for whom we find it almost impossible to secure free homes which will be comparable to the homes from which the children have come both as to background and orthodox tradition'.[78]

Thus, during the first two years of operation, the German-Jewish Children's Aid organization found itself facing opposition on several fronts: Jewish social workers in Germany were still not attuned to the large-scale project of selecting the children and the management of the many requirements. In addition, the program that would separate children from their families attracted protests from several German Jewish bodies. In the United States, the resources needed for the maintenance of each child ($500) were difficult to collect. And to cap it all, even with the meager number of children signed up for the project, there were not enough free foster-families to take the children in. Among various reasons for the lack of foster-homes, the fact that no large-scale public appeals were being made for fear of giving the project too much publicity, which might cause an increase in the existing antisemitism in the United States, no doubt further hindered the project.[79] However, with good will on both sides, by 1941 these misunderstandings were eventually resolved and cooperation went on amicably, solving together grave problems, and in the process developing close and friendly relationships.[80]

The bureaucratic process was complicated and called for creative thinking. Children from Germany were usually selected through the Berlin office that took care of thorough preliminary physical examinations, and prepared a personal file for each child, which included a detailed history, photographs, evaluation by social workers and the family's social status. All this information was transferred to the New York headquarters for final confirmation and to make travel arrangements. The bureaucratic process in the United States involved the Departments of Labor and State, provision of affidavits, location of any existing relatives, finding proper foster parents and arrangements in the port of arrival, which included sending women to welcome the children and to take care of their transfer to the various cities where they were supposed to be met by foster-families or social workers. Dr Rosenheim, who worked tirelessly in Berlin, often sent requests concerning specific children to Razovsky, for example a request for a foster home for Margot Joseph in New York City, where she had friends, rather than to send her to relatives in Brooklyn.[81]

The program proceeded in an orderly fashion until early in 1937 when Dr Lowenstein gave up his chairmanship and Mrs Maurice L. Goldman, former National President of NCJW, was elected chairman.[82] Up till then, Miss Mary Boretz and Miss Lotte Marcuse acted as consultants, but, as the work increased, it became advisable to have Miss Lotte Marcuse accept full-time responsibility at headquarters to supervise the child placement agency.[83] Marcuse dedicated all her efforts to finding suitable homes for the children. In 1938 Chamberlain praised '[H]er knowledge of Germany, her knowledge of the child placement work, her capacity for understanding the psychology of children and for knowing what kind of a child belongs to what kind of home.'[84]

Miss Razovsky continued to take responsibility for the pre- and post-immigration work for the children. Selecting the children and collating their documents, as well as dealing with the American consuls with regard to visas and making all travel arrangements, came under the auspices of the German Jewish organization. But it was Razovsky whose knowledge and confirmation were necessary in order to complete the project in Germany. By the close of the 1937 fiscal year, 250 children had been brought in and a request was made to the government to agree to the admission of a further 120, at the rate of ten children per month, for the fiscal year 1937/8.[85] By 1 March 1938, GJCA had 351 children under its auspices and its directors contemplated terminating the program.[86]

By now the procedure was moving along more smoothly and this was a noticeable improvement, in contrast to the early years of the project. It became easier to make plans because the German agency had gained a deeper understanding and was therefore able to submit more accurate documents. The children's histories contained more pertinent data and gave a better evaluation of their individual personalities, so that the local agencies in the United States found it easier and quicker to interest prospective foster families. Moreover, there was a growing awareness in the US as to the situation in Germany and therefore a growing tendency by American Jewish families to accept refugee children. Experience accumulated with regard to receiving the children and was felt especially in the ports of arrival. The children's painful experiences in Germany had made them suspicious of anyone in uniform, and on arrival they had often been upset by confusion at the pier head, long hours of waiting, the customs inspection, and dispatch of luggage, all of which were now rendered unnecessary. Further, whereas in the first years the children had travelled without an official escort, usually under the supervision of adult immigrants who agreed to care for them during the sea voyage, it was now decided to engage experienced professional workers.

These escorts, who made the trip repeatedly, were able to comfort the scared and homesick children, telling them stories 'about the new country ... and even describe the persons who would greet them on their arrival'.[87] After the first three years, during which the children were sent directly to foster-parents, most groups of refugee children arriving in the United States were now allowed to go through a few days of reception care. This process followed recommendations from social workers and aimed to enable the children to recover from their ordeal before having to meet their foster-families and acclimatize to life in America. It also enabled psychologists and social workers to observe the children in a friendly and stress-free environment and look for special problems. Throughout this reception period, the children underwent medical examinations and had time to relax and orient themselves. They were temporarily placed in and around New York City in institutions such as the Clara de Hirsch Home,[88] the Gould Foundation, the Seaman's Church Institute, the Academy, the

Hebrew Orphans Asylum and the Pleasantville College School. This was particularly helpful for groups arriving after the outbreak of war and whose members were much more traumatized than those from the early 1930s. Many efforts were made during the transit stay in New York to relieve the children's stress so as to enable them to proceed to their final destination with the greatest ease possible. They were encouraged to ask questions and to express their anxieties. It was imperative for the Jewish women in charge to reassure the children and to make them feel welcome.

Most of the children in the United States were ultimately placed in large cities, with approximately 27 per cent in the greater New York area.[89] Once the children were settled, the local childcare agencies became responsible for them, together with their foster-parents. Each child maintained contact with a social worker until his or her discharge at the age of 21. Contact was usually on a monthly basis. GJCA main office in New York maintained constant connection with the social workers in each community. The latter had to send in regular reports on each child and to point out specific problems concerning the child's adjustment at home and at school.[90] GJCA's growth necessitated the expansion of its placement department to include a total of seven supervisors who maintained contact with accredited local agencies throughout the United States.[91]

As the children's files demonstrate, Razovsky's concern for them went far beyond the call of duty. She extended personal attention to each child, attending to its medical and behavioral problems as well as to minor issues. A case in point is that of a 16-year-old boy who developed schizophrenia two years after his arrival. Razovsky not only had him hospitalized immediately in a New York sanitarium, but also made frequent visits to provide support during his darker moments. Or the case of an 11-year-old boy who missed his mother desperately, 'literally driving [his foster-family] crazy with his weeping and wailing to be sent home to his "mommy"'.[92] Razovsky visited the boy, brought him to New York where she could keep a close watch on him and found a therapist for him, who reported to her personally.

Another case concerned a 14-year-old girl who, according to Razovsky, was 'very mature and well developed and was adolescing ... violently ... her wild temper' such that Razovsky felt she must be 'closely watched'. Another 13-year-old girl insisted on using make-up, smoked, wanted to go out with boys and was 'very disobedient and willful'. Razovsky's reports indicate that she was well informed and took special care with every child, trying to find the proper solutions.[93] She made field trips, met with the children and local social workers handling the children, searched for foster-homes and encouraged local women to volunteer and raise money for the project.[94] She was constantly seeking future events for the children, debating possibilities of summer camps, locating sources for camp scholarships for children whose foster-parents could not afford them, organizing English tuition with the help of local Boards of Education and planning special programs for vocational training, especially for youngsters who were reaching working age.[95] In all these she was helped by Jewish volunteer women who contributed their work and experience to that of professional workers all around the country, who answered directly to Razovsky.[96]

There were also cases of children who had trouble at school; some were lonely and had difficulty integrating into their new surroundings. As Michael Werner confessed, sixty years after his arrival in the United States, 'I belonged nowhere'.[97] Due to their interrupted education and language difficulties, some of the children were initially put back several grades or placed in a combined class for foreigners of all ages. Within a short period, however, most of the Jewish children entered their regular grades.

Notwithstanding the existence of certain problems, most of the children adjusted well and were happy with their foster-families; many of them were even awarded prizes for exceptional scholarship. Glowing reports were received about the first group of children who had arrived in the winter of 1934. A letter from one family stated: 'If your placements are as successful as the one with us, you will be doing really great work. We are already very fond of the boy and he is helping to bring us great happiness. Your selection shows good judgment.'[98] Another letter from foster-parents in Philadelphia explained that 'their girl' was being tutored in English, taking piano lessons and was attending Sunday and Hebrew School and in general was doing 'very nicely'.[99] On the whole, most children wrote to their parents joyfully and happily about their experiences in the United States, which delighted their parents and made the German Jewish organizations satisfied. [100] In 1941, Razovsky reported to the GJCA Board of Directors:

> They live a happy, normal life in 103 American communities. Several of the children have reached the age of 21 and are naturalized American citizens. Many of them are already self-supporting and a few others are contributing toward their own

support. Nine have married and 105 are reunited with their own parents.[101]

While the program concentrated on refugee children from Germany, the *Anschluss* – the incorporation of Austria into the Reich – on 18 March 1938 and the Nazi persecution of Austrian Jews, raised the question of the fate of Austrian Jewish children.[102] Beginning in April 1938, an avalanche of letters from panic-stricken Jewish parents in Austria arrived at the New York office of GJCA, pleading to take Jewish children into the United States.[103] Apart from the problems involved in finding enough foster-homes, the issue was complicated by various professional difficulties. As there were not enough trained social workers in Vienna, GJCA considered establishing a suitable network to organize the program from the European end in Vienna or using the already existing one in Berlin, even though the Berlin center expressed its concern that additional children from Austria might be 'deducted from Berlin'.[104] Moreover, the occupation of the Sudetenland brought more pleas from parents in Czechoslovakia, and the GJCA was thus faced with a growing refugee problem, with the need to find more foster-homes, and what proved to be even harder, to recruit more funds. In the words of Dorothy Thompson, 'For settling people successfully in new homes, one needs money, money and again money.'[105] Another obstacle was the fact that since 1938 the quota from Germany and Austria was oversubscribed and refugee children had to wait their turn along with adults. The results were felt immediately. Whereas in September 1938 the Department of Labor had given GJCA permission to bring in twenty children each month, ten to come from Germany and ten from Austria, an annual total of 240,[106] the quota regulation brought the number of children actually arriving during 1938 down to seventy-four.[107] Moreover, since the quota from Germany for 1939 was filled (for the first time), instead of receiving 240 children during 1939 as had been hoped, only about fifty children received their visas.[108] However, it should be emphasized that, although the consuls generally continued to limit the issue of visas, 'they expressed still a very interested attitude toward children below 16'.[109] Rosenheim, experiencing personally the terrible events in Germany, strongly urged GJCA headquarters in New York 'to utilize the possibilities of help in every possible way, since', she argued, 'the principles which govern the limitation of adult immigration do not apply to children'.[110] and, 'To us every single child whom we can help to emigrate presents a very important case and no difficulties ... could possibly prevent us from following up the plan.'[111]

Notwithstanding Rosenheim's observation, the most urgent problem was the need for affidavits. In order to receive a visa, a potential immigrant – including unaccompanied minors – had to secure an affidavit from American relatives that would guarantee that s/he would not become a public charge. However, most applicants could not get such affidavits. Matters became worse in 1939 and, especially after war broke out, when American consuls in Nazi-occupied territories became stricter and tried to reduce the numbers of visas, mainly by imposing more stringent affidavit standards. They refused to accept affidavits from non-relatives unless they had substantial means, and even then in many cases the sponsors in the United States had to place cash deposits for the refugees in American banks.[112] This ruling, together with the fact that Germany refused to allow for transportation to be paid in German currency, meant that even eligible children were unable to leave when their quota numbers eventually came up.[113] Here, too, Razovsky made a difference. She initiated a successful program among American Jewish women to undertake the signing of such affidavits. She appealed to all Jewish women's organizations, urging them 'as women and mothers [who] have special interest in *children of Germany*' (original emphasis) to save them from 'degradation'.[114] Although men, too, participated in this operation,[115] Razovsky emphasized her preference for married women.[116] In cases where people were concerned about their responsibility for the children for whom they were being asked to sign affidavits and refused to do so, Razovsky stepped in and assured them of the GJCA's backing.

In 1939, as part of its role of successor to the NCC, the NRS undertook the administration of GJCA and responsibility for the following departments: Migration, Resettlement, Employment, Special Categories, Relief and Casework, Information and Research, Comptroller and Central Office. Each was administered by a departmental head responsible to the executive director. The Migration Department, headed by Cecilia Razovsky, dealt with affidavits, sponsorship, visas and other legal aspects of the immigration process.[117] Razovsky also communicated with the US government on matters relating to immigration legislation and special cases.[118]

During the war years, agreements with both the NRS and the new United States Committee for the Care of European Children affected the responsibilities and finances of GJCA. A July 1941 cooperative agreement requiring annual renewal stated that children would be brought to the United States on a corporate affidavit of the United States Committee which would be responsible for the children's immigration and transportation. GJCA's responsibility would begin only from the point of disembarkation. Reception care and follow-up costs would be born by the two organizations.[119] In November 1942, to accommodate federal government refugee legislation and coordinate with the US Committee for the Care of European Children, GJCA changed its name to the European-Jewish Children's Aid.[120] During the war, GJCA undertook the care of Jewish children evacuated from Great Britain in the summer of 1940 and of Jewish refugee children from central Europe from 1941 onwards. From its inception in 1934 until the end of 1943 GJCA was responsible for a total of 942 children.[121]

One of the most active agencies supporting the program of the GJCA was the National Council of Jewish Women[122] and its local Sections contributed generously towards financing. Since the foundations which contributed to the GJCA in 1934 stopped doing so in 1937 and 1938, the organization needed to look for other sources and made an offer to the NCJW.[123] In 1938 the Allocations Committee of the NCC invited the NCJW to take over complete responsibility for financing the administrative cost of the national project and for maintaining children placed in the New York area on a paid basis. In addition, the NCJW was invited to provide for the maintenance of all new children who might arrive after 1 January 1938. A resolution adopted at the Triennial Convention of the National Council of Jewish Women, held in Pittsburgh on 25 January 1938 declared that 'the National Council of Jewish Women obligates itself to assume full responsibility for the project now being undertaken by the German-Jewish Children's Aid, Inc'.[124] It was agreed that the NCJW should continue to serve in a fund-raising capacity and in finding homes for children. It was further agreed that the GJCA would continue to be an administrative and policy-making group, functioning with and through the cooperation of child-placement agencies, locating and investigating potential homes and undertaking periodic supervision of the children. From 1 January 1938 until 1 January 1941, the NCJW assumed full responsibility for the financial requirements of the national office of GJCA, including the care of children in paid homes in the New York area.[125] In undertaking financial responsibility for the total budget of the GJCA, the NCJW had set up a special group known as the Children's Aid Committee, functioning under the auspices of Mrs   Samuel R.

Glogower. A quota had been assigned to each local Section of the NCJW which was asked to raise that quota from its own membership, in order not to conflict with other fund-raising activities in the community.

Funds collected by local sections were sent to its national office and then redistributed among sections caring for the refugee children.[126] A grand total of $209,079 was raised during the period that the Council was responsible for this project.[127] The NCJW offered to continue not only the financing but also the administration of the project, but the incorporators of the GJCA voted to turn it over to the National Refugee Service, which was already administering the project.

During the latter part of 1939 doubts arose as to whether the GJCA should continue as an independent agency, because of the activities of the Non-Sectarian Committee for Refugee Children which later merged with the United States Committee for the Care of European Children. Both these organizations indicated a desire to take over and absorb this project. However, it was evident by 1 January 1941 that the GJCA would continue to function. While there might be further discussion with the United States Committee, it was the consensus of opinion of the Executive Committee at a 3 June 1941 meeting that the GJCA should maintain its identity as a corporate body, although it might well turn to other organizations to accept responsibility for financing and for certain phases of administration.[128]

Finally, although when compared with the *Kindertransports* to England that brought about 10,000 Jewish children into the UK,[129] the GJCA's achievements might seem less impressive, it was nevertheless a grand rescue operation, providing over one thousand Jewish children with a safe haven in the United States.

NOTES

1. Harold Fields, Chairman, Committee on Migration, American Jewish Congress, to Mr Meyer Bloomfield, 30 August 1933. German-Jewish Children's Aid (hereafter GJCA) Inc. Collection, Folder 3. Yivo Archives, New York.
2. Mr Bloomfield was a personal friend of Acting Secretary of State Phillips. Harold Fields to Bloomfield 13 September 1933. GJCA Collection, Folder 1. Yivo Archives, New York.
3. Bloomfield immediately sent a request for an interview with the Secretary of State. Bloomfield to Mr Phillips, Department of State, 31 August 1933. GJCA Collection, Folder 3. Yivo Archives, New York.
4. William Carr to Bloomfield, 2 September 1933. Ibid. Bloomfield had no intention of

answering this letter, but was going to wait for Mr Phillips' return to discuss the matter with him.

5. Fannie Hurst, Chairman, American Committee for the Relief of Victimized German Children, to Max Kohler, 11 November 1933. GJCA Collection, Folder 3. Yivo Archives, New York.

6. Members of the Committee: Dr Maurice Karft, Mr Harry Lurie of the Bureau of Jewish Social Research, Mr Joseph C. Hyman, Congressman Nathan Perlman, Mr Max Kohler, and Cecilia Razovsky. Present also were: Mr Paul Baerwald, Dr Bernard Kahn, American Joint Distribution Committee, Mr Eric Warburg, Mr Charles Liebman and Mr Morris Waldman, who were invited to attend the meeting as guests. Minutes of the Meeting of the Committee on Aid to German-Jewish Children, 3 January 1934. GJCA Collection, Folder 3. Yivo Archives, New York.

7. At that stage, the Joint Distribution Committee (hereafter JDC) was not ready to actively participate, though it offered the use of its facilities to the new organization.

8. Dr I.M. Rubinow, Secretary, B'nai B'rith, Cincinnati to Max Kohler, 9 and 10 October 1933. GJCA Collection, Folder 3. Yivo Archives, New York.

9. Razovsky, Executive Director, GJCA to *Zentrale fuer jued, Pflegestellen u. Adoptionvermittlung*, 6 January 1936. GJCA Collection, Folder 64. Yivo Archives, New York.

10. However, at a meeting of the Board of Directors, GJCA, in December 1935, the question of adoption was raised again. Razovsky reported that a few families asked to adopt children at present in Germany. It was agreed that a letter would be written to Dr Kahn to inquire whether there were children in Germany whose parents would be willing to offer them over for legal adoption in the United States. Mr Eric Warburg pointed out the importance of such an inquiry as he felt that the situation had changed greatly since the matter of adoption had been considered two years before. The Board decided to apply to the State Department for permission to bring additional children for adoption. See Minutes, Meeting of the Board of Directors, GJCA, 17 December 1935. GJCA Collection, Folder 22. See also, Razovsky to Rosenheim, 6 January 1936: 'the only way in which we can arrange for adoption will be to find out which of the children who have been sent to the United States, are available for adoption'. GJCA Collection, Folder 64, and Meeting Board of Directors GJCA, 13 February 1936: 'Dr Lowenstein reminded the Committee that with regard to adoption we must stand by the original proposal not to take children with living parents'. Ibid. Folder 10. Yivo Archives, New York. The records indicate that the question of adoption was raised several times from 1937 to 1941, but there seems to be no correspondence regarding actual adoption of children.

11. Dr Kahn was the liaison between the American organizations and leasers and social workers among the Jews of Germany. Max Kohler to Frances Perkins, 6 April 1934. Warburg Papers, File 298/6: American Jewish Committee, 'Aiding German Jewish Children', American Jewish Archives (hereafter AJA), Cincinnati. Dr Kahn proposed to start with 250 children. See Razovsky and Lowenstein, 'Interview with Mrs. Stephen S. Wise', Women's Division, American Jewish Congress, 2 February 1934. GJCA Collection, Folder 3. Yivo Archives, New York.

12. Minutes of Meeting, Committee on Aid to German-Jewish Children, 3 January 1934. GJCA Collection, Folder 3. Yivo Archives, New York.

13. To mention only a few: The American Jewish Committee, the American Jewish Congress, B'nai B'rith, Committee on German-Jewish Immigration Policy, the Committee on Aid to German-Jewish Children and the National Council of Jewish Women (NCJW). See, for example, the pamphlet published by NCJW, 'The National Council of Jewish Women and the German Situation', in which the functions of the organization are detailed. 20 March 1934. GJCA Papers, Folder 21. Yivo Archives, New York.

14. Meeting of representatives of Jewish and non-Jewish organizations to work out a plan for possible coordination of the work of various organizations in the United States in connection with the German refugees. Minutes, Board of Directors. CNN Collection, File 16. Yivo Archives, New York. Present were: James G. McDonald, Professor J. Chamberlain, Representatives of American Christian Committee on Refugees, American Friends Service Committee, American Jewish Committee, B'nai B'rith, Committee on German-Jewish Immigration Policy, American Jewish Congress, American Jewish Distribution Committee, Child Adoption Bureau, Emergency Committee for Musicians, Emergency Committee in

Aid of Displaced Foreign Physicians, Emergency Committee in Aid of Displaced Foreign Scholars, Federal Council of Churches of Christ in America, Hebrew Sheltering and Immigrant Aid Society, Hospites, International Migration Service, Joint Clearing Bureau, International Student Service, Jewish Agricultural Society of America, Musician Emergency Fund, INS, National Council of Jewish Federation and Welfare Funds, National Consul of Jewish Women, OSE – International Health Association, Zionist Organization of America. Professor Chamberlain was Chairman and Cecilia Razovsky acted as Secretary.

15. The original members of the corporate group were Judge Irving Lehman, Judge Joseph M. Proskauer, Dr Solomon Lowenstein, Max J. Kohler, Mrs Blanche B. Goldman, Mr Louis Fabricant, Joseph C. Hyman, Mrs Louise Wise, Maurice J. Karpf, Henry Moskowitz, ex-Congressman Nathan Perlman, Paul Felix Warburg, John Bernstein, Edgar J. Kohler, Isaac L. Asofsky and Miss Razovsky. Dr Solomon Lowenstein was appointed as Chairman and Miss Razovsky as Secretary and Executive Director.

16. Several other organizations were also interested, notably the National Conference of Jewish Social Service and the American Jewish Congress. It was finally decided to amalgamate all the groups into one committee to be known as the German-Jewish Children's Aid. A Meeting of the sub-Committee on Plan to Bring German Jewish Children to the United States, 3 April 1934. GJCA Collection, Folder 4. Yivo Archives, New York.

17. Commissioner MacCormack to Isaac Landman, editor, *The American Hebrew*, 24 August 1933, File 119: Bureau of Immigration.

18. Verbatim Minutes of sub-Committee meeting, 26 October 1933. FWP Collection, Box 303, AJC. See also Simmons to Carr, 21 November 1934. NA 150.623 J/123. National Archive, Suitland, Maryland.

19. Concerning the difficulties in advancing the plan see Max Kohler to Senator Alfred M. Cohn, 22 September 1933. Max Kohler Papers, Box 1, American Jewish Historical Society Archives (hereafter AJHS), New York.

20. 'Aiding German Jewish Children', Max Kohler to Secretary Perkins, 6 April 1934. GJCA Collection, Folder 21, Yivo Archives, New York. See also Warburg Papers, Box 269/8. AJA, Cincinnati.

21. Minutes, Meeting of the Executive Committee of NCC, 22 February 1934. NCC Collection, Folder 1. Yivo Archives, New York.

22. Opinion of the Attorney-General of the United States, 26 December 1933, and the opinion by Charles E. Wyzanski, Jr, Solicitor of the Department of Labor, 3 November 1933, in 'Frances Perkins: Immigration-Public Charge Bonds', NA. See also Secretary of Labor to the Attorney-General, 4 November 1933, NA 150.01/2151 1/4.

23. Sec. 3 of the Immigration Act, 1917, U.S. Code, Title 8, Sec. 13, subs. M., pursuant to Sec. 21 of the same Act.

24. 'Memorandum', Cecilia Razovsky, 12 April 1934. GJCA Collection, Folder 265. Yivo Archives, New York.

25. Ibid., pp. 2–3. See also Razovsky to Dr Solomon Lowenstein, 12 April 1934: 'I want to say that the plan ... was received with much sympathy by all the officials who feel that it is conservative and at the same time constructive, and that it will appeal to many Americans as a fine gesture of friendship.' GJCA Papers, Folder 490, Yivo Archives, New York. G. Messersmith, Consul-General in Berlin, also found the plan acceptable and promised full cooperation with the organization. G. Messersmith to Mr Baerwald 3 May 1934. Ibid. Folder 316.

26. Meeting of the Committee on German-Jewish Immigration Policy and the Committee on Aid to German-Jewish Children, 18 April 1934, p. 4. GJCA Papers, Folder 4, Yivo Archives, New York. See Bylaws of German-Jewish Children's Aid, Inc. Folder 1. Ibid.

27. Razovsky to NCJW Branches, 18 April 1934. GJCA Collection, Folder 3. Yivo Archives, New York.

28. It is interesting that all the bodies he mentioned were organizations with female membership, such as: NCJW, Women's Division of the American Jewish Congress, the local Federation of Philanthropic Societies, Temple Sisterhoods, Women's League of the United Synagogues of America, Women's Division and Union of Orthodox Jewish Congregations of America. See Fannie Brin, National President, NCJW to Presidents of each Section, 'Urgent', 16 March 1934: 'While the need for immediate relief among the Jews in Germany is great, we, as women and mothers have a special interest in the *children of Germany*. [as original] ... It is generally agreed that our organization because of its long

record in immigration and social service work, and its technical equipment for this work, is the logical women's organization to assist in this project.' GJCA Collection, Folder 3. Yivo Archives, New York.

29. Dr Lowenstein to Mrs Brin, 24 April 1934, Folder 21. See also identical letter to Max Kohler, Committee on German-Jewish Immigration Policy, 24 April 1934. GJCA Collection, Folder 3. Yivo Archives, New York.

30. Alfred Cohn, President, B'nai B'rith, to Lodge Secretaries, 18 April 1934. GJCA Collection, Folder 21. Yivo Archives, New York.

31. MacCormack to Dr Lowenstein, Chairman, GJCA, 14 July 1934. Chamberlain Papers, Folder 16: Correspondence; Lowenstein to Chamberlain, 26 July 1934, ibid., Yivo Archives, New York.

32. Max Kohler to Professor Chamberlain (cable), 19 July 1934. Ibid.

33. Chamberlain to Dr Lowenstein, 31 July 1934. GJCA Collection, Folder 265. Yivo Archives, New York.

34. 'Memorandum', Cecilia Razovsky to Dr Henry Moskowitz, 30 July 1934. GJCA Collection, Folder 3. Yivo Archives, New York.

35. Simmons to Carr, 17 July 1934. NA 150.626/94.

36. Simmons, 'Memorandum for File', 23 August 1934. NA 150.626 I/117.

37. Simmons, 'Memorandum', 23 August 1934; Simmons to Phillips, 30 August 1934, NA 150.626 J/101; Under-Secretary Phillips to the Secretary of State, 13 September 1934, NA 150.626 J/97; Secretary of State Hull to Secretary of Labor, 30 November 1934, NA 150.626 J/117.

38. Razovsky to Lowenstein, 17 August 1934. GJCA Collection, Folder 265. Yivo Archives, New York.

39. Razovsky to Dr Kahn, AJC, Paris, 17 August 1934. Ibid., Folder 316.

40. Reference in Simmons to Carr, 8 October 1934. NA 150.626 J/101.

41. In accordance with immigration regulations, no organization in the United States was permitted to contribute towards underwriting these expenses. Mr Paul Felix Warburg therefore opened a special account and Mr Stephen Koshland was appointed agent for the donors to the account, known as the Koshland Fund. Mr Koshland would be responsible for purchasing the steamship tickets for the children. Between 1936 and 1939 Jewish money from Germany was used by the *Reichsvertretung der Juden in Deutschland* to finance the children's emigration, but with the exception of this period, all expenses connected with the transfer of refugee children were paid through the Koshland Fund. It was closed in late 1942. See Solomon Lowenstein to Kohler, 2 May 1934; Kohler to Lowenstein, 3 May 1934. GJCA Collection, Folder 490; Lowenstein to Razovsky, 12 June 1934, ibid., Folder 621; Razovsky to Schweitzer, *Hilfsverein der Deutschen Juden*, 19 October 1934, ibid., Folder 490; Razovsky to Simmons, 7 November 1934, ibid., Folder 631; Chamberlain to Razovsky, 10 November 1934, ibid., Folder 490. Yivo Archives, New York.

42. MacCormack to Chamberlain, 28 August 1934. Chamberlain Papers, Folder 16: Correspondence 1934. Yivo Archives, New York.

43. MacCormack to Chamberlain, 4 September 1934, ibid.

44. Razovsky to L.J. Schweitzer, *Hilfsverein der Deutschen Juden*, 19 October 1934. Folder 490, ibid. It should be noted that immigration officials were 'very helpful' in the reception of children arriving from Germany. See Report of the Executive Director, NCC, 13 November 1934. NCC Papers, p. 1640. Yivo Archives New York.

45. Resolution adopted by the Board of Directors of GJCA, 4 September 1934. GJCA Collection, Folder 15. Yivo Archives, New York.

46. 'Memorandum' by James Houghteling and Katharine F. Lenroot, INS, to the Secretary of Labor, 22 July 1939. GJCA Collection, Folder 16: 'The experience of the GJCA under arrangements worked out with the Department of Labor, has demonstrated the possibility of constructive accomplishment in this field.'

47. Until 1939 GJCA brought over children only from Germany; from 1939 until 1941 children from Austria, Czechoslovakia, and later refugee children in transit countries such as England, Holland and Belgium joined the German children on their journey to the United States. Refugee children from central Europe coming via France, Spain and Portugal were cared for by GJCA from mid 1941. On 15 December 1942 GJCA was renamed European-Jewish Children's Aid (GJCA) until its dissolution in 1952.

48. GJCA Incorporation Amendment, 23 April 1941. GJCA Collection, Folder 2. Yivo Archives, New York.

49. Incorporation Report, 3 April 1934. GJCA Collection, Folder 1. Yivo Archives, New York.

50. Mary Boretz was a member of the executive group of the National Conference of Jewish Social Workers. Lotte Marcuse, a former student of political history, philosophy and economics at the universities of Berlin and Heidelberg, received a diploma in social work from the Prussian Ministry of the Interior in recognition of her services aiding military families. After migrating to the United States in 1921, she gained wide and varied experience in the field of social services for children. She played an active role in GJCA's placement committee almost from its inception. In 1937 she became the official placement director of GJCA; she was recognized as an authority not only on the placement committee but in all activities dealing with the transfer and resettlement of refugee children through GJCA. However, despite her commendable devotion to what she called 'her children', her argumentative and opinionated personality did not endear Marcuse to many of her colleagues. Both Boretz and Marcuse acted in a volunteer capacity up to 1937. See Report, 'The German-Jewish Children's Aid, Inc.', Confidential, 8 March 1935, p. 3. GJCA Collection, Folder 199. Yivo Archives, New York.

51. Bylaws of GJCA Inc., April 1934, GJCA Collection, Folder 1. Yivo Archives, New York.

52. Ibid.

53. Undated letter from the Commissioner to Dr Lowenstein, Chairman of the GJCA, Correspondence 1934. Chamberlain Papers, Folder 16. Yivo Archives, New York.

54. The coalition represented ninety-eight individual organizations and claimed a vast membership. Its anti-immigration propaganda was often tinged with antisemitism.

55. American Coalition of Patriotic, Civil and Fraternal Societies to 'All officers of Societies represented on the Board of the American Coalition, members of their organization, and other individual associates in patriotic endeavor', December 1934. Chamberlain Papers, Folder 16: Correspondence 1934. Yivo Archives, New York.

56. GJCA Board of Directors, Minutes, 14 February 1935. Chamberlain Papers, Folder 249. Yivo Archives, New York.

57. Barbara McDonald Stewart, *United States Government Policy on Refugees from Nazism, 1933–1940* (New York and London: Garland Publishing, 1982), pp. 208–9.

58. The Treasury Department declared on 3 July 1935 that contributions made to GJCA were tax deductible. Leob and Troper to Ittleson, 14 October 1938. GJCA Collection, Folder 114. Yivo Archives, New York.

59. GJCA Board of Directors Meeting, 28 February 1938. Chamberlain Collection, Folder 14. Yivo Archives, New York.

60. See Razovsky's correspondence with *Hilfsverein der Deutschen Juden*, November 1934 to March 1935 (in German). GJCA Collection, Folder 63. Yivo Archives, New York. See, for example, letter to Razovsky, 21 November 1934: '*Wir halten es aber für richtig, in nächster Zeit keine weiteren Anmeldungen mehr anzunehmen, schon um keine vergeblichen Hoffnungen zu erwecken.*' (It is better not to engage new requests now and not to raise full hopes.)

61. Razovsky, 'Report – GJCA', 19 September 1935, GJCA Collection, Folder 10. Yivo Archives, New York.

62. Almost all the thousands of Jewish women across the social spectrum – from homemakers to professionals – who were actively involved in refugee rescue and aid operations, were volunteers.

63. *Hilfsverein der Deutschen Juden*, Berlin, to Razovsky, 27 November 1934 (in German). GJCA Collection, Folder 63. Yivo Archives, New York.

64. The *Hilfsverein* was established by German Jews in 1901 as an independent agency until 1939, when it became a section of the *Reichsvereinigung der Juden in Deutschland*, controlled by the Nazi régime. It operated until 1941. Kaethe (Kate) Rosenheim, the daughter of a famous Berlin surgeon and a trained social worker, was Director of the Children's Emigration Department of the Central Organization of German Jews in Berlin, which sought and coordinated rescue of German Jewish children from 1933 to January 1941, when she left for the States. Rosenheim worked with organizations around the world and is credited with saving thousands of children, including over 600 children who came to the United States through the offices of the GJCA. See Kaethe Rosenheim, 63 (27) Oral History Division, Institute for Contemporary Jewry, Hebrew University, Jerusalem. Also

Gudrun Maierhof, *Selbst-Behauptung im Chaos. Frauen in der Jüdischen Selbsthilfe 1933–1943* (Frankfurt and New York: Campus Verlag , 2001), pp. 204–7.

65. For a detailed report of the Jewish German organization, see Maierhof, *Selbst-Behauptung im Chaos.*

66. Judith Tydor Baumel, *Unfulfilled Promises. Rescue and Settlement of Jewish Refugee Children in the United States* (Juneau, Alaska: The Denali Press, 1990), pp. 105–6.

67. 'Report on Children', 10 January 1938. Chamberlain Collection, Box 4, Folder 95. Yivo Archives, New York.

68. Rosenheim to Marcuse, 8 August 1938, GJCA Collection, Folder 381; Rosenheim to Marcuse, 17 December 1938, ibid. Folder 335. Yivo Archives, New York.

69. Many women volunteers, especially those speaking German or Yiddish, spent many hours with the children. Among the social workers were Sara Egelson of the Hebrew Orphans Asylum, Kate Rosenheim (from 1941) and Dr Ernest Papanek. On the problems faced by social workers, see Report, 21 June 1941; Report on Children Arriving May–October 1943. GJCA Collection, Folder 485. Yivo Archives, New York.

70. Razovsky to *Hilfsverein der Deutschen Juden,* 19 December 1934. GJCA Collection, Folder 63. Yivo Archives, New York. For the parents' complaints, see Razovsky, 'Report 1935', GJCA Collection, Folder 10, pp. 8–9. Razovsky, nevertheless, changed her mind in later years. In a meeting with foster parents she asked them to take into account the children's misery and their worries.

71. Razovsky to Dr Epstein, 7 January 1935. GJCA Collection, Folder 63. Yivo Archives, New York; *Zentralwohlfahrsselle der Deutschen Juden* to Razovsky, 28 June 1935, ibid. Folder 64; Kate Rosenheim to Razovsky, 8 January 1936, ibid.

72. Lotte Marcuse, on behalf of Razovsky, to S. Lifschitz, *Hilfsverein der Deutschen Juden,* Berlin, 3 March 1935. GJCA Collection, Folder 63. Yivo Archives, New York.

73. Razovsky, 'Report – 1935', 15 May 1935. GJCA Collection, Folder 10, p. 10. Yivo Archives, New York.

74. Rosenheim to Razovsky, 3 July 1936. GJCA Collection, Folder 64. Yivo Archives, New York. Judith Tydor Baumel argues that Lotte Marcuse, the person in charge of resettlement in GJCA, had a strong bias against orthodoxy and did not always place children in observant homes, even when they were available. I could not find evidence for this in GJCA sources. See Baumel's 'Introduction', *Don't Wave Goodbye,* Philip K. Jason and Iris Posner (eds) (Westport, CT: Praeger Publishers, 2004), p. 10.

75. Razovsky to Rosenheim, 9 June 1936. GJCA Collection, Folder 64. Yivo Archives, New York; Razovsky, 'Report', 15 May 1935, ibid., Folder 10.

76. Bureau of Jewish Social Research, 'State Laws on Interstate Child Placement', 22 November 1933. GJCA Collection, Folder 169. Yivo Archives, New York. See also, Baumel, 'Introduction', *Don't Wave Goodbye,* Jason and Posner (eds), pp. 1–18.

77. Razovsky, 'Report – 1935'. GJCA Collection, Folder 10, pp. 9–10. Yivo Archives, New York.

78. Solomon Lowenstein to Rabbi Joseph H. Lookstein, 28 February 1935. GJCA Collection, Folder 15. Yivo Archives, New York.

79. Bat-Ami Zucker, *In Search of Refuge: Jews and US Consuls in Nazi Germany 1933–1941* (London and Portland, OR: Vallentine Mitchell, 2001), pp. 170–80.

80. See, for example, correspondence (in German) between Dr Kate Rosenheim in Berlin and Razovsky and Lotte Marcuse, GJCA, New York, February, March 1935. GJCA Collection, Folder 64. Yivo Archives, New York.

81. Rosenheim to Razovsky, 25 March 1935, GJCA Collection, Folder 63. Yivo Archives, New York. It should be stressed that the GJCA preferred to place children with relatives in the United States, if these were willing to accept them. Rosenheim's request was therefore against the usual procedure; Razovsky, nevertheless, took care of it. See Razovsky to Rosenheim, 29 March 1935, ibid.

82 . In 1937, Dr Lowenstein was elected to the Board of the Department of Social Welfare, and was therefore not permitted to serve on the board of any welfare organization under its supervision and had to resign. Mrs Goldman was elected chairman. See Minutes of the Meeting of the GJCA, 15 December 1936; GJCA Collection, Folder 9, p. 1; 'Annual Report – 1938', GJCA, 31 December 1938. GJCA Collection, Folder 10, p. 3. Yivo Archives, New York.

83. See n. 50.

84. 'Report on Children', 10 January 1938. Chamberlain Collection, Box 4, Folder 96. Yivo Archives, New York.

85. During the first half of 1937 the GJCA was granted permission to sponsor an additional five non-Aryan children per month. See Minutes GJCA, 14 May 1937, 20 January 1938. Chamberlain Collection, Folder 14. Yivo Archives, New York.

86. Meeting, Board of Directors GJCA, 1 March 1938. GJCA Collection, Folder 10. Yivo Archives, New York. It should, however, be mentioned that on 7 December 1937 the Board of Directors of the NCC had recommended the continuation of the work of the GJCA. See Goldman, 'Referendum to Members of the Board of Directors', ibid.

87. Maurice L. Goldman, Chairman, GJCA, Cecilia Razovsky and Lotte Marcuse, 'Annual Report – 1938'. GJCA Collection, Folder 10, p. 8. Yivo Archives, New York.

88. The Clara de Hirsch Home for Working Girls in New York on East 63rd Street was the temporary home of a number of the refugee children in 1934 and 1935, waiting for placement with foster-families. Dr Gabrielle Kaufmann was their much beloved house-mother and escort on the first ship in 1934 to bring unaccompanied children to the US under GJCA.

89. Other cities included Chicago, Philadelphia, St. Louis, Los Angeles, Cleveland, Detroit, Baltimore, Boston, Newark, Atlanta, Pittsburgh, Cincinnati and Kansas City. Cities receiving between two and ten children included Albany, Bridgeport, Buffalo, Columbus, Dallas, Hartford, Indianapolis, Louisville, Milwaukee, Minneapolis, New Haven and Washington, DC, Wilmington El Paso, Houston, Manchester, Nashville, Oklahoma City, Providence, San Antonio, Shreveport, Spokane, and Stockton had one refugee child each.

90. Razovsky, 'Report', 16 June 1941. GJCA Papers, Folder 29. Yivo Archives, New York.

91. Razovsky, 'Report', 8 March 1935. GJCA Collection, Folder 10. Yivo Archives, New York.

92. Razovsky, 'Report', 16 June 1941. GJCA Papers, Folder 29. Yivo Archives, New York.

93. Razovsky, 'Report – 1935', GJCA Collection, Folder 10, p. 8. Yivo Archives, New York. It is interesting to note Razovsky's resentful comment when referring to the girl: 'Contrary to the ideas of the German people our American girls of that age who were well brought up do not act this way.' See also, Razovsky, Minutes of the Meeting of the GJCA, 20 November 1936, GJCA Collection, Folder 9, p. 2. Yivo Archives, New York: 'We have kept in New York all the children who presented difficulties and in fact took back from other communities children who were not able to adjust there.'

94. See for example, Razovsky's report, cited in Minutes of a Meeting of the GJCA, 16 April 1936. GJCA Collection, Folder 9, p. 3. Yivo Archives, New York.

95. At a meeting of the Board of Directors, 20 January 1938, Razovsky reported that arrangements had been made with the Employment Division of the Greater New York Coordinating Committees to assign a special worker to meet with the children and make vocational and work plans for them. See Meeting of the Board of Directors GJCA, 20 January 1938, GJCA Collection, Folder 9, p. 3. Yivo Archives, New York.

96. See for example, Minutes of the Meeting of the Board of Directors, GJCA, 19 September 1936; Minutes of Meeting, 4 November 1937, GJCA Collection, Folder 9. Yivo Archives, New York.

97. Cited in Susan Levine, 'Beyond Hitler's Reach', *The Washington Post*, 5 January 2003, p. W12.

98. See for example, Marcuse to Razovsky asking for her approval before distribution, 'Procedures of GJCA' – including a proposed change in the procedure of placing children by Razovsky. 11 July 1939. GJCA Collection, Folder 16. Yivo Archives, New York.

99. Cited in 'Meeting', Board of Directors of the GJCS, 13 December 1934, pp. 1–2. GJCA Collection, Folder 9. Yivo Archives, New York.

100. See, for example, Minutes of the Meeting of the Board of Directors, GJCA, 19 September 1936, ibid., pp. 3–4.; Razovsky to Mr Henry Siegbert, the Hofheimer Foundation, 22 October 1936. Yivo Archives, New York.

101. Razovsky, 'Report', 16 June 1941. GJCA Papers, Folder 29. Yivo Archives, New York. See, also J. C. Hyman to Arthur D. Greenleigh, National Refugee Service, Inc., 16 July 1941, ibid. See also, Rosenheim's enthusiastic report of her visit, while on vacation in the US, to the different locations where the children were placed, cited in Minutes of the Meeting of the GJCA, 20 November 1936. GJCA Collection, Folder 9, pp. 1–2. Yivo Archives, New York.

102. Sources for the number of Jews in Austria cite different figures. Bauer lists the Jewish population of Austria as 185, 246 at the time of the *Anschluss*. See Yehuda Bauer, *My*

Brother's Keeper; a History of the American Jewish Joint Distribution Committee 1929-1939 (Philadelphia: Wayne State University Press, 1981), p. 223. All sources agree that the majority lived in Vienna. About 30,000 were schoolchildren under the age of 12. See Baumel, *Unfulfilled Promises*, p. 19.

103. After the German annexation of Austria, the situation in Vienna worsened. The American consul there reported that, between March and July 1939, more that 40,000 Jews filled out waiting-list questionnaires. See Consul-General John C. Wiley to Secretary of State, 14 July 1938, NA 150.626 J/444. It should also be mentioned that the United States combined the German and Austrian quotas, bringing them to a total of 27,370, thus enabling the GJCA to include Austrian refugee children in its program. About the situation in Vienna, see the unpublished doctoral thesis by Melissa Jane Taylor, "'Experts in Misery'?: American Consuls in Austria, Jewish Refugees and Restrictionist Immigration Policy, 1938–1941', University of South Carolina, 2006.

104. Kate Rosenheim to Razovsky, 8 August 1938. GJCA Collection, Folder 331. Yivo Archives, New York.

105. Dorothy Thompson, *Refugees: Anarchy or Organization* (New York: Random House, 1938), pp. 90–1.

106. For formal requests by GJCA, see Solomon Lowenstein, Chairman, GJCA to Col. MacCormack, 29 September 1938; Mrs Maurice L. Goldman, (new) Chairman, GJCA to James L. Houghteling, Commissioner, Immigration and Naturalization Service, Department of Labor, 6 December 1936 (a copy also to Col. MacCormack on the same date), and the Commissioner's reply, see Edward J. Shaughnessy, Deputy Commissioner, to Razovsky, Executive Director, GJCA, 9 December 1936. GJCA Collection, Folder 265. Yivo Archives, New York.

107. Razovsky to Pickett, American Friends Service Committee (hereafter AFSC), 10 July 1939, Files Foreign Service – Refugee Service. AFSC Archives, Philadelphia.

108. 'Annual Report – 1940', GJCA Collection, Folder 10, p. 2, GJCA Collection, Yivo Archives. See also, Razovsky to Dr Carter Alexander, Library Professor, Teachers College, Columbia University, New York, 22 December 1938. Razovsky Papers, Box 3, Folder 4: Correspondence. AJHS Archives, New York.

109. Kate Rosenheim to Lotte Marcuse, 12 August 1940. GJCA Collection, Folder 16. Yivo Archives, New York.

110. Ibid.

111. Ibid.

112. For a detailed analysis see Chapter 3.

113. 'Informal Report on Immigration from Germany to the United States and Other Countries', mimeograph, 21 November 1939, pp. 1–2. AFSC, Central Files, 1939, Foreign Service, Folder: Quaker Delegation to Germany, AFSC Archives, Philadelphia.

114. Razovsky to NCJW branches, 16 March 1934, 13 March 1940. GJCA Collection, Folder 16. Yivo Archives, New York.

115. See for example, J.C. Hyman to Lotte Marcuse, 'Memorandum', 24 January 1941. GJCA Collection, Folder 16, Yivo Archives, New York. Hyman agreed to sign affidavits for eight children in Camp de Gurs and Germany.

116. Razovsky to NCJW branches, 16 March 1934, 13 March 1940. GJCA Collection, Folder 16. Yivo Archives, New York.

117. 'NRS Board Meeting', 24 October 1939. Razovsky Papers, Box 3, File: NRS Relief Work, September 1939–1940, AJHS Archives, New York; Harry Greenstein, Executive Director, Associated Jewish Charities, Baltimore, 'National Coordinating Committee Recast', reprint from *Notes and News*, 5 June 1939. NRS Collection, Folder 120. Yivo Archives, New York.

118. Officers of the NRS: Joseph Chamberlain – Chairman of the Board; William Rosenwald – President; Paul Felix Warburg – Secretary; Albert Abramson, Arthur D. Greenleigh. The Executive Committee included Harry Greenstein, William Haber; and Joseph C. Hyman. Executive Officers: William Haber, Ann S. Petluck, Cecilia Razovsky, Albert Abramson, Stella Baruch, Milton Feinberg, Arthur Greenleigh, Augusta Mayerson, Ephraim Gomberg. In 1946 the NRS became the US Service for New Americans.

119. On 20 May 1941 the NRS formally accepted administrative responsibility for GJCA, resulting in the supervision by NRS of the Personnel and Accounting Division, formerly part of the GJCA. See NRS Annual Report 1942, GJCA Collection, Folder 162. Yivo

Archives, New York.

120. Kathryn Close, *Transplanted Children, A History* (Prepared for the United States Committee for the Care of European Children, Inc., 1953), pp. 25–6.

121. By May 1943, 1,193 children from Great Britain, France and Spain had been brought to the United States under the corporate affidavit of the United States Committee for the Care of European Children (USC). Of these, 735 were Protestant, 113 Catholic and 320 Jewish. The remainder were children of mixed parentage. See USC Report, 12 May 1943, GJCA Collection, Folder 174. Yivo Archives, New York.

122. The National Council of Jewish Women was formed in 1893 to offer community and education services to children – especially girls – the elderly and the destitute. With the arrival of refugees from Nazism, a variety of immigration services were provided by local sections of the NCJW. The national office, under the associate directorship of Cecilia Razovsky from 1932, centralized these services in a Department of Immigrant Aid, originally know as the Committee on Service to Foreign Born.

123. Lotte Marcuse, Director of Placements, GJCA to Blanche Renard, Committee on National Jewish Agencies, Council of Jewish Federations and Welfare Funds, 1 February 1940. GJCA Collection, Folder 169. Yivo Archives, New York.

124. 'A Statement Regarding the Status of the German-Jewish Children's Aid, Inc.', by Mrs Maurice L. Goldman, Chairman. GJCA Collection, Folder 197. Yivo Archives, New York.

125. NCJW to Goldman, President GJCA, 13 February 1939. GJCA Collection, Folder 239. Yivo Archives, New York. Between 1938 and 1940 over $200,000 was given to GJCA. See NCJW to GJCA, 18 July 1941. GJCA Collection, Folder 34. Yivo Archives, New York.

126. The largest part of the cost of the program was carried by the local Jewish communities throughout the United States. See H. L. Lurie, Executive Director, Council of Jewish Federations and Welfare Funds, Inc., to Razovsky, 16 May 1938. GJCA Collection, Folder 169. Yivo Archives, New York. On 2 August 1943 the NCJA contributed $20,624,81 to GJCA to cover maintenance of refugee children. See *Contemporary Jewish Record*, 6 (October 1943) p. 505.

127. Mrs Maurice L. Goldman, President, NJCW, 'Report, National Council of Jewish Women', 16 June 1941. GJCA Collection, Folder 29. Yivo Archives, New York.

128. Resolution adopted by the Executive Committee GJCA, 3 June 1941. GJCA Collection, Folder 8. Yivo Archives, New York. See also, Alan M. Stroock, Chairman, GJCA, 'Statement on German-Jewish Children's Aid, Inc.', 19 August 1941. GJCA Collection, Folder 29. Yivo Archives, New York.

129. On 21 November 1938, following *Kristallnacht*, the British government decided to take in Jewish children from Germany, and offer them refuge from Nazi persecution. The Jewish communities in Germany, and relief organizations abroad, such as the World Movement for the Care of Children from Germany, organized the rescue operation. On 2 December 1938, the first *Kindertransport* arrived in the East Anglian port of Harwich, England. Between December 1938 and the beginning of September 1939, around 10,000 children were brought to England by ship. Only Jewish children were given refuge. They had to separate from their parents; the majority of the children never saw their parents again. See, Jonathan Harris and Deborah Oppenheimer, *Into the Arms of Strangers: Stories of the Kindertransport* (London: Bloomsbury, 2000).

3 The Search for Affidavits

Anyone requesting an immigration visa for entry into the United States was obliged to overcome numerous obstacles. The main problems stemmed from State Department policy, which aimed at keeping immigration numbers below the quota, difficulties in obtaining the required documents and, what turned out to be hardest of all, the need to convince the consul that the applicant would not become a public charge.

The 1917 and 1924[1] immigration laws specifically excluded 'persons likely to become a public charge' from admission as immigrants into the United States.[2] But neither the laws nor the instructions provided the consuls with any real guidance. It was simply stated that certain persons were inadmissible for immigration, and the rest was left to the consulate officer's discretion. There was no 'open sesame', no rule of thumb to be followed, nor were general observations provided, to be applied to any kind of case that might arise.[3] In short, in the absence of definite guidelines for enforcing the public charge clause (hereafter LPC), the consular officers, who had to decide at their own discretion whether or not a specific applicant was likely to become a public charge, were faced with general confusion. It was thus the consul's interpretation of the law at a given time or place which eventually determined the individual applicant's fate. The same consul could even make conflicting decisions in different cases. Malcolm C. Burke, Vice-Consul in Hamburg, reported to the Secretary of State in February 1934, that:

> [T] he interpretation of the 'public charge' provision ... has not only varied somewhat as between one consular officer and another ... but it has varied strikingly from one year to another, even in the hands of the same officials. In many instances, the

examining officer is thrown back largely upon intuition and instinct, and cannot avoid forming in his own mind an opinion – favorable or unfavorable – which he is later unable fully to justify by analysis and argument.[4]

In order to establish that he or she was not likely to become a public charge, the applicant had either to prove to the consular officer that they themselves had sufficient assets to ensure self-support, or to provide an affidavit filed by a relative or friend in the United States.[5] The affidavit contained a detailed list of the affiant's assets and included his or her official guarantee to support the applicant in the United States. A 1931 memorandum from the Quota Control Office in Washington instructed the consuls to grant visas to non-preference applicants only if they were in possession of funds or property sufficient to support themselves for an indefinite period without having to resort to labor[6] or to the assistance of others.[7] In the 1930s, against a background of Nazi persecution, such instruction created a vicious circle for the Jews, and a trap for Jewish refugees, who had to steer 'artfully between the rock and the whirlpool'.[8] On the one hand, applicants had to prove they were not likely to become a burden on the community; on the other, if they admitted to having work waiting for them, they were rejected outright. In Hamburg, Vice-Consul Burke was hard put to understand the logic behind it: 'I fail to perceive any reasonable explanation why an alien should be expected to seek employment the day *after* [original emphasis] he lands in New York, and strictly forbidden to seek it the week or the month before he lands.'[9]

Given the new German restrictions, according to which the transfer of funds from Germany by emigrants was reduced from the original 15,000 Reich marks to 2,000 and, after October 1934, to 10 marks – not to mention the adoption of the Nuremberg laws in 1935, which resulted in intensified anti-Jewish measures – it was almost impossible to consider emigration based on personal assets. All Jewish assets were frozen; Jews were denied the right to hold assets and a ban was placed on taking money out of the country. Potential immigrants were now financially crippled by the need to meet the requirement of the public charge clause on their own.[10] Consul-General Honaker, reporting from Stuttgart in fall 1936, stated that, due to the governmental restrictions on the transfer of funds from Germany, 'nearly all applicants for immigration visas at this office depend for their initial support in the United States upon relatives or other connections rather than upon personal resources.'[11] Reacting to criticism in the United States targeted at the consulate in Berlin in 1934 for issuing only a few visas to German Jews because of the strict implementation of the LPC, Consul Geist explained that the large mass of Jews in Germany could not afford emigration. This was, he said,

> partly due to the fact that they cannot get their property out of the country and partly due to the fact that a large mass have not even the means to pay for ocean transportation, not to mention the necessity of having certain funds to defray expenses even for a short time when arriving in a foreign country.[12]

It remained, therefore, for relatives or friends in the United States to guarantee support so that the applicant could meet the requirement. However, each affidavit had to be evaluated by the American consuls in Germany, who more often refused to credit affidavits from distant relatives. The prevailing notion was that distant relatives or friends were not as obligated to extend indefinite support to future immigrants as were close relatives. And since the consul felt that the Department expected them to restrict immigration, it was safer for them to deny immigrant visas to such applicants. Assistant-Secretary Carr stated clearly that in spite of the pressure to make concessions with regard to the public charge clause, 'consular officers are bound to enforce it ... faithfully'.[13] When asked by the Committee on Immigration of the House of Representatives in 1934 for his opinion on bills to restrict immigration, Carr replied that there was no immediate need because 'the existing application of the public charge clause is being continued ... and so long as that is done ... there is no chance of any material increase in immigration'.[14] The likelihood of an immigrant becoming a public charge was indeed taken as the chief and easiest grounds for refusing to grant visas, especially when the consul legally need not justify his decision to limit the acceptance of affidavits for support only from near relatives.[15]

In an answer to Governor Lehman, who was inquiring about immigration into the United States, President Roosevelt stated that '[a] promise of support made by a close relative will naturally be given more weight than one from a distant relative upon whom [the] legal or moral obligation to support the applicant will not ordinarily be as great as in the case of a close relative.'[16] While there was a consensus among consuls and within the State Department that affidavits from near relatives carried more weight than those sent, for example, by a cousin or a friend, the consuls differed in their evaluation of the affidavit itself. Since most applicants in the 1930s had to count on affidavits, either because they could not take money out of Germany or because they had none, the danger of arbitrary decisions in the evaluation of the affidavit was evident. The issuing of affidavits, therefore, became a central bone of contention both in the applicant's negotiations with the consul and in criticism of the consuls in the United States. The question of the legal status of affidavits was never completely resolved.[17] Jewish jurists as well as government legal experts tended to agree that they imposed only a moral obligation.[18] An expert on international law, Albert F. Coyle, stated in an elaborated opinion that 'the moral obligation' promised by the affidavits 'will not pass inspection': 'The "moral obligation" involved is a very vague and indefinite thing and is of no use whatsoever, either to the government or the immigrant, if the maker of the affidavit chooses to ignore it.' Moreover, he was advised by the Department of Labor that the average affidavit of support 'is worthless legally and cannot be enforced, and that the Department makes no effort to enforce it.'[19]

In another opinion given to the American Jewish Committee, Harry Schulman, Professor of Law at Yale University, stated that:

> The affidavit does not give rise to any legally enforceable obligation on the part of the affiant. The representation in the affidavit is a solemn avowal of responsibility, and doubtless creates a moral obligation which the affiant is expected to perform ... [He or she] is subject to criminal penalties if he makes knowingly false representation.[20]

Such legal opinions appeared to justify, to some degree, the government's preference for affidavits from close relatives. However, even State Department officials agreed that the case of German Jewish immigrants was different. In late 1936, the State Department dispatched Klahr Huddle, a Foreign Service Inspector, to Germany to review visa procedures. His report recommended a more lenient approach to the affidavits given to Jewish applicants from friends and more distant relatives since, he argued, 'Jews have a sincere desire to assist ... so that the likelihood of their becoming a public charge is very remote'.[21] Referring to Huddle's report, Eliot B. Coulter of the Visa Division also recommended a change of course with regard to affidavits from second-preference applicants. He suggested that 'the Jewish people often have a high sense of responsibility towards their relatives, including their distant relatives ... and ... they feel keenly the difficult lot of their kin in Germany'. In such cases, he concluded, a sincere expression of willingness to furnish such support should be sufficient.[22] Coulter's recommendations were indeed included in Carr's letter to Consul-General Jenkins in Berlin in 1936: 'The mere fact that a person promising support is not closely related to the applicant or that he is not under a legal or moral obligation towards him is not sufficient to warrant the rejection of the evidence of support as inadequate.'[23]

Most Jewish applicants had no close relatives in the United States, and faced with the increasing perils for Jews in Nazi Germany, Jewish leaders and organizations claimed that affidavits of support should be accepted for what they were – a sworn promise from a relative or friend in the United States to support the alien after his or her arrival for as long as necessary and a guarantee that she or he would not be allowed to become a public charge.[24] The new approach, if accepted by the consuls, could have opened a window to applicants with relatives in the United States, when those relatives or friends were willing and able to support the aliens 'regardless of the relationship and in spite of the absence of any direct obligation'.[25] Unfortunately, the consuls were reluctant to utilize this opening and continued to cast doubts on affidavits from distant relatives.[26]

Nevertheless, Jewish as well as non-Jewish organizations, individuals and philanthropists joined in efforts to persuade the consuls to acknowledge such affidavits. They continued to urge families in the United States to secure affidavits for distant relatives or friends in Germany. In June 1937, Albert Martin, representative of the AFSC in Germany, felt that there was still some hope of convincing the consul that the affidavits from distant relatives or friends were as good as affidavits from near relatives:

> All you need to do is to get three or four affidavits, i.e., *more* than required, for each family, and send them over and then see the proper people in Washington and tell them that you need quick action on them. If Washington writes to Berlin, things will go through right away. I have seen this happen here in several cases.[27]

However, this did not happen in practice. After holding discussions with the consulate in Berlin, Martin himself reported that same year and again a year later that, according to Consul Geist, 'since they [the applicants] have no near relatives in America, no affidavit would be acceptable at present'.[28]

In many cases, several distant Jewish relatives or friends in the United States sent joint affidavits of support hoping that 'their number

would make up, to some extent, at least, for the distance in consan-
guinity'.[29] But records indicate that, notwithstanding the instruction
from Washington, American consuls seldom accepted affidavits from
distant relatives or friends as sufficient evidence to counter the LPC
clause.[30]

With conditions in Nazi Germany deteriorating, Cecilia Razovsky,
in her capacity as Executive Director of the NCC, sought some practical and satisfactory method by which the consul could give credence
to an affidavit presented by a person without moral or legal obliga-
tions for support. After many discussions with her colleagues,
Razovsky had a long conference with George L. Warren, Secretary of
the President's Advisory Committee, who suggested using statements
issued by local social agencies or other accepted authorities.
According to his plan, which was eventually sent to the Department
of State, supporting statements made by responsible local welfare
agencies attesting to the sincerity of the affiant might be considered.
The relevant local welfare agency would interview the affiant, determine the circumstances of his relation to the applicant, discuss with
him all the implications of his affidavit and reach a judgment as to the
likelihood of the affiant's commitment to the applicant. If the local
welfare agency found that the affiant had only a casual interest in the
applicant and was executing the affidavit irresponsibly, no supporting
statement would be sent to the consul. If, on the other hand, the local
social agency was convinced that the affiant had a serious interest in
the applicant based on previous contacts or ready sympathy with the
applicant's situation, and had a serious purpose and intention to
assist the applicant to avoid public relief, a report to this effect would
be sent to the consul to assist in appraising the dependence which
might be placed upon the affidavit of support. The agencies Warren
had in mind were those accredited by the government such as the
NCC, the American Red Cross, the National Catholic Welfare
Conference, the NCJW, the International Migration Service, the
National Travelers Aid Association, the Child Welfare League of
America and the Family Welfare Association.[31]

The NCC was one of the organizations that played an active role
in the campaign to bring German refugees into the United States.[32]
The anti alien atmosphere in Congress and in the country at large, the
rising antisemitism and the economic situation prevented any immediate change of the immigration laws. Jewish leaders in fact feared
such a change and also agreed that any attempt to alter the situation
might result in more restricted laws. The hope for German Jewish

refugees rested therefore with the possibility to achieve the number of immigrant visas permitted by the quota – 25,957 for Germany and 1,413 for Austria [33] – which, except for the 1939 fiscal year, was never filled.[34] In effect, American consuls used the LPC as an efficient safety valve to restrict the immigration of Jewish refugees from Europe.

As Executive Director of the NCC, Cecilia Razovsky had already decided in 1934 that in order to bypass the LPC, American Jews should be urged to send as many affidavits as possible, even to people with whom they were unfamiliar.[35] Only by understanding the ponderous bureaucratic machinery of rescue is it possible to comprehend the difficulty of implementing her goal. There can be no doubt that her mission faced enormous obstacles. First, given the harsh economic conditions in the United States, people were reluctant to guarantee the well-being of German Jewish families or individuals for an indefinite period, merely because they shared the same religion and, especially, when they were distant relatives or complete strangers.[36] Second, such a large-scale operation called for a highly organized system. It was necessary to establish efficient headquarters and to create a network of thousands of branches throughout the United States. It involved handling pre- and post-emigration problems ranging from obtaining affidavits to providing recreation and resettlement, and contacting existing Jewish organizations to ask for their financial and administrative cooperation, through their local connections. It meant organizing local liaison committees embracing all the local agencies involved in refugee work. Moreover, it was necessary to locate, recruit and train the right people to work at the centers.[37] In other words, it required much paper work, good will and devotion to what Razovsky considered 'a sacred mission' – the rescue of Jewish refugees from the hell that was Germany and bringing them to safety. It was therefore urgent and essential to secure affidavits of support. However, given the anti-immigration and antisemitic atmosphere in the United States, it was feared that publicity would boomerang and provoke criticism in the country. To overcome 'bad publicity', NCC treasurer, Mr Paul Warburg, put forward a plan in January 1936 – which was eventually agreed upon – and according to which private individuals would be approached discreetly and asked for their assistance by supplying affidavits to affect the emigration of worthy refugees from abroad, such as musicians, scholars and other professionals.[38]

An additional difficulty rested with the law that stated that organizations were not permitted to submit affidavits in their own name.[39] Organizations, nevertheless, were permitted to advise and assist interested persons to prepare such affidavits. This meant that even an established organization such as the NCC could do all the preparation work behind the scenes but would not publicly guarantee support or be responsible in their own right. Razovsky with her volunteer Jewish women did their utmost to ensure that affidavits obtained from individuals were fully and correctly completed according to the requirements. Since the affidavits required to prove to the American consul that the would-be immigrant would not become a public charge, it was imperative that they be corroborated by irrefutable proof of the financial stability of the signer. Moreover, when an individual signed an affidavit, the ultimate obligation was his or her own personal responsibility. Should one relative not be able to furnish a very satisfactory affidavit, Razovsky sought a supplementary affidavit from other relatives, as the more proof of material help that could be given, the better the chance that they would satisfy the consul's requirements.

On 11 July 1939, Razovsky – then head of the Migration Department – with the encouragement of the National Refugee Service (NRS),[40] devised a plan whereby guarantee committees were allowed to make affidavits for very urgent and special cases such as those involving the reunification of families, or where the imminent danger of being sent to a concentration camp could be avoided by the possession of an affidavit. According to that plan, special guarantee committees were established with special guaranty funds to be utilized in aiding providers of affidavits. Such a guaranty fund constituted a method whereby the responsibility incurred was satisfactorily covered and, at the same time, would benefit those who were most vulnerable.[41]

As a general rule, all routine requests for contacting and locating relatives in order to obtain affidavits for families abroad were referred to the National Council of Jewish Women (NCJW) and its various sections or to the HIAS. Specific cases, however, were handled by Razovsky in her capacity of Executive Director of the NCC. These involved:

a. Cases of men in concentration camps, whose release depended on affidavits.
b. Cases of failed routine procedure due to technical problems, raised by the overseas consuls abroad, that needed to be brought to the attention of the visa office or other departments in Washington.

c. Cases where the person concerned had some special qualifications in his field, but had no relatives in the United States and efforts were made to obtain affidavits through other sources. These usually involved scholars, scientists or other renowned persons who could not be referred to NCC's special committees such as Scholars and Physicians, because, technically, they were ineligible.[42]

d. Situations referred by special persons in the community who demanded individual attention, but who could not be referred through routine channels.[43]

Thousands of pleas for affidavits reached Miss Razovsky's office from affiliated organizations and individuals; each of them received her full attention. To mention one example – the case of Dr Jacobi, his wife Else and his child, Ursula Ruth, a minor. They were refused affidavits because the cousin who made the affidavit was only his second cousin, and therefore considered a distant relative. Dr Jacobi visited the American consul in Rotterdam eight times, only to realize that he could not fulfill the consul's demands. He brought to the consul proof of his own finances and two supplementary affidavits from relatives in Holland, but the consul denied him a visa, each time finding fault with the affidavits provided, reaching the conclusion that the applicants had

> no funds of their own; that Doctor Jacobi had been unable to support his family in the Netherlands, that he would probably encounter difficulty in earning a livelihood for himself and his family in the United States; and that the evidence furnished by the interested relatives was insufficient to establish that the applicants would have assured means of support in the United States for an indefinite period.[44]

Especially urgent were requests for persons imprisoned in concentration camps, whose release could be facilitated by an immigration visa or an affidavit. In December 1938, Razovsky sent an urgent call to all affiliated committees to send her sufficient information about those cases so that they might be referred forthwith. She asked for full information about the person, including his or her age, occupation, names of relatives in any European country and also the addresses of the persons in the United States who had submitted affidavits and the date of submission. Committees were urged to scour their communities for help and to forward the relevant information as soon as possible.[45]

To mention only a few cases: young Ludwig Lechner had been

imprisoned in a concentration camp since April 1938.[46] A few weeks
later he was transferred from Dachau to Buchenwald ('the worst concentration camp in Germany'). His sister's former employer, Dr
Ungvari, a dentist, newly arrived in the United States, had already
submitted affidavits on behalf of two close relatives and since he
could show no income at the time, 'another [affidavit] would be not
effective'. He stated, however, that once the young man reached the
United States, 'he will undertake the sole responsibility for all his
needs'.[47] A typical private promise of support that illustrates the procedure is the case of Mr Emil Auspitz from Vienna, whose friend
Kalman Friedmann of New York could not legally sign an affidavit
'which would satisfy the American consul', but who nevertheless
pledged that '[he] will receive his friend on his arrival ... [and] take
care of him in any way. He can stay and live with me until he will
become self supporting.'[48] Or the case of three Jewish heads-of-fam-
ily imprisoned in concentration camps, all of whom would be
released if their departure were vouched for. Ferdinand Gutmann, an
American citizen had already given affidavits for so many and felt
that the government 'may delay matters through investigation, and as
"time" was the important matter in those cases to relieve them from
being held in concentration camps', he pleaded for affidavits on
behalf of these families. He promised to send each signer of an affidavit a letter to the effect that he would guarantee 'to support these
prospective immigrants so that they [would] not become public
charge'.[49] Another urgent request concerned the Meyer family from
Frankfurt am Main, who had obtained an affidavit from a relative
indicating he owned real estate worth over $60,000,000. The consul
rejected the affidavit since the signer did not indicate his income
because he had changed his business connections. Mr Meyer was
imprisoned and the family 'seems to be quite desperate, especially
since they would be able to leave Germany very soon after their
papers [were] in order', due to the fact that they had made applications at the American consulate at a very early date.[50] Or the case of
Dr Borchardt, who had come to the United States on a visitor's visa
and wished to bring over his wife and two children, who were still in
Germany. Borchardt had a distant relative and friend in Ann Arbor,
Michigan whom he had approached for affidavits but who refused to
help. Dr Borchardt had no other contacts in the United States and
had no possibility of obtaining an affidavit of support. Furthermore,
his German passport had expired and in order for him to obtain an
extension of his visitor's visa it was necessary for him to get a United

States certificate of identity, which precluded 'absolutely any possibility of his return to Germany'.[51] Each case reveals a tragedy. Husbands imprisoned; families separated – one of them already in the United States and spouse and children still in Germany; young people suffering from police pressure – all in urgent need of affidavits.

The case of the Bobker family is especially interesting since Mrs Bobker was an American citizen living in Germany with her husband and four children. She was pregnant with her fifth child and had left for the United States with one of the other four children. The consul in Berlin had refused to allow Mrs Bobker to leave with her husband and three other children, but assured her that he would 'definitely' issue them immigrant visas on receipt of satisfactory affidavits. Mrs Bobker had a few distant relatives in the United States, but these had arrived only six months earlier and, on a weekly income of only $15, were unable to support another family.[52]

It should also be mentioned that not only was an affidavit a way out of Germany, but no less important, it provided some relief from local police interrogation and, at times, even helped to avoid imprisonment or internment in concentration camps. Furthermore, in some European countries, such as Belgium, Sweden, Norway, Holland and others, holders of affidavits were able to obtain permits for temporary stay. Countries which permitted temporary asylum to such people usually required evidence of guaranteed support. An affidavit clearly showed the responsibility of the affiant and his intention of guaranteeing for the care of the prospective immigrant.[53] NCC was called to help.

Razovsky's office was busy sending out affidavit blanks and information to countrywide branches,[54] to be filled by volunteers – preferably married women[55] – locating relatives and collecting funds from them.[56] Razovsky kept sending letters to prospective signers[57] and recruiting signers from her own office, urging all to sign supplementary affidavits of support for those whose original affidavit did not furnish a very satisfactory obligation, and on behalf of applicants who had no acquaintances in the United States.[58] Specially qualified volunteers were standing by, ready to help with preparing the affidavit, making sure that it was correctly completed and that the required substantiating proof was provided. Different types of affidavits were used, depending upon the relationship between the prospective emigrant and the person filling out the affidavit.[59] Since the problem mainly involved affidavits by friends or distant relatives, it was agreed at a conference called by the NCC on 17 September 1938 that Professor Chamberlain would appoint a small committee to meet and formulate some plan which might be acceptable to the consuls and for adoption by the various committees and agencies throughout the country.[60] Since preparing an affidavit was time-and labor-consuming, twelve requirements were called for, including:

1. If the signer was in business he or she had to include a statement from a certified credit-rating agency indicating income, investments, assets and liabilities. If such a statement was not available, an auditor's statement or letters should be secured from firms or persons with whom the petitioner dealt. A statement from the landlord where the business was conducted could be helpful.

2. If the petitioner was employed, a letter from the employer witnessed by a notary indicating the occupation, salary, length of time employed, the permanency of the position and general responsibility.

3. If the petitioner was a professional, such proof as was available. A statement or professional letterhead might furnish proof. Showing a notarized copy of the most recent income tax return could prove income, or a photostatic copy of a cancelled check (front and back) showing payment of income tax.

4. A statement from the life insurance company as to the amount of insurance carried and cash surrender value.

5. Statements from savings banks as to deposits and statements from commercial banks regarding the account in general.

6. A notarized statement from brokers could prove possession of stocks and bonds or a notarized statement from the man in charge of the safe-deposit room to whom the securities had been shown.

7. If the affiant was in possession of real estate, tax receipts were considered prima facie evidence of ownership. If possible, outstanding mortgages by receipts or letters of the mortgages.

8. If monetary help was sent to the person in whose behalf the affidavit was made, receipts for same, or a statement from the bank through which they were sent abroad should be added to the application.

9. Proof of payment of income tax, especially where the stated income was above $1,000 (single), $2,500 (head of family). If no tax was paid, notarized copy of tax return should be produced. If tax was paid, the notarized copy of tax return or photostatic copy of cancelled check showing payment of last federal or state tax should be produced.

10. The relationship should be explained in detail, with full names and statement as to whether the relationship was on the maternal or paternal side. When the relationship was distant or if the application was made by a close friend, detailed proof had to be given showing the friendship was of long standing and that the tie had been as close as a blood tie.
11. Letters of recommendation from prominent citizens or businessmen testifying as to character and responsibility of the petitioner.
12. Where the person making the affidavit was a friend it was important to add a letter to the American consul asking favorable consideration of the application for the visa, summarizing reasons why the applicant was being supported by the affiant, describing petitioner's home, and that he was prepared to give a home to the immigrant if necessary.[61]

It should also be stressed that an affidavit was valid for one year only. That meant that if paperwork at the consulate took longer – and often it did – and the affidavits had not yet been reviewed, new affidavits had to be forwarded. In practice, it meant that the NCC had to make out two sets of affidavits for each case.[62] Towards 1939, the consuls' demands grew stricter, asking now for proof that, 'in some concrete way' givers were not only able but also 'willing and ready to support the person who was coming in on those affidavits'.[63] Two examples will suffice to indicate the consuls' new approach. In a letter to Mr Mark Brunswick in New York, Leland S. Morris, consul-general in Vienna, suggested that, since the person for whom he had made an affidavit was not a relative, he should 'inform [the consul] as to the exact reasons for undertaking the support of the applicant and also the number of applicants for whom [he has] already executed affidavits of support'.[64] What's more, since March 1939 the consuls had been demanding that trust funds be opened in the United States for each applicant.[65]

The provision of affidavits raised many technical difficulties. Since immigration visas were given on the basis of the quota allotted to a certain country, it was important to make sure that the place of birth supplied by the potential immigrant was accurate. However, with regard to applicants from Austria it was not always easy to determine the 'country of birth'. For instance, those persons born in what was formerly Austria and which, in the 1930s, was Romanian territory, were given visas under the Romanian quota despite the fact that those people had never been Romanian, never considered themselves to be

Romanian, and at all times had been Austrian subjects. Those persons, however, who at the time of division stayed in what was Austrian territory and maintained their Austrian nationality, could hardly have been classified as Romanian by birth simply because a part of the territory where they were born had been taken over by Romania. The law states that, 'For the purposes of this Act nationality shall be determined by the country of birth, treating as separate countries the colonies and dependencies of self-governing dominions for which special enumeration was made in the US census of 1890.'[66] Accordingly, the attitude of the NCC was that the country of birth of those people at the time of their birth was Austria. To judge their nationality by a subsequent Act was contrary to the intent of the Statute. The Statute specifically states that the country of birth is the governing country and not the country of citizenship.[67] Since the quota for the new east European countries was small, it was important to dispute the Department of State approach and to enable refugees from former parts of Austria to be included in the Austrian quota, which after the *Anschluss* was included under the German quota.[68]

To sum up, although there were numerous obstacles to overcome on the way to obtaining an immigration visa, procuring an affidavit was the main concern. Without an affidavit there was no chance of ever obtaining the life-saving visa. However, the issue of the content and credibility of the affidavit, and the decision as to who would be considered sufficiently close as a relative to supply it, raised major difficulties, especially for all those who had no relatives or friends in the United States,[69] or for those whose friends were reluctant to vouch for them indefinitely. This, again, was where Razovsky, as Executive Director of the NCC and Head of Migration, NRS, together with her volunteer Jewish women, made a difference. Not only did Razovsky scour the United States to find available relatives or friends but she appealed to Jewish communities and to Jewish philanthropists to persuade them to assist in sending affidavits even to people they had not known. By establishing an efficient routine in major Jewish communities, Razovsky and 'her women' dedicated long hours to help interested people fill out the complicated forms, and locate the necessary documents, all in order to speed up the procedures and to bring into the United States as many Jewish refugees as possible.

NOTES

1. Immigration Act, February 1917, 39 Stat. 891, United States Criminal Code; Immigration Act of 1924, 43 Stat. 153, United States Code.
2. It should be noted, however, that, 'A consular officer has no authority to refuse a non immigrant visa to an alien on the ground that the alien is likely to become a public charge.' See John F. Simmons to Theodore G. Holambe, 13 March 1934. 150.01/2234/1/2. United States Department of State, Central Decimal Files, Record Group 59. National Archives, Suitland, Maryland.
3. Avra Warren to Hooker A. Doolittle, American Consul, Tangier, Morocco, 27 April 1939. 811.111 Refugees/48. National Archives, RG 59.
4. Malcolm C. Burke, American Vice-Consul, Hamburg, 'Memorandum Regarding the Immigration Situation as Discussed in an Article in the Weekly *To Day*', 20 January 1934. 150.626 J/93. National Archives, RG 59.
5. There were two different kinds of affidavit. One promised to employ the refugee in household service for a period (to be filled in by guarantor) at a salary (to be filled in by guarantor). The second affidavit was to be completed by either a blood relative or a 'friend' of the refugee. It assured the consul that the guarantor 'will properly receive and care for' the immigrant upon his arrival and 'will not permit him to become a public charge upon any community or municipality'. On both types of affidavit, guarantors had to give detailed information as to their income, insurance, savings, etc., which had to be sworn to before a notary public.
6. 'The contract labor clause' in the Act of 1917 forbade an immigrant to the United States to have employment in advance of his entry into the country unless he belonged to one of the exempted occupations. Such a prohibition had in fact already been incorporated in the Alien Contract Labor Law of 1885, which was designed for the prevention of abuses such as the importation of foreign labor to drive down wage rates. The Act stipulated that it was unlawful to assist the entry of aliens under a prior contract for labor.
7. 'Memorandum' from the Quota Control Office to offices receiving allotments under the German quota, 5 February 1931. 811.111 RHG – G Box 163. National Archives, RG 59.
8. Malcolm C. Burke, American Vice-Consul, Hamburg, 'Memorandum Regarding the Immigration Situation as Discussed in an Article in the Weekly *To Day*', 20 January 1934. 150.626 J/93. National Archives, RG 59.
9. Ibid.
10. Consul James P. Moffitt, Stuttgart, to Secretary of State, 'Removal of Capital from Germany by Emigrants', 29 May 1934, 150.626 J/90; Vice-Consul William Ware Adams, 'Current Immigration to the United States from the Consular District of Berlin, Germany', 1 November 1934. 811.111 Quota 62/468. National Archives, RG 59.
11. Consul-General Honaker to Secretary, 'Status of Visa Work at the American Consulate, Stuttgart, Germany, with a Summary of the Work for September 1936', 5 October 1936. 811.11 Quota 62/468. National Archives, RG 59.
12. Consul Geist to Secretary, 5 March 1934, 150.626 J/74. See also Geist to Secretary, 5 February 1934, 150.626 J/60. National Archives, RG 59.
13. Assistant-Secretary of State Carr to Consul-General Messersmith, 1 June 1933. 150.626 J/9a. National Archives, RG 59. Secretary of State Hull admitted in spring 1934 that consuls were instructed 'to be particularly careful in requiring proof that an alien applying for an immigration visa will not become a public charge'. Hull to Mrs Carrie Chapman Catt, Chairman, Committee of Ten, 12 March 1934, Morris Waldman Papers, Box 19: Aliens, Folder 9: Immigration – Refugees, 1933–35; 1938–39. Yivo Archives, New York.
14. Statement of Wilbur J. Carr, Assistant-Secretary of State, before the Committee on Immigration of the House of Representatives, 12 March 1934. 150.01/2200. National Archives, RG 59.
15. Geist to Secretary of State, 2 February 1934, 150.626 J/56; Memorandum to Simmons from an unidentified person in Visa Division, 21 November 1934. 811.111 Quota 62/468. National Archives, RG 59.
16. President Roosevelt's answer reflected the Department's views. The draft was apparently prepared by John Farr Simmons of the Visa Division since Roosevelt had asked the State Department to prepare a reply. See FDR memorandum for the State Department, 17 June 1936; Carr to Roosevelt with attached draft, 27 June 1936. 150.626 J/208. National Archives, RG 59.

17. Clarence Pickett to Mac Maser, 23 November 1934. General Files 1934. Folder: Letters to Germany. AFSC Archives, Philadelphia.
18. Max Kohler to Morris Waldman, 28 August 1933. Morris Waldman Records, RG 347.1, Box 18: Germany, Folder 6: Immigration 1933. Yivo Archives, New York.
19. Albert F. Coyle to Professor Chamberlain, 6 June 1938. Chamberlain Papers, File 18. Yivo Archives, New York.
20. Harry Schulman to Carl Austrian, 11 January 1939. Morris Waldman Records, RG 347.1, Box 19: Aliens, Folder 9: Immigration – Refugees, 1933–35, 1938–39. Yivo Archives, New York.
21. Attached to Visa Instructions from State to Diplomatic and Consular Officers, 12 January 1937. 150.626/J242. National Archives, RG 59.
22. Coulter to Carr, 30 November 1936. 150.626 J/242. National Archives, RG 59.
23. Carr to all American Diplomats and Consulate Officers, 5 January 1937. 150.626 J/242. National Archives, RG 59.
24. Meeting at the Committee on German-Jewish Immigration Policy, 26 January 1934, American Jewish Joint Distribution Committee Records. AR 1033–1934, File 683: Emigration into the United States, 1933–1934. American Jewish Joint Distribution Committee Archives, New York.
25. Consul Hodgdon to Consul-General Wiley, Vienna, 11 January 1937. John Wiley Papers, Boxes 6 and 7. FDR Library, Hyde Park.
26. For details see Bat-Ami Zucker, *In Search of Refuge: Jews and US Consuls in Nazi Germany 1933–1941* (London and Portland, OR: Vallentine Mitchell, 2001), pp. 144–56.
27. Emphasis in original. Albert Martin to Pickett and Hertha Kraus (consultant to AFSC on refugee matters), 9 June 1937. General Files, 1937, Foreign Service – Germany, Folder: Letters from Germany. AFSC Archives, Philadelphia.
28. Martin to Pickett, 16 November 1938. General Files 1938. Folder: Letters from Germany; for the earlier letter, see Martin to Pickett, 16 May 1937. General Files, 1937, Folder: Foreign Service – Refugee, 1937. AFSC Archives, Philadelphia.
29. Eliot B. Coulter, Acting Chief, Visa Division Department of State to Razovsky, 21 July 1936, p. 2. VD 811.111, Jacobi, Curt, in Warburg Papers, Box 329, Folder 4. American Jewish Archives, Cincinnati; Read Lewis and Marian Schibsby, 'Status of the Refugee under American Immigration Laws', *The Annals of the American Academy of Political and Social Science*, 203 (May 1939), p. 79.
30. Report by Hertha Kraus (signed on her behalf by Barbara L. Cary), fall 1938. General Files 1938, Foreign Service – Refugee Services, Folder: Refugee Services – General Files 1938, and Clarence Pickett to Howard Elkinton, AFSC representative in Berlin, 12 December 1938, General Files 1938, Folder: Letters to Germany, 1938. AFSC Archives, Philadelphia.
31. George L. Warren to Chamberlain, ' Statement Attesting the sincerity of Affidavits of support Executed by Distant Relatives or Friends of Applicants for Visas to be Issued by Local Social Agencies or Other accepted Authorities', 22 June 1938. Chamberlain Papers, Folder 18. Yivo Archives, New York.
32. The four most important organizations were: the National Coordinating Committee for Aid to Refugees and Emigrants Coming from Germany; the American Committee for Christian-German Refugees; the Committee for Catholic Refugees from Germany; the National Council of Jewish Women. All four were located in New York City. For the structure and activities of the NCC, see Chapter 1.
33. After the *Anschluss*, March 1938, both quotas were combined and the total quota for Greater Germany was 27,370.
34. See Statement Issued to Press Representatives on 12 September 1939. Chamberlain Papers, Folder 16. Yivo Archives, New York.
35. Cecilia Razovsky, Associate Director NCJW to Presidents and Chairmen of all Branches, 17 October 1934, NCC Records, File 3: Correspondence File of Cecilia Razovsky when she was Associate Director of the NCJW. Yivo Archives, New York.
36. In May 1938, it was suggested that an affidavit form be prepared which would limit the liability of the signer until such a time as the immigrant became a citizen, instead of the existing form which stated that the signer would at no time permit the proposed immigrant to become a public charge. See William Rosenwald to Chamberlain, 6 May 1938. Chamberlain Papers, Folder 18. Yivo Archives, New York. See also Louis Fabricant, Vice-President, B'nai B'rith to

Lotte Marcuse, GJCA, 14 December 1939. GJCA Records, Folder 143: Correspondence with Field Agencies Regarding Affidavits. Yivo Archives, New York.

37. Erika Mann and Eric Estorick, 'Private and Governmental Aid to Refugees', *Annals for the American Academy of Political and Social Sciences*, 203 (1939), p. 143.

38. Meeting of the NCC, 6 January 1936. Warburg Papers, Box 329, Folder 5, p. 2. American Jewish Archives, Cincinnati.

39. Cecilia Razovsky to Professor Chamberlain, 6 September 1938: 'there have been no new rulings which permit consuls to accept affidavits from organizations'. NCC Records, File 6: Correspondence between Razovsky and Chamberlain, 1 June–30 December 1938. Yivo Archives, New York.

40. See Chapter 1: American-Jewish Rescue Organizations.

41. Chamberlain, NRS Chairman to all Cooperating Committees, 'Statement Regarding Responsibility of Affidavit Makers Supplementing Letter from NRS, Inc', and 'Statement of Methods to be Used by Professional Workers for the Purpose of Interpreting Responsibility of Affidavit Makers', STRICTLY CONFIDENTIAL, (original emphasis) 11 July 1939. NCC Records, File 16: Informational Memos from Razovsky to Constituent Groups. Yivo Archives, New York . A guarantee by a group was extremely important in cases where 'friendship affidavits' were concerned. In such cases, a Guarantee Fund Committee with a fund to act as a cushion for the affidavit maker added support to an individual affidavit.

42. For a detailed analysis concerning scholars and physicians, see Chapter 4: Professionals' Rescue Committees.

43. See for example, the case of Dr Schocken, a leading merchant in Dresden, who proposed to organize the Brotherhood of the Reform Temples in the United States and have them set up committees that would furnish affidavits and so enable a large number of immigrants to enter the United States. It was his belief that thousands of German Jews could be located in the United States who would be interested in sending for distant relatives from Germany. He had already made contact with the Union of American Hebrew Congregations with regard to this matter. Miss Razovsky advised that Dr Schocken's brother had sent 400 of his employees in Germany to South America and South Africa and wanted the NCC to provide affidavits for 200 of their employees who were still in Germany. Miss Razovsky and Dr Billikopf promised to look into the matter. See Minutes of the Board of Directors of the NCC, 27 October 1937. Chamberlain Papers, Folder 8. Yivo Archives, New York.

44. Eliot B. Coulter, Acting Chief, Visa Division, Department of State to Razovsky, 21 July 1936, and Rita Rosenberg to Mrs Florence Kahn, Member of Congress, 23 April 1936. Warburg Papers, Box 329, Folder 4. American Jewish Archives, Cincinnati.

45. Razovsky to All Cooperating Committees, 28 December 1938. NCC Records, File 16: Informational Memos from Razovsky to Constituent Groups. Yivo Archives, New York.

46. Miss Taubenblatt was in charge of affidavits in the New York Section, NCJW. She was the liaison with the Humane Refugee Aid Society (HRSA), which was one of the rescue organizations functioning through the NCJW, affiliated with the NCC. It was established in 1938 and proved quite efficient. On 1 March 1939 it reported to Miss Cohen, Statistician in the NCC, that '[we] have procured and furnished 149 affidavits for 325 people for the months of January and February 1939. From the formation of our society (July 1938) up to December 1938 we have procured 282 affidavits for 752 people.' See NCC Records, File 90: Correspondence between New York Section of the NCJW and the Humane Refugee Aid Society on Individual Refugee Cases, 1938–1939. Yivo Archives, New York. The procedure was simple. The Humane Refugee Aid Society asked the NCJW to investigate a case directed to them and, after being properly checked, an affidavit was obtained from people who were ready to sign it, even if they had not known the person involved. See Laura Grant, Assistant Secretary HRAS, to Mayerson, 25 October 1938; Mayerson to Ella Courlander, 18 November 1938. NCC Records, File 89: Interoffice Memoranda of the National Refuge Center. Yivo Archives, New York. See also Razovsky's reply to a question at a conference, September 1938: 'If you notify the NCC [that there are people ready to make affidavits] we will send you a full history and description of half a dozen deserving and urgent cases and we will be delighted to do it. We have had hundreds of requests of cases already investigated in Europe.' NCC Records, File 2: A Report on the Proceedings of Conference called by NCC, 17 September 1938, p. 20.   A 'Memo' by

Mayerson confirms that it was agreed in a meeting with Miss Courlander that the 'NCJW will take care of cases from their community ... where an affidavit is already sent and supplementary is needed and the party is not yet 45 years old.' Ibid., File 92. For people in Germany for whom information was needed, the *Hilfsverein der Juden in Deutschland* investigated all these persons carefully and wrote fully about all the details required as to their qualifications, character, ability and so on, and forwarded it directly to the NCC, whose task was to procure affidavits for those who had no relatives or friends in the United States. See Max M. Warburg to Miss Alice Emanuel, secretary to Paul Warburg in New York, 1 March 1936. American Jewish Archives, File: Warburg, Box 329, Folder 5. Cincinnati. List of officers in the HRSA – President – Hon. Judge Lois B. Brodsky; Joint Vice-President – Samuel I. Cohen, Mr William Infield; Secretary – Mr Leopold Spira; Treasurer – Samuel Redllich; Office Staff – Mrs Gisela Scheuer, Miss Vera Kari Schwab, Miss Evelyn Schlage.

47. Miss Taubenblatt, New York Section, NCJW, to Mrs Ella Courlander, Assistant Supervisor to Mr Leopold Spira, Humane Refugee Aid Society, (NCC), 9 January 1939, NCC Records, File 91: Correspondence between New York Section of the NCJW and the Humane Refugee Aid Society on Individual Refugee Cases, 1938–1939. Yivo Archives, New York.

48. Kalman Friedmann to Humane Refugee Aid Society, 31 August 1938. NCC Records, File 90: Correspondence between NY Section NCJW and HRAS on individual cases. Yivo Archives, New York.

49. Ferdinand Gutmann to Augusta Mayerson, New York Section, NJCA, 5 December 1938, concerning Franz Marcus, Hamburg, Arthur Mann, Hamburg and Dr Norbert Cassel, Berlin. NCC Records, File 91: Correspondence between New York Section of the NCJW and the Humane Refugee Aid Society on Individual Refugee Cases, 1938–1939. Yivo Archives, New York.

50. L. Teutsch, NCJW, to Ella Courlander, 3 January 1939, NCC Records, File 91: Correspondence between New York Section of the NCJW and the Humane Refugee Aid Society on Individual Refugee Cases, 1938–1939. Yivo Archives, New York.

51. Augusta Mayerson, NY Section, NCJW, to NCC, 25 October 1938. NCC Records, File 90: Correspondence between the NY Section, NCJW and the Humane Refugee Aid Society on Individual Refugee Cases, 1938–1939. Yivo Archives, New York.

52. Berta Taubenblatt, New York Section, NCJW, to Ella Courlander, transferred to Razovsky, 14 April 1939. NCC Records, File 90: Correspondence between the NY Section, NCJW and the Humane Refugee Aid Society on Individual Refugee Cases, 1938–1939. Yivo Archives, New York.

53. See collection of requests for affidavit, NCC Records, Files: 90, 91, 92, 93. Yivo Archives, New York. For the protection affidavits gave to refugees, see Zucker, *In Search of Refuge*, pp. 104–5. See also Razovsky, Executive Director NCC to All Cooperating Committees, 11 May 1939, p. 2. NCC Records, File 16: Informational Memos from Razovsky to Constituent Groups. Yivo Archives, New York.

54. See for example, Ann Petluck, Secretary to Razovsky, to Miss Ruth Benedict, Department of Anthropology, Columbia University, 21 September 1938. NCC Records, File 19: Correspondence between Razovsky and Joseph Chamberlain. Yivo Archives, New York. See also Fainberg, NCC, to Miss Marion Katz, 'Form letters re affidavits', 29 July 1938. NCC Records, File 10: Correspondence between Razovsky and Moses Fainberg, (NCC). Yivo Archives, New York.

55. Edith L. Lauer, the Jewish Family and Children Bureau to Lotte Marcuse, 31 October 1939; Lotte Marcuse to Mrs E. Bercovich, Detroit, 28 December 1939. GJCA Records, Folder 143: Correspondence with Field Agencies Regarding Affidavits. Yivo Archives, New York.

56. Chamberlain to Razovsky, 30 December 1939. NCC Records, File 8: Correspondence between Razovsky and Chamberlain, p. 2. Yivo Archives, New York.

57. Felix M. Warburg was especially involved in finding new signers. Razovsky kept a direct line to him through his secretary, Miss A. R. Emanuel. See Warburg Papers, Box 329, Folders 4, 6 and Box 316, File 2, for the correspondence between Razovsky and Warburg with regard to affidavits. See for example, Warburg letter to the American consul in Stuttgart offering himself as guarantee for support, 12 March 1936. Ibid. American Jewish Archives, Cincinnati.

58. See for example, Razovsky, NCC, to Mrs Schwartz, 9 January 1939: 'Rabbi David

Pearlman of Connecticut has telephoned that he had organized a group of people in his congregation who were willing and able to give affidavits.' NCC Records, File 92. Yivo Archives, New York.

59. For the different types of affidavits, see NCC Records, File 84: NCC's Manual on Immigration. Yivo Archives, New York .

60. Saturday Afternoon Session, Conference Called by NCC, 17 August 1938. NCC Records, File 2: Report on the Proceedings of Conference Called by NCC, 17 August 1938, p. 9. Yivo Archives, New York.

61. Razovsky, NCC, 'Advice to a Prospective Quota Immigrant, April 11, 1939'. NCC Records, File 84: NCC's Manual on Immigration. Yivo Archives, New York.

62. Mayerson to Razovsky, 28 October 1938. See also, Razovsky Director of Migration NRS, to William Haber, Executive Director, 19 April 1940. NCC Records, File 88: Correspondence of the NCC regarding US visa application procedures and affidavits of financial support. Yivo Archives, New York.

63. Razovsky, NCC, to Mrs Gisela Scheuer, Humane Refugee Aid Society, 27 June 1939. NCC Records, File 91: Correspondence between the NY Section, NCJW and the Humane Refugee Aid Society on Individual Refugee Cases, 1938–1939. See also, Chamberlain, Chairman NRS, to All Cooperating Committees, 11 July 1939, File 16: Informational Memos from Razovsky to Constituent Groups. Yivo Archives, New York .

64. Leland B. Morris, American Consul-General, Vienna to Mr Mark Brunswick, 1 December 1938. NCC Records. See also Ann S. Petluck to Razovsky, copy of a letter sent by Albert Tugendhat, 2 February 1939. File 88: Correspondence with State Department. Yivo Archives, New York.

65. See correspondence between Razovsky and Sophie Shaffer, New York Section, NCJW, 6 and 9 March 1939. NRS Records, Folder 89: Coordinating Committee. Yivo Archives, New York.

66. Section 12A, Act of May 26, 1924.

67. See Miss Petluck to Razovsky, Re: Quota Nationality, 7 June 1938. Chamberlain Papers, Folder 21. Yivo Archives, New York.

68. After the *Anschluss*, the combined quota for Germany and Austria was 27,370.

69. There could be no doubt that a state of emergency prevailed and, as constantly indicated by Jewish claims, most applicants did not have near -relatives in the United States. See for example, Meeting of the Committee on German-Jewish Immigration Policy, 26 January 1934, American Jewish Joint Distribution Committee Records, AR 1933–1944, File 683: Emigration into the United States, 1933–1944. American Jewish Joint Distribution Committee Archives, New York.

4 Professionals' Rescue Committees

Following the advent of the Hitler regime in Germany in 1933 and, especially after the enactment of the Nuremberg Laws in 1935, increasing numbers of German Jewish scholars and professionals, banished from German universities, hospitals and other academic institutions and denied the pursuit of their scientific work, sought refuge in the United States. Though scarred by their recent experiences, they were full of hopes for a better, even a glorious, future. They soon discovered that their aspirations encountered obdurate constraints imposed by American culture and the American social structure. Their ambitions tended to be high, but their attainments during the period of adjustment and acculturation were often disappointing. In addition to the usual problems facing new immigrants, most intellectual refugees suffered from the fact that their status in the new country was inferior to that to which they had felt entitled in Germany. Whereas refugees with extraordinarily high international status like physicists Albert Einstein or Kurt Goedel found no obstacle to assuming positions in the United States commensurate with their previous status, things were difficult for intellectuals below this rank. For them, previous positions could not so readily be translated into their American equivalents. Scholars who had already attained the rank of professor in their homeland soon found that they had relatively few chances to join the faculties of major American universities.

In order to centralize efforts to facilitate the entrance of refugee academics into the US and to pursue available positions, Jewish rescue organizations in the United States created specific committees, among them The Emergency Committee in Aid of Displaced Foreign Physicians and The Emergency Committee in Aid of Displaced

Foreign Scholars. These were closely allied with the National Coordinating Committee for Aid to Refugees and Emigrants Coming from Germany (henceforth NCC), to whom funds had been granted to cover the cost of the work either in part or in whole by the National Coordinating Committee Fund, Inc.[1]

The Committee for Displaced Foreign Physicians attempted to deal with problems facing German doctors in their efforts to find positions in medical research and practice. From the outset, Professor Joseph Chamberlain, with the continual assistance of Cecilia Razovsky, participated in the organization and development of these agencies. They took care of applicants before and after their arrival in the United States, making connections with academic and medical institutions all around the country. Razovsky, who in her capacity as Executive Director of the NCC, was in charge of relations with government authorities, made endless efforts, especially in cases of Jewish scholars and physicians in the United States on visitor visas, attempting to change their status, or at least prolong their stay.[2] Razovsky also maintained special campaigns among Jewish philanthropic associations to raise money for the upkeep of these people, as well as conducting extensive correspondence with medical centers.

One of many such letters reflects her connections. In spring 1938 Dr Lawrence Kubie of the American Psychoanalytic Association told her of his suggestion to certain officers of the American Medical Association, the American Psychiatric Association and the American Neurological Association that, at the next general meeting, they launch an appeal for contributions to a relief fund on behalf of refugee colleagues. He felt that this 'might carry some weight as a dignified protest'. Since the large majority of the physicians at these congresses were not Jews, it would enable them to be in a position to say 'that the funds so gathered would be used in a non-sectarian way, for all sufferers under Nazi oppression'.[3] Although non-sectarian by definition, Razovsky's efforts in the committees for the aid of physicians and scholars focused on Jewish refugees.

In a report dated November 1933, the NCC defined the three main aims of the Emergency Committee in Aid of Displaced Foreign Physicians as follows, and called for the committee to be created along these lines.[4]

1. To attempt to place preeminent research workers in medical schools and laboratories by supplying some of the necessary funds as stipends to be used for their maintenance.

2. To establish a bureau of information for other refugee physicians which would sympathetically and intelligently advise them concerning the rules governing medical licensure and the opportunities for medical or special practice.[5]
3. To find temporary volunteer employment in local institutions and hospitals for those in the US so that they may familiarize themselves with American methods of medical practice.[5]

One of the signs that the American public was becoming increasingly interested in the fate of refugees was the growing number of relief committees that sprang up in the US. In the fall of 1939 there were 208 organizations collecting money on behalf of European refugees. As the war continued, the number of foreign war-relief agencies mushroomed, reaching 700 by October 1941. Most of them fell into one of four categories: professional bodies dealing with specific problems; organizations based on national origin; religious groups and church committees; and community services. In summer 1934, Dr Sachs of the Committee in Aid of Displaced Foreign Physicians invited Razovsky to share 'part or all work to any other agency, if in the opinion of NCC another agency [was] better equipped to handle the work'. He argued that if a similar statement were to come from other agencies, such as the Physicians Committee of the American Jewish Congress, which would also abide by the decision of the NCC, 'we shall make more rapid progress toward unifying or coordinating our efforts'.[6] In reality, the two committees did not get along. In a letter to Chamberlain dated 6 July 1934, Razovsky complained that both Dr Baehr, secretary of the Committee in Aid of Displaced Foreign Physicians and Dr Jablons, chairman of the Committee of the American Jewish Congress, disagreed completely on the question of authority. Dr Jablons refused to 'be a tail to a kite' and demanded 'an equal footing with the other committee'.[7]

The forced mass migration of intellectuals, physicians, artists and skilled workers during the 1930s greatly intensified the usual difficulties experienced with the integration of immigrants in their new country, in particular when they reached America in the midst of the country's gravest economic depression. The placement, vocational training and case treatment of certain categories of newcomers with unique problems, necessitated the establishment of professional committees. Thus, committees were founded for social workers, physicians, psychologists, dentists, pharmacists, scholars and other professionals. These committees dealt with specially selected groups of outstanding and prominent professionals, for whom teaching appointments and other related posts had been secured in American universities. Although designed as a non-sectarian committee, by far the largest number of its beneficiaries was Jewish or non-Aryan.[8]

One group of refugees whose situation was a source of concern from the beginning was the physicians. Between 1934 and 1938, a total of 1,528 physicians entered the US from Germany and Austria, of whom 1,399 were Jewish;[9] 766 foreign physicians were admitted from all countries over the six months between July and December 1938. Of this number, 639 were Jewish.[10] In view of the fact that 5,500 doctors graduated annually from American medical schools and that in 1939 there were about 170,000 physicians throughout the country to provide medical care for a steadily increasing population, the entry of a few hundred immigrant physicians every year should not have presented a problem.[11] The fact was, however, that immigrant Jewish doctors faced enormous obstacles. In addition to the usual difficulties in adjusting to a foreign country, the physicians had to obtain a license to practice which was contingent on several requirements. As licenses to practice medicine in the United States were issued individually by the states, it depended on each state to establish its regulations. All states granted licenses only after examinations, although a state required physicians to pass its own local examination; most states, however, recognized and endorsed licenses secured by examination in those other states with which they had reciprocal relations;[12] and a few states accepted for license the diploma granted – upon examination – by the National Board of Examiners.[13]

In all states the pre-medical and medical educational requirements were similar: usually four years of secondary school, two years of college science and the equivalent of a four-year course in medicine. The National Board examination was divided into three parts. It was necessary to pass Parts I and II in order to gain an internship in an approved hospital. It was also necessary to serve an internship in an approved hospital before taking Part III. However, the most difficult condition for getting a license was the requirement of US citizenship.[14] In spite of the ruling by Texas Attorney-General Gerald C. Mann in summer 1939, that 'US citizenship as a condition precedent to the practice of medicine in Texas is invalid and unconstitutional ... and a denial of right guaranteed by the 14th amendment and of article 1, section 3 of the state's fundamental law', most states demanded that the candidate at least pass the stage of first papers toward citizenship before practicing medicine.[15]

The fact that refugee physicians were concentrated in New York posed yet another obstacle.[16] Although the regulations of the New York State Board of Medical Examiners were more lenient than those of the medical institutions in other states, it was nevertheless more difficult to find a position there.[17] Moreover, very few states endorsed a license issued by New York State. The concentration of thousands of refugee doctors in one city aroused the wrath of the local physicians – including Jewish physicians – who feared competition.[18] The NCC was aware of the antagonism expressed by medical sources. In a meeting of the Board of Directors of the National Coordinating Committee, on 6 January 1936, Mr Eric Warburg, who was on a visit from Germany, expressed his feeling that, as the only country still open to physicians, at least 1,000 more physicians might have to come to the United States from Germany. Every effort was made at the meeting to impress upon Mr Warburg that it would be very dangerous to flood the country with German physicians and that so far it had been very difficult finding places for even the 350 émigré physicians who were already in the US.[19]

Although newcomers had also found it desirable to take their medical examinations in New York because of the training units that existed there to help them prepare, a report published in January 1939 advised Jewish immigrant doctors not to take their examination in New York and especially not to establish themselves permanently in New York State: 'Any more immigrant physicians settling in New York would find great difficulty in building up practices and at the same time increase the danger of blocking the port of entry.'[20] The same report emphasized that, besides New York, there were five states in which examinations could be taken without long preliminaries: Connecticut, Maryland, Massachusetts, New Jersey and Ohio.[21] In these five states training units similar to the ones in New York were established with the assistance of the NCC, and local committees were formed to help physicians prepare for their examination and to help doctors find places to practice once they had secured licenses.[22]

When it became obvious that the great majority of the refugee physicians were Jews, the atmosphere of hostility toward the refugees became tinged with antisemitism. In 1941 an article in *The Journal of the American Medical Association* (hereafter *JAMA*) stated, that 'Much gossip and false generalizations can be traced to prejudice, unfriendliness and an unwillingness to make allowance for the period of adaptation.'[23] Although, on investigation, the majority of complaints against Jewish physicians proved baseless, the Emergency Committee saw fit to remove 180 Jewish physicians from its list and to advise them to change their profession.[24] An editorial in February 1939 complained that 'some of the refugees are poorly trained or of low ethical standing [and] some find it difficult to adapt themselves to American ways in the practice of medicine'.[25] At the same time, the Emergency Committee in Aid of Displaced Foreign Physicians strongly denied the accusations that Jewish physicians competed with non-Jewish doctors [26] or that they were poorly trained.[27]

Toward the late 1930s, more and more critical voices were heard from antisemitic groups, which resulted in stricter regulations regarding the issue of medical licenses.[28] In 1938 and 1939, thirty-seven states adopted new measures which ranged from the obligation to work as an intern for a year to the condition that a candidate had to become an American citizen before he could apply for examination by the local medical association.[29] Where once a medical degree from any noted European university was considered proof of outstanding scholarship, in the late 1930s there was a deplorable tendency to swing in the other direction. Retreating to an incomprehensible isolation, legislators and others built bars around their own small domains, arbitrarily cutting off those valuable immigrants whose professional ability could have contributed to the health of the United States. It was not the European physician who had changed; it was, at least partially, the American attitude. And surely it was not the universities which they represented which had changed, except in the years since the Nazis had crushed culture in one European country after another. This reversal of attitude had become a major problem to the Committee and hampered its work. There was an urgent need to persuade the American medical authorities that the immigrant physicians – especially the Jewish doctors – would eventually integrate and contribute to the benefit of American society and its health.[30] Unfortunately for the refugees, the new restrictions further reduced their prospects of finding suitable positions and reflected the need for an efficient professional organization to deal with specific problems.

Already in mid-1934 there were five organizations assisting physicians: the Emergency Committee in Aid of Displaced Foreign Physicians, with Bernard Sachs as chairman; the Physicians' Committee of the American Jewish Congress, with Benjamin Jablons as chairman; the German Jewish Physicians' Committee, with Ernst Gundelfinger as chairman; the Physicians' Committee of the

Conference on Jewish Relations, with Reuben Ottenberg as chairman; and another committee under the chairmanship of Dr Auslander.[31] The duplication of several physicians' committees caused confusion, inefficiency and needless suffering to the refugees.[32] After the NCC started to operate as the umbrella organization, Razovsky undertook responsibility for the professional committees.[33] A report by Razovsky, as Executive Director of the NCC, dated 13 November 1934, described several meetings with representatives of the various physicians' committees in order to clarify and coordinate the activities of the committees and prevent duplication. It was decided to centralize all assistance for physicians with the Emergency Committee in Aid of Displaced Foreign Physicians, which received funds from the NCC.[34]

The Committee was established on the initiative of a non-sectarian group in order 'to facilitate the placement of a limited number of specially qualified foreign medical men in non-competitive positions'.[35] From the outset it limited its activities to finding positions for outstanding physicians in research institutes, hospitals, laboratories and universities. An additional aim was to establish a national card index with comprehensive data on the refugee physicians. The card index was made available to hospitals, universities and research institutes, which were thus able to choose the researcher most suited to fulfill their particular needs.[36]

In principle, the Committee agreed to deal with physicians regardless of their religion, but since the clear majority of the doctors were Jews, most of their beneficiaries were also Jews.[37] It was 'non-sectarian' only in as far as it professed to provide assistance to persons of all faiths without distinction, although due to the nature of the immigration itself most of the aid went to Jews. Those who did the practical work, like the secretary, George Baehr, and the chairman, Emanuel Libman, were Jews. The funds came from Jewish sources, such as the JDC, the Hofheimer Foundation, the Rosenwald Family Foundation and the New York Foundation via the NCC. In other words, the Physicians' Emergency Committee was affiliated with the NCC and, since 1939, with the NRS, in both cases under the responsibility of Cecilia Razovsky, through which it received its annual budget of tens of thousands of dollars.[38] Cecilia Razovsky was in charge of all direct communication with medical centers nationwide and with the Committee and its local branches that sent to her all changes and information concerning the licensure of foreign physicians.[39] She gathered and published the relevant information with regard to each state, including the Panama Canal Zone, and the fees needed for registration[40] and forwarded it to the various centers.[41] Not only was Razovsky interested in changing the regulations, but she surveyed the work of each state legislature to identify suggestions for new bills which might affect Jewish physicians, sending her recommendation to the local committee. In October 1938, when news about a new bill to modify requirements for foreign physicians applying for licenses in Oregon reached her, she immediately sent an urgent message to the local Émigré Committee, 'to see to it that this bill is not presented before any state Legislature ... Our feeling is that just such suggestions are likely to cause more stringent laws to be passed ... It is our opinion that the introduction of bills of the nature described will not be helpful to the cause.'[42]

Whenever she heard of an available opening, Razovsky searched for the right physician. A letter to the committee in Iowa indicated that she had received a request from the University of Iowa for two physicians and she asked them to allocate the $600 they had promised previously for a stipend to be paid to a physician, who would be placed at the disposal of the university.[43] When the New York Committee for Clinical Pathology allocated a $500 stipend to a newly-arrived refugee ophthalmologist to work in an institution, she arranged for the NCC to match that sum.[44] In a report summarizing the activities of the NCC in 1937, Razovsky informed the Board of Directors, NCC, that Jewish physicians were placed in universities and hospitals as a result of the efforts of the Emergency Committee in Aid of Displaced Foreign Physicians and her department. She also stated that paid positions were found for many physicians in laboratories, institutions and Departments of Health. A number of physicians were also placed in various hospitals' Out-Patient Departments in order to acquire American training and experience.[45]

In a report covering the activities of the NRS in the fall of 1941, Razovsky stated that a notable increase had taken place in the assistance extended to refugee professionals whose skills could be utilized in the US. This was particularly true of physicians, with more than forty a month being placed in positions or in practice. In all, she stressed, 'about 75 professionals a month were being placed'. In addition the Capital Loan Committee of the NRS had helped Jewish physicians establish themselves in practice.[46] Especially interesting was her correspondence with Professor Albert Einstein.[47] Not only had Einstein contributed several small sums, but he often asked for her assistance in bringing into the United States famous physicians and scientists, or in finding positions for those who were already in the US, with which she was happy to comply.[48] In a letter dated May 1938, while acknowledging his help in finding a position for one doctor and his wife in Arrowhead Spring Hotel, she sent Einstein the names of four more physicians and asked him to contact his friend, Mr Harry S. Ward, who was managing director of the Arrowhead Springs Hotel, to find jobs for 'these physicians with excellent experience'.[49]

In contrast to Razovsky, who dealt with all Jewish refugee doctors, the Committee limited its activity to research institutes and universities in which to locate positions for what it considered outstanding physicians, which unfortunately left many other refugee physicians, outside its scope.[50] Consequently, a new committee, The National Committee for Resettlement of Foreign Physicians, under the aegis of the NCC, was established to arrange for the placement of less-well-known doctors in minor hospitals around the country or in private practices.[51]

Its objectives were few but vital:

1. To evaluate the eligibility of individual émigré physicians to practice medicine in the United States.
2. To assist those who were found competent in preparing for examinations and for American medical requirements.
3. To further their resettlement in those parts of the United States where medical services are needed.[52]

In other words, the new committee's aim was to review all the required qualifications in order to help medical authorities examine the medical associations by collecting data on regulations in different states and, finally, to take care of the resettlement of doctors outside the New York area where they were really needed; at the same time they aimed to protect American physicians from possible unfair competition. The objective was the complete integration of the émigré physician into the American system.[53]

With the encouragement and assistance of the NCC/NRS, the Committee set up local committees and voluntary boards in each state.[54] Several physicians were chosen from each of the state bodies to serve on the national committee. Within each state the special committees acted in an advisory capacity, liaising between the émigré physicians, the state licensing boards and local medical societies. They also located rural employment opportunities and internships and evaluated individual émigrés considered for placement in practice or institutional work.[55] To exclude unfit persons from assistance, the national committee required proficiency in English and a favorable professional evaluation by its advisory committee, which was composed of American physicians. Between 1933 and 1941, 700 male and female physicians had been placed in hospitals throughout the United States. From among them only five had to be relocated, and complaints had been made concerning only three.[56]

During the process of sponsorship and resettlement the committee provided the refugee physician with facilities which could enable him or her to adjust to American conditions. The NRS placed special emphasis on the preparation for general practice, especially in small communities. The physicians were recommended to take a retraining course in American medicine by placing them in internship. In addition to her work with the committee, Razovsky was constantly on the alert to find available openings. In 1941, about 500 physicians had been successfully resettled in small towns or villages in Ohio, California, Colorado, Maryland, New Jersey and Virginia. After interviewing forty physicians who had been settled in small communities, a field secretary concluded that 'Assimilation of the foreigner may be said to be complete when he is "in" as well as "of" his community.'[57] Most of them did indeed adjust and, after a short period, had integrated into American society, contributing professionally as well as socially. A report published in 1941 by The Émigré Physician in America Organisation concluded that the National Committee for Resettlement of Foreign Physicians had succeeded in 'assisting and placing between twelve and fifteen hundred émigrés in internship or practice during the two and a half years of its existence', and that 'no serious complaints or maladjustments have occurred among 95 to 98 per cent of such placements'.[58]

Similarly, The Emergency Committee in Aid of Displaced German Scholars,[59] organized by President Livingston Farrand of Cornell University, with the cooperation of Felix M. Warburg, Dr Alfred E. Cohn, Mr Fred M. Stein, Mr Bernard Flexner and others, had, since its inception in early May 1933 (long before the establishment of other refugee committees), granted aid through American universities to a number of scholars for a period of one or more years.[60]

Expulsion from German academic institutions left thousands of scholars and scientists unemployed and unable to continue their research, not to mention being bereft of any source of income. By mid 1934 there were already 7,500 academicians, teachers and students desperately in need of assistance.[61] Many of those who eventually.

succeeded in getting into the United States faced monumental difficulties in finding suitable positions.[62] The main reason given for the rejection of German scholars from American institutions was the fear that German professors 'would bloc teaching positions for young American scholars and could prevent and/or hamper their careers'.[63] Although the Emergency Committee had been convened in defense of the dignity of mankind regardless of race, creed or political opinion and was guided by a determination that there should be no place for a spirit of intolerance and repression, in reality, a different picture emerged. It should be remembered that when the Emergency Committee was organized in 1933, the United States was in the midst of the Great Depression. Colleges and universities lacked resources. Enrollment of students dropped and contributions to endowments were much diminished. Under such conditions, any integration of foreign scholars would naturally have caused resentment among faculty members. However, when the issue involved Jewish scholars, the stated economic reasons were in fact an excuse and a cover-up for plain and simple antisemitism. For example, when, in the summer of 1933, American universities promoted a plan to permit the entry of German refugee scholars and asked US consuls in Germany for information about available Jewish professors, George Messersmith, then Consul-General to Germany, went out of his way to prove that Jewish professors were dangerous individuals, holding ideas which, 'while designated as "liberal", are in reality in direct opposition to our own social order'. Messersmith gave several reasons for his objection to the admission of Jewish professors; for example, Jews differed from American professors in their lack of interest in everything which was not directly relevant to their field. His strongest objection, however, was focused on what he deemed an established fact, that 'many of the Jewish professors were socialists of an advanced type' and would contaminate young students.[64] A less sweeping view was expressed by Dr Stephen Duggan, chairman of the Emergency Committee, according to whom antisemitism was found in some places, but they were very few. He mentioned only one flagrant case, which had occurred in an eastern college where a scholar was dropped because of 'incompatibility with the head of the department'. A professor who investigated the matter and reported his findings to the Emergency Committee concluded that the reason for the dismissal of the émigré professor can be traced to 'his outspoken and determined criticism of Nazi Germany'.[65]

Very much like the Emergency Committee in Aid of Foreign

Physicians, the Scholars' Committee restricted its activity to helping only outstanding scholars, whose research could serve the advancement of American civilization.[66] In Stephen Duggan's words: 'Not all can be saved. The Emergency Committee in Aid of Displaced German Scholars must not *only* (original emphasis) confine itself to displaced German scholars but also *only* (original emphasis) to the ablest and most distinguished among them'.[67] Certain definite regulations shaped the Committee's program:

1. The Committee has refused to urge the employment of specific scholars by colleges and universities. An institution wishing to invite a professor to its staff with the help of the committee must take the initiative in applying for aid. Such institutions ... must feel free to select candidates and follow the technique they would normally employ in calling members to their faculties.
2. Observance of this policy has kept the committee free of commitments to individual scholars. In no case can it undertake to place them. Its true function is to work with universities, assisting institutions that wish to call displaced foreign professors but require help during the initial year. The Committee has made a practice of placing its files of displaced scholars at the disposal of colleges, universities and other qualified parties at their request.
3. It has been the policy of the Committee to make grants only to institutions which expect to give tenure to the scholar in question provided the grantee proves his acceptability during a trial period and the arrangement is otherwise satisfactory.
4. Individual grants made by the Committee have ranged in amount from \$450 to \$2,000 ... the Committee is reluctant to make grants covering the total salary of any displaced scholar, preferring to assist in cases where the institution has either been able to provide part of the salary from its own budget or has succeeded in securing a grant for the scholar's partial support from outside sources.[68]
5. There has been no sectarian basis for the Committee's grant. No record is kept of the religion or race of scholars aided. Stipends have been given, for example, to Protestant and Jewish theological seminaries alike, and a number of Catholic colleges and universities have received assistance.
6. The Committee adheres to the policy ... that it must not give encouragement to displaced foreign scholars who will compete with American teachers. It will encourage ... scholars of preeminence because they compete with no one.[69]

In other words, the Committee's help was limited to scholars who had been professors or at least *Privatdozenten* (senior lecturers) in European universities. It also decided that it would not provide grants for refugee scholars under 30 years of age or over 60. The Emergency Committee offered the scholars no relief services. Due to its financial difficulties, and out of principle, the Committee considered relief to be a personal matter. Jewish scholars were referred mostly to NCC/NRS agencies according to the nature of their problem. Although the NCC/NRS did their utmost to help the émigré Jewish scholar and his family who had been receiving a grant for two years from the Emergency Committee and who could not find employment or was ill, they had their own financial difficulties. An 8 February 1936 meeting of the Executive Committee of the NCC discussed the responsibility for providing relief to persons brought to the United States under grants given by special committees. After discussion, it was agreed that the NCC 'cannot assume to handle relief cases of persons that have been placed by special committees'. It was suggested that these special committees be advised to keep a certain reserve on hand to take care of their clients if they were unable to find permanent posts for them. It was eventually agreed that in such cases a definite time should be set for the NCC to discontinue relief and turn the scholar's case over to the Emergency Committee.[70] The cases of individual scholars not under the responsibility of the Emergency Committee were, however, different. A special relief committee operated under the NCC, taking care of needy scholars and their families.[71]

In a 1 May 1937 report of the Emergency Committee in Aid of Displaced German Scholars, John Whyte, Assistant Secretary for the Executive Committee, called for more efforts to be made to save émigré scholars and stated categorically that:

> Not only are such efforts to be considered purely humanitarian gestures or, in these troubled times, merely valuable reaffirmation of our faith in the fundamental importance in universities of the spirit of free inquiry and the search for truth; enlightened self-interest demands that we save for ourselves and the world the distinguished German scholars who have served, and with our help will continue to serve, the highest causes of scholarship, science and humanity.[72]

Most universities appeared to agree and even encouraged a plan to bring prominent scholars into the US, in order to enrich higher learning; yet, with the dearth of available positions, the reduced resources and the unbalanced budgets of American colleges and universities, it is no wonder that young American scholars feared competition. The request for grants for displaced scholars and the subsequent provision for placing them permanently in university faculties threatened such young American scholars who could find no openings in their field of scientific interest.

It all began in early May 1933, when news of the persecution of German scholars – mostly Jewish or of Jewish descent – reached the United States. A group of prominent American scientists and philanthropists – Dr Alfred E. Cohn, a distinguished scientist of the Rockefeller Institute for Medical Research, Bernard Flexner, an eminent lawyer and philanthropist, Felix M. Warburg, a celebrated New York lawyer and philanthropist and Fred M. Stein, a leader in philanthropic work in New York City – looked for a method for extending aid to scholars who had fled to the United States. An organizing committee, Emergency Committee in Aid of Displaced German Scholars,[73] consisting of Dr Cohn, Dr Flexner, Mr Stein and Dr Duggan of the Institute of International Education, was formed. The Committee functioned as an agency for twelve years, raising funds on behalf of displaced scholars and making these funds available primarily through a program of grant-in-aid to colleges, universities and other institutions of learning. Its first act was to send letters announcing its objectives to American colleges and universities asking for their cooperation.[74] The letters of acceptance were nearly always accompanied by expressions of great satisfaction, offering their help and cooperation. The universities were therefore invited to send their representatives to serve on the General Committee. Dr Livingston Farrand, President of Cornell University, became chairman of the Committee, Dr Stephen Duggan its secretary and Mr Fred M. Stein its treasurer. Professor Nelson P. Mead of the College of the City of New York and Professor L.C. Dunn of Columbia University were added to Messrs Cohn, Farrand, Flexner, Stein and Duggan to form an Executive Committee.[75] In 1940, Dr Frank Aydelotte of the Institute for Advanced Study, Dr Hertha Kraus of the American Friends Service Committee, Dr Alvin Johnson of the New School for Social Research, Dr Henry Allen Moe of the Guggenheim Foundation and the Oberlaender Trust, Charles A. Riegelman of the NRS and Professor Harlow Shapley of Harvard University all joined the Executive Committee.

Stephen Duggan, who served as the Committee's secretary and

later as its chairman until 1945, when it was disbanded, maintained in 1942 that the entrance of German scholars would be for the benefit of the United States, urging American institutions to grasp the unique opportunity afforded them.[76] The Committee distributed a list of available refugee scholars along with their curricula vitae and their achievements in respective fields, so that interested universities could select the most qualified candidate. At the same time the Committee allocated a grant to each institution which invited a scholar, on the assumption that after a trial period of a year or two, the scholar would be offered a permanent job.[77] Young scholars, who had not yet made a name for themselves, were naturally left out, unable as yet to prove their talents. The fact that they could not apply directly to the universities limited their prospects of finding work. Razovsky, who dealt with individual refugee scholars, made endless efforts to help them, not only in locating positions but also in providing recommendations, which she obtained from well-known scientists, among them Professor Albert Einstein.[78] It has already been mentioned that, after arriving in the United States, Professor Einstein maintained close contact with Cecilia Razovsky and praised her successful efforts. He brought to her attention names of worthy Jewish scientists, whom she tried to bring in as non-quota immigrants, by locating for them academic positions.[79] The NCC and later the NRS had circularized colleges and universities, asking them to offer appointments to refugee German scholars. But soliciting jobs for refugees was a procedure that contradicted the principles of the Emergency Committee. At a conference between representatives of the two organizations in early 1935, it was agreed that the NCC would no longer consider the placement of émigré scholars as part of its activities.[80] But such an agreement was not fully implemented. The Committee helped only prominent scholars and excluded young scholars who did not meet its requirements, or scholars who had been granted a temporary position as visiting professor but whose appointment had not been made permanent by their university; these were left without the backing of the Committee.[81] Razovsky, who centralized all pleas for positions from foreign scholars, had to use her own personal connections, especially with Jewish institutions.[82] To mention but two cases: Dr S had been an art historian in Germany. Due to Razovsky's efforts he was granted a stipend covering one year, and was eventually placed as art historian with the Detroit Institute of Art, with the understanding that at the end of one year he would be employed as a regular member of staff and have his salary paid by the Institute. Similar arrangements had been made for Dr R., a philologist, who had good prospects of becoming a permanent member of staff at Columbia University.[83]

Felix Warburg, a member the Provisional Committee of the Emergency Committee in Aid of German Scholars and of the Executive Committee, was also the treasurer of the NCC. He was in constant touch with Razovsky during the 1930s and 1940s. They corresponded frequently concerning Jewish scholars and scientists who were in need of affidavits or stipends to enable them to obtain a position in US institutions of higher learning.[84] Notwithstanding Warburg's activities in the Emergency Committee, he was always open to Razovsky's pleas for assistance. While Warburg supplied the funds, Razovsky was the middle-woman, liaising with the relevant institutions.[85]

The difficulties facing German Jewish professors, although in many instances not dissimilar to those facing their non-Jewish counterparts, were nevertheless better handled by American Jewish rescue organizations. The most effective was the NCC/NRS under the responsibility of Cecilia Razovsky, NCC Executive Director, and, since 1939, Director of Migration, NRS. Although cooperating with the Emergency Committee which was, at least by definition, non-sectarian, her special attention was focused on Jewish scholars and especially those who did not meet the requirements of the Emergency Committee. Locating a position in the US for a German Jewish professor still in Germany provided a way out of the Nazi hell – a life saver. The Immigration Law of 1924 permitted the movement of professors to the United States as non-quota migrants. Under Category (d) such applicants had to establish that they had been employed continuously as professors in a college, academy, seminary, or university for at least two years prior to their entry into the United States. In addition, such an applicant had to provide proof that s/he has been offered a permanent teaching position in an American institution of higher learning.[86] However, it should be stressed that under employment procedures in American universities, teaching positions were approved only for a limited period of time. Tenure was granted, if at all, only after several years and only after the candidate had established himself or herself as a scholar and been approved by academic committees and university authorities. Jewish professors – among them renowned scholars and scientists – often could not comply with all these requirements. Nazi anti-Jewish legislations made it impossible for them to practice their professions in Germany, especially since the enactment of the 1935 Nuremberg laws. Many of them had been out of work for over two years and hence were disqualified as potential non-quota immigrants under this provision. In fact, their inability to gain employment was one of the reasons for their desire to emigrate. Victor Klemperer, Professor of Romance Literature, for example, who had converted to Christianity in 1912 and was married to a non-Jewish woman, was denied a non-quota immigration visa because he had been dismissed in 1935 and therefore could not meet the requirement of holding an academic position for two years prior to his application. The case of Professor Werner Winter was similar. He was denied a non-quota visa, because he 'has not been actively engaged as a professor during the last two years'.[87] The main problem remained finding positions in the United States. Well connected with academic institutions and scientific laboratories, Razovsky started to search for possible positions that could be filled by Jewish professors and scientists. Two projects in which she was involved were especially renowned. The first, the New School in New York City, was headed by Alvin Johnson and known as the 'University of Exile', when it became a professional home for the many German Jewish professors who joined its faculty.[88] The second, the Hebrew Union College (HUC) in Cincinnati, was headed by Dr Julian Morgenstern and established a Jewish scientific foundation with the help of European Jewish professors.[89] In the fall of 1934, at a joint meeting of faculty and Board of Governors, the Hebrew Union College (HUC) made its initial commitment to appropriate $4,000 for the purpose of bringing two Jewish German scholars to the college, Julius Lewy and Guido Kisch, who were already in the United States; and to invite Michael Wilensky, who was still in Lithuania, for a year in order to catalogue Hebrew manuscripts. This project, carried out in addition to the program initiated by the Emergency Committee, had done a great deal by way of saving for the world the outstanding contribution of distinguished scholars and intellectuals.[90] Yet, whereas the Emergency Committee operated as a non-sectarian committee, the project of the HUC was focused on helping Jewish scholars. Between 1935 and 1942, the Hebrew Union College in Cincinnati succeeded in bringing into the United States eleven scholars.[91] While Kisch, a historian of law, did not join the HUC faculty, becoming instead a visiting faculty member at Stephen Wise's Jewish Institute of Religion, Lewy and Wilensky came and joined the college as permanent scholars.[92]

The significance of this project was well summarized in the words of Michael Guttmann, Head of the Jewish Seminar in Budapest, to Morgenstern on 23 April 1939: 'What you are doing is a deed which has its unique historical value and will remain memorable for all times. It is a noble rescue, not alone of the Jewish teacher, but also of the Jewish teaching.'[93]

On the whole, the relationship between Razovsky and the Emergency Committee proved fruitful, especially in the later 1930s. In a letter to Razovsky, now director of the Migration Department, NRS, Betty Drury, assistant secretary to the committee, acknowledged that 'there was a complete cooperation between the two organizations [in working] together to find employment and aid the refugee scholars'.[94]

These efforts on behalf of the foreign scholars – both Jewish and non-Jewish – required funds. From the outset in 1933 it was agreed that, since the economic conditions in the country were reflected in the universities and colleges, the rescue organizations would contribute to the maintenance and/or salary of the scholars admitted to these institutes. The original announcement from the Provisional Committee of the Emergency Committee to the Universities on 27 May 1933 declared clearly that 'because of the financial condition of our own institutions of higher education, they ought not to be called upon in any way for financial assistance ... The funds necessary to carry out any program must be raised from sources outside the universities'.[95]

During the first years of its existence, the Committee was financed almost exclusively by Jewish foundations and institutions. The New York Foundation, the Nathan Hofheimer Foundation, the Rosenwald Family Foundation[96] and, especially, the JDC contributed the lion's share of the budget. From 1934 to 1936 the JDC allocated $297,000. Over the entire period of the Committee's existence, the New York Foundation contributed a total of $339,851 and the Hofheimer Foundation $67,000. All the funds were transmitted through the NCC and afterwards through the NRS.[97] It should be emphasized that, although two-thirds of the displaced scholars who were placed by the Emergency Committee were Jewish, it was not only Jewish sources that contributed to the Emergency Committee. The Rockefeller Foundation, for example, supported a total of 303 scholars with aid amounting to $1,410,778. The Carnegie Corporation awarded twenty grants to scholars which totaled $110,000;[98] and, since 1939, the Oberlaender Trust, whose grants to scholars totaled, by 1945, $300,000.[99]

Although the number of scholars admitted to US universities and colleges was limited,[100] the Emergency Committee in Aid of Displaced Foreign Scholars not only helped foreign academics to escape the Nazi hell, but also provided opportunities for a wide range of American scholars and students to benefit from the abilities of excellent German professors. There can be no doubt that the Emergency Committee plan had worked well. There are scores of American institutions whose intellectual life has been greatly enriched by the distinguished scholars brought by the Emergency Committee. In the words of Stephen Duggan and Betty Drury:

> We believe that the displaced scholars have kept the faith and have contributed largely to the spiritual life of our country; and we believe also that our country as symbolized by its institutions of learning has realized at least in part the spirit of its great Declaration in extending, 'life, liberty, and the pursuit of happiness' to this group of splendid scholars.[101]

It was also evident by the late 1930s that the efforts of American organizations had paid off. In a July 1938 memorandum Joseph Chamberlain stated that:

> It is needless to recite the cultural contribution which many of the intellectuals have brought into the country, or the benefits America will derive from them and their children ... and this is true not only of the half dozen or more Nobel prize winners whom we have been fortunate enough to secure for this country – exiles from Germany – but of hundreds of first-rate scientists, authors, artists, musicians and professors who, in loyalty to this country which has given them refuge, will repay America manifold.[102]

In retrospect, it may be concluded that the Emergency Committee achieved a great deal by way 'of saving for the world the outstanding contribution of distinguished scholars and intellectuals'.[103]

NOTES

1. See Chapter 1.
2. Augusta Mayerson, NCJW, New York Section, Service to Foreign Born, to NCC, Subject: Dr Fritz Borehardt, 24 October 1938. NCC Records, Folder 90. Yivo Archives, New York.
3. Lawrence Kubie M.D., The American Psychoanalytic Association, New York to Razovsky, 21 April 1938. Chamberlain Papers, Folder 16. Yivo Archives, New York.
4. Dr Emanuel Libman was chairman of the Emergency Committee; Laurence Farmer was its executive director.
5. 'Report', NCC Records, Folder 34: Correspondence with the Emergency Committee in Aid of Displaced Foreign Physicians, November 1933. Yivo Archives, New York.
6. Dr Sachs to Razovsky, 3 July 1934, Re: Displaced Physicians. NCC Records, Folder 34:

Correspondence with the Emergency Committee in Aid of Displaced Foreign Physicians. Yivo Archives, New York.

7. Razovsky to Chamberlain, 6 July 1934. Chamberlain Papers, p. 2762. Yivo Archives, New York.

8. Cecilia Razovsky, 'Memorandum', 21 October 1938. Razovsky Records, Box 3. AJHS Archives, New York.

9. 'Organization Section, Immigration of Alien Immigrant Physicians', *The Journal of the American Medical Association* (hereafter JAMA), (25 February 1939, 112, 8), p. 737.

10. United States, Department of Justice: Immigration and Naturalization Service, 'Immigrant Physicians Admitted to the United States', and 'Statement Issued to Press Representatives on 12 September 1938', Prepared by Henry W. Levy, NRS. Chamberlain Papers, Folder 96. Yivo Archives, New York.

11. Lawrence Farmer, Executive Secretary, Emergency Committee in Aid of Displaced Foreign Physicians, to Razovsky, 31 August 1938: 'I think one can state categorically that it is not true that the German Jewish doctors are occupying so many posts in New York hospitals that it has become difficult for Christian doctors to obtain appointments. Few, if any of these German doctors have obtained appointments to staffs in hospitals. Many are working as assistants in dispensaries. I believe that relatively few are working at the non-Christian hospitals.' NCC Records, Folder 32. Yivo Archives, New York.

12. The regulations governing reciprocity were complicated and difficult to interpret; every state has its own regulations covering its relations with every other state. For the various regulations, see, 'Regulations Covering the Admission of foreign Physicians to the Medical Licensing Examinations in the Various States of the Union', Chamberlain to Laurence Farmer, Executive Director of the Emergency Committee in Aid of Displaced Foreign Physicians, 14 December 1938. Chamberlain Papers, Folder 16. Yivo Archives, New York.

13. Dr Laurence Farmer, Executive Secretary, Emergency Committee in Aid of Displaced Foreign Physicians, to Razovsky, NCC, 28 September 1938, 'Information on the Procedure for Securing Medical Licenses by Foreign Physicians', January 1939. Chamberlain Records, Folder 16, and also in NCC Records, Folder 32. Yivo Archives, New York. It should be mentioned, however, that these regulations did not give complete information about reciprocity (that is, the acceptance and endorsement by one state of a license granted in another state after examination). Every state had its own regulation covering its relations with every other state.

14. The states that demanded full American citizenship: Arizona, California (as of 1 January 1939), Arkansas, Delaware, Florida, Georgia, Idaho (as of 1 January 1939), Iowa (as of 1 January 1939), Kansas, Kentucky, Michigan, Missouri (as of 1 January 1939), Montana, Nevada, Nebraska, Oklahoma, Oregon (as of 1 January 1939), North Carolina, South Carolina, Tennessee, Texas, West Virginia, Wisconsin, Wyoming. See 'Regulations Covering the Admission of foreign Physicians to the Medical Licensing Examinations in the Various States of the Union', Chamberlain to Laurence Farmer, Executive Director of the Emergency Committee in Aid of Displaced Foreign Physicians, 14 December 1938. Chamberlain Papers, Folder 16. Yivo Archives, New York.

15. 'Banning of Aliens as Doctors Held Illegal', *Austin Chronicle*, 10 June 1939. See also the rulings of the Attorney-Generals of South Dakota in 1926, and of Utah in 1939, who also held such legislation to be unconstitutional. Similar requirements were also demanded of émigré dentists who wished to practice in the United States. They, however, were also required to attend dental school in the US, even if they had graduated from dental schools in Germany. The reason was that training in the US took longer than in Germany. Razovsky was responsible for the émigré dentists, informing them about the different requirements in every state and using her connections to find a proper position for them. See NCC Records, Folders 19, 25. See also Attorney-General W. H. Wright to Ziegler, Dunn and Becker, Attorneys at Law, Omaha, Nebraska, 16 September 1936, Chamberlain Papers, Folder 16. Yivo Archives, New York.

16. In 1941 about 1,500 doctors were in practice and 1,500 unlicensed. See 'Report of the National Committee for Resettlement of Foreign Physicians, 1941', p. 4. Chamberlain Papers, Folder 16. See also 'Information on the Procedure for Securing Medical License by Foreign Physicians', ibid., 1 January 1939. Yivo Archives, New York.

17. Minutes, Executive Committee of NCC, 13 November 1934: 'A Study of the Adjustment of 282 Émigré Physicians Living in Greater New York, March 1945–August 1945'. NRS

Papers, pp. 1639–41. See also Chamberlain Papers, Folder 26. Yivo Archives, New York.

18. See Boris Fingerhood, Superintendent, Israel Zion Hospital, Brooklyn, N.Y. 'The Refugee Physician in America, A Medical Refugee Settlement Plan', 5 January 1939. Chamberlain Papers, Folder 16. Yivo Archives, New York.

19. Meeting of the Board of Directors, NCC, 6 January 1936. Chamberlain Papers, Folder 2. Yivo Archives, New York. The Warburg family was a German-Jewish family of bankers since 1789. The family was traditionally divided into two prominent lines, the Alsterufer Warburgs and the Mittelweg Warburgs. One of the members of the family in the United States was Felix Warburg. He was a banker and philanthropist. Another American Warburg was Paul Warburg. The German branch of the family included Max Warburg, one of the founders of the IG Farben industrial conglomerate. At the outbreak of the Second World War all Jewish members had been expelled from the board of IG Farben. Virtually all members of the Warburg family had fled to the United States or Great Britain in 1938. However, two cousins, mother and daughter Gerta and Betty Warburg were captured by the Nazis and died in the concentration camp at Sobibor. Max, Paul and Felix M. Warburg were brothers; Eric Warburg was their cousin. For more details of the family see Ron Chernow, *The Warburgs: the Twentieth-century Odyssey of a Remarkable Jewish Family* (New York: Random House, 1993).

20. Information on the Procedure for Securing Medical Licenses by Foreign Physicians', January 1939. Chamberlain Records, Folder 16. Yivo Archives, New York.

21. In fact, there were other states which did not raise legal bars against foreign physicians, but they nevertheless found other methods of blocking admission to examinations. See, ibid., p. 1.

22. For a detailed list of all requirements needed according to states, see ibid., pp. 2–14. See also earlier draft of 'Regulations Governing the Admission of Foreign Physicians to the Medical Licensing Examinations in the Various States of the Union', 14 December 1938. Chamberlain Records, Folder 16. Yivo Archives, New York.

23. 'The Émigré Physician', *JAMA*, 117 (29 November 1941), pp. 1881–2.

24. Cited in ibid.

25. Editorial, 'The Problem of the Refugee Physician', *JAMA*, 112 (25 February 1939), p. 735. See also Chamberlain to Bernard Sachs, Chairman of the Physicians' Emergency Committee, 1 November 1934. Chamberlain Papers, Folder 9. Yivo Archives, New York.

26. See for example, Jesse H. Steinhart, Attorney, to Jerome Michael, General Jewish Council, discussing the situation in California where bills were introduced to restrict the number of foreign physicians: 'Figures showing the total number of émigré doctors admitted to practice in California within the last five years indicate first, that competition by émigré doctors is not sufficient to justify the attempt to pass these bills, and second, that the number of émigré doctors who may seek admission to practice, judging from past figures, is not of tremendous import.' However, his conclusion is that the bills 'are objectionable from the standpoint of the spirit behind the bill and the possibility of the extension of that spirit to other fields'. NCC Records, Folder 19. Yivo Archives, New York.

27. Farmer to Razovsky, 31 August 1938. NCC Records, Folder 32. Yivo Archives, New York.

28. Jerome Michael, General Jewish Council, to Razovsky, NCC, 2 May 1939 and Razovsky's reply on 5 May 1939. NCC Records, Folder 19. Yivo Archives, New York.

29. D. L. Edsall, 'Émigré Physicians', *JAMA*, 117 (29 November 1941), reprinted on p. 13. Chamberlain Papers, Folder 16. Yivo Archives, New York.; See, also, 'Regulations Governing the Admission of Foreign Physicians to the Medical Licensing Examinations in the Various States of the Union', 14 December 1938. Chamberlain Papers, Folder 16. Yivo Archives, New York.

30. 'Report of the National Committee for Resettlement of Foreign Physicians', 1941, p. 3. Chamberlain Records, Folder 16. Yivo Archives, New York. In January 1939, Dr Boris Fingerhood of the Israel Zion Hospital sent 'A Medical Refugee Settlement Plan' to Chamberlain, with the suggestion of locating the physicians in rural areas where they were most needed. Such a plan, he argued, would accomplish 'the double purpose of benefiting the refugee physicians themselves and at the same time prove a real boon to the people of the country at large'. Dr Boris Fingerhood, Superintendent, Israel Zion Hospital, Brooklyn, N.Y., 'The Refugee Physician in America – A Medical Refugee Settlement Plan'. Chamberlain Papers, Folder 16. Yivo Archives, New York.

31. Cecilia Razovsky, Memorandum, 'Refugee Physicians in the United States', July 1934 and

Razovsky to Chamberlain, 6 July 1934. Chamberlain Papers, Folder 29. Yivo Archives, New York; George Baehr to Razovsky, 3 July 1934. Ibid. Yivo Archives, New York.

32. For the confusion and power struggles among the various committees, see Razovsky to Chamberlain, 6 July 1934. Razovsky Papers, Box 3, Folder 1. AJHS Archives, New York.

33. See Chapter 1.

34. See Chapter 1.

35. James G. McDonald Papers, General Correspondence Files. School of International Affairs, Columbia University, New York.

36. It should be noted that it was not confined to the US. It also helped resettle refugee doctors in Honduras, Paraguay, Mexico and Bolivia. See George Baehr to Razovsky, 26 March 1935. Razovsky Papers, Box 2, AJHS Archives. See also *Emergency Committee in Aid of Displaced Foreign Physicians*, pamphlet, 1934. CNN Papers, Folder 34. Yivo Archives, New York.

37. Sources do not agree on the exact percentage of Jews among refugee physicians. According to government statistics about 66% of the doctors who migrated into the US in the years from 1933 to 1943 were Jews. See U.S. Department of Justice, Immigration and Naturalization Service, Chamberlain Papers, Folder 34. Yivo Archives, New York. Another study initiated by the NRS placed the figure at 89.4% for Jewish physicians. See Central Index of Refugees, Physicians, Dentists and Medical Scientists. 31 August 1944. NRS Records, Folder 564. Yivo Archives, New York.

38. JDC, 'Report: Sources of Income of Refugee Aid Organizations in the United States', April 1935. Chamberlain Papers, Folder 97. Yivo Archives, New York.

39. See for example Laurence Farmer, Executive Director, Emergency Committee in Aid of Displaced Foreign Physicians to Razovsky, 1 November 1938, Re: Requirements. NCC Records, Folder 32. Yivo Archives, New York.

40. See for example Razovsky's letter to Miss Hanna Hirshberg, San Antonio, Texas, 3 November 1938: 'We have been informed that by 1 January there will probably be only two states who will allow physicians to take their examinations to practice before they become citizens of this country. All the other states will require American citizenship.' Razovsky Papers, Box 3, Folder 1. AJHS Archives, New York. See also a letter of thanks from Dr Feibes and his wife: 'you certainly helped many of us in establishing a new existence ... Nobody will ever be able to reward you for your work but I thank you nevertheless'. 21 December 1938. Ibid., Box 3, Folder 6.

41. See for example Laurence Farmer, Executive Director, Emergency Committee in Aid of Displaced Foreign Physicians to Razovsky, 1 November 1938, Re: Requirements. NCC Records, Folder 32: Correspondence with the Emergency Committee in Aid of Displaced Foreign Physicians. Yivo Archives, New York.

42. See Razovsky to Max Hirsh, Chairman Oregon Émigré Committee, 18 October 1938, re: Bill to modify requirement for foreign physicians applying for licenses. NCC Records, Folder 32. Yivo Archives, New York.

43. See Razovsky to Farmer, 7 October 1938: 'I understand that the Brooklyn Jewish Hospital is ready to consider the application of an ophthalmologist. Do you know of anyone who might be available for this appointment?' Razovsky to Mr George P. Frenkel, 7 October 1938. NCC Records, Folder 32. Yivo Archives, New York.

44. Ibid.

45. Razovsky, 'Summary of the Activities of the NCC, 1937'. NCC Records, pp. 1163–73. Yivo Archives, New York.

46. 'Activities of the NRS, Fall 1941', NRS Records, p. 1773. Yivo Archives, New York.

47. NCC Records, Folder 9. Yivo Archives, New York.

48. Razovsky Papers, Box 3, Folder 6. AJHS Archives, New York.

49. Razovsky to Professor Albert Einstein, 17 May 1938. NCC Records, Folder 9. Yivo Archives, New York.

50. From 1934 to 1942 only about 225 out of approximately 6,000 refugee physicians benefited from the Emergency Committee's help. See 'Report of the Emergency Committee in Aid of Displaced Foreign Medical Scientists', 27 January 1942. NRS Papers, p. 829. Yivo Archives, New York.

51. Report on the Emergency Committee, 22 November 1938 'Since March 1938, positions have been found for 15 physicians in widely scattered communities of this country as follows: Chicago, White Plains Maryland, Detroit, Missouri, San Francisco, Worcester,

Brooklyn, Boston and Newark.' NCC Records, Folder 11. Yivo Archives, New York.

52. David L. Edsall, chairman, and Tracy J. Putman, vice-chairman, the Émigré Physician in America, 1941, 'Report of the National Committee for Resettlement of Foreign Physicians', 1941, p. 1. Chamberlain Records, Folder 16. Yivo Archives, New York.

53. 'Summary of a Meeting of Representatives of Emergency Committee. NCC and Greater New York Committee', 5 December 1936. Chamberlain Papers, Folder 16. Yivo Archives, New York. See also, 'Placement of Physicians in Private Practices', May 1944. NRS Papers, pp. 828, 831. Yivo Archives, New York; 'Minutes, Executive Committee of NRS,' 7 January 1941, Chamberlain Papers, Folder 16. Yivo Archives, New York. The Committee also sent doctors and dentists to Indian reservations, to territories of Alaska, Hawaii and the Virgin Islands.

54. See Emanuel Libman, Emergency Committee in Aid of Displaced Foreign Physicians to Dr Charles J. Kaufman, Medical Director, National Jewish Hospital, Denver, Colorado, 10 August 1938: 'We are very glad to learn of the deep interest which your group has in aiding the medical refugees in establishing themselves here ... May I suggest that you form a state-wide committee with branches in the large cities. I would urge that you have as many non-Jewish members as possible. It is expected that groups constituted in such fashion will meet with less opposition than such as are headed by Jewish men, or such as are composed of Jews only. It is important that all groups work quietly ...'. NCC Records, Folder 32. Yivo Archives, New York.

55. In 1941, 700 men and women had been located in American hospitals throughout the United States. See, 'A Report of the National Committee for Resettlement of Foreign Physicians, 1941', p. 6. Chamberlain Records. Yivo Archives, New York.

56. Ibid.

57. Ibid., pp. 7–8.

58. Ibid., p. 21.

59. On 9 November 1938, the Committee changed its name from the Emergency Committee in Aid of Displaced German Scholars to the Emergency Committee in Aid of Displaced Foreign Scholars. Betty Drury, Assistant Secretary, The Emergency Committee in Aid of Displaced Foreign Scholars, to Razovsky, Executive Director, NCC. NCC Records, Folder 35. Yivo Archives, New York.

60. In 1939 a Rockefeller Foundation report showed that at least 1,500 had been forced to leave Germany since 1933 because of the situation that suppressed intellectual and spiritual life.

61. High Commissioner for Refugees, Press Release, 7 July 1934. James G. McDonald Papers, Folder: High Commissioner for Refugees, Columbia University, New York.

62. Report by Cecilia Razovsky, Executive Director, NCC, 10 October 1935, states that at a meeting in London on 13 July 1935, she had found out that the number of displaced scholars still remained approximately 1,300 'and that the problem for these people is far from being solved'. Warburg Papers, File 316/2. American Jewish Archives, Cincinnati.

63. Consul-General Messersmith, private letter to Assistant-Secretary Carr, 27 July 1933, 150.626J/17. United States Department of State, Central Decimal Files, Record Group 59, National Archives, Suitland, Maryland.

64. Messersmith to the Secretary of State, 'With Reference to the contemplated Emigration to the United States of Certain Professors who have been Displaced from their Positions in Germany', 21 July 1933, 811.11/800; Messersmith's private letter to Assistant-Secretary Carr, 27 July 1933, 150.626J/17. United States Department of State, Central Decimal Files, Record Group 59, National Archives, Suitland, Maryland.

65. Stephen Duggan and Betty Drury, *The Rescue of Science and Learning: The Story of the Emergency Committee in Aid of Displaced Foreign Scholars* (New York: the Macmillan Company, 1948), pp. 189–90.

66. For the contribution of German intellectuals to the United States, see: Norman Bentwich, *The Rescue and Achievement of Refugee Scholars: The Story of Displaced Scholars and Scientists, 1933–1952* (The Hague: Martinus Nijhoff, 1953); Lewis A. Coser, *Refugee Scholars in America: Their Impact and Experiences* (Yale: Yale University Press, 1984); Duggan and Drury, *The Rescue of Science and Learning*.

67. The Emergency Committee in Aid of Displaced German Scholars, 1 May 1937, p. 4. NCC Records, Folder 222. Yivo Archives, New York.

68. Due to the limited funds, the committee decided in the beginning of 1936 to make grants for a single year and only to such institutions as could offer some assurance of permanent

appointment. See The Emergency Committee in Aid of Displaced German Scholars, 1 May 1937, p. 7. NCC Records, Folder 222. Yivo Archives, New York.

69. 'Fifth Annual Report', The Emergency Committee in Aid of Displaced German Scholars, December 1938, pp. 1–2. NCC Records, Folder 35. Yivo Archives, New York.

70. Minutes of the Executive Committee of the National Coordinating Committee, 8 February 1936. NCC Records, Folder 15. Yivo Archives, New York.

71. See Chapter 1.

72. The Emergency Committee in Aid of Displaced German Scholars, 'Report', 1 May 1937, p. 5. NCC Records, Folder 222. Yivo Archives, New York.

73. On 9 November 1938, the Committee's name was changed into Emergency Committee in Aid of Displaced Foreign Scholars to include refugee professors from all the countries of western Europe that had been occupied by the Nazis.

74. Institute of International Education to Universities, 27 May 1933. Cited in Duggan and Drury, *The Rescue of Science and Learning*, pp. 173–4.

75. In November 1937, Charles I. Liebman, then vice president and later president of the Refugee Economic Corporation also joined the Executive Committee. He was responsible for a plan to place European scholars in Venezuela and the Philippines.

76. Stephen Duggan, 'Report of the Emergency Committee in Aid of Displaced German Scholars' 31 January 1942. Cited in Duggan and Drury, *The Rescue of Science and Learning*, pp. 1–2.

77. Confidential Report of the Emergency Committee in Aid of Displaced German Scholars, 1 February 1935, and Report of the Emergency Committee, 1 January 1934. Chamberlain Papers, Folder 29. Yivo Archives, New York. Annual Report of the Emergency Committee in Aid of Displaced German Scholars, 1 December 1938. NCC Records, Folder 4. Yivo Archives, New York.

78. Correspondence between Professor Einstein and Razovsky, NCC Records, Folder 9. Yivo Archives, New York.

79. Razovsky to Einstein, 17 and 26 May 1938 and Einstein to Razovsky, 27 April, 17 May, 28 September 1938. NCC Papers, Folder 9: Correspondence of Cecilia Razovsky, 25 June 1938–31 May 1939. Yivo Archives, New York.

80. Duggan and Drury, *The Rescue of Science and Learning*, p.184.

81. In May 1937, the Committee declared that 'it can take no responsibility' for scholars whose appointment was not renewed: 'The problem of these individuals ceases to be one of scholarship in the narrower sense which alone is within the province of the emergency Committee, and becomes one of relief ... The initiative in establishing new relations with other universities and colleges must, however, be taken by the German scholar and his colleagues and friends'. The Emergency Committee in Aid of Displaced German Scholars, 1 May 1937, p.7. NCC Records, Folder 222. Yivo Archives, New York.

82. Razovsky also sought positions outside the United States. See for example, a request from Canada offering positions for professors in pathology, physiology and biochemistry. S. Belkin, Secretary, Canadian Committee for Jewish Refugees, to Razovsky, 2 February 1939. NCC Records, Folder 7. Yivo Archives, New York.

83. Meeting of Board of Directors, NCC, April 1937. NCC Records, Folder 7. Yivo Archives, New York.

84. Warburg Papers, Box 321, Folder 7; Box 327, Folder 3; Box 329, Folders 4, 5, 6. American Jewish Archives, Cincinnati.

85. See Miss Emanuel (Warburg's secretary) to Razovsky, 5 August 1936, with regard to Dr Gruenhut: 'I am sending [Dr Gruenhut's résumé] to you rather than to the Scholars Committee, as I hardly believe they will do anything for him.' Another letter concerning his case asked Warburg to secure a fellowship for him, 20 August 1936. See also the case of Dr Edinger, an expert in religious education, for whom Razovsky asked Warburg's financial assistance. Razovsky to Warburg, 12 March 1936. Re: Dr Dora Edinger and her 13-year-old son, Lujo, see Warburg Papers, Box 329, Folder 4. American Jewish Archives, Cincinnati.

86. Section 9(a) Immigration Act 1924, Category (d). In 1939 Secretary Hall allowed the waiver of the requirement for the two-year employment if such a professor had been forced to discontinue his academic activities 'for reasons beyond his control, such as discrimination on account of race, religion, or political opinion'. Secretary Hull to Dr Harold Dodd, 27 January 1939. NA, 150.626 J/594.

87. Victor Klemperer, *Ich will Zeugniss ablegen biz zum letzten. Tagebücher 1933–1941* (Berlin: Aufbau Verlag, 1995), 8. Aufl. 1996. See also Consul Maurice Q. Altaffer, Zurich, to Leland Harrison, American Minister, Bern, 4 April 1938. NA, 811.11–850.
88. On the University in Exile, see Bentwich, *The Rescue and Achievement of Refugee Scholars*, pp. 48–52.
89. Michael A. Meyer, 'The Refugee Scholars Project of the Hebrew Union College', in Bertram Wallace Korn, (ed.), *A Bicentennial Festschrift for Jacob Rader Marcus* (New York: KTAV, 1976), pp. 359–75.
90. Emanuel Libman, Chairman, Emergency Committee in Aid of Displaced Foreign Physicians, to Dr Charles J. Kaufman, Medical Director National Jewish Hospital, Denver, Colorado, 10 August 1938. NCC Records, Folder 32. Yivo Archives, New York.
91. Michael Meyer, 'The Refugee Scholars Project of the Hebrew Union College', in Korn (ed.), *A Bicentennial Festschrift*, p. 359.
92. So did other Jewish scholars, including Fritz Bamberger and David Baumgard, philosophy, Nahum Glazer, history, Martin Plessner, Semitics, and Joseph Fijs, bibliography and history. HUC Records, Box 732. American Jewish Archives, Cincinnati.
93. Cited in Michael Meyer, 'The Refugee Scholars Project of the Hebrew Union College', in Korn (ed.), *A Bicentennial Festschrift*, p. 372.
94. Betty Drury, Assistant Secretary, the Emergency Committee in Aid of Displaced Foreign Scholars, to Razovsky, Director of the Migration Department, NRS, 21 November 1939. See, for example, a letter from Drury to Razovsky's Secretary, 29 March 1939: 'We have an opportunity to suggest candidates to teach at a Protestant mission school for southern mountain girls for the remainder of the school year. The school would provide room and board but not traveling expenses. The candidate must be a woman ... If you have anyone to suggest, won't you please let us hear.' See also Drury to Razovsky, 16 January 1939. NCC Records, Folder 35. Yivo Archives, New York.
95. Cited in Duggan and Drury, *The Rescue of Science and Learning*, pp. 173–4.
96. The Rosenwald Fellowships were founded in 1942 by William Rosenwald and the Rosenwald family. The fellowships were intended for the benefit of younger émigré professionals: artists, musicians, architects, men of letters and others who gave promise of creative work. From the list of 147 applicants, forty-seven were chosen. The fellowships had good results. Of the forty-seven, eighteen became established in universities, colleges and other research institutions. Several of the fellows held highly successful art exhibitions in New York galleries; others published books, which were well regarded by the critics. For a full account on the Rosenwald Plan see Duggan and Drury, *The Rescue of Science and Learning*, pp. 72–4.
97. The Scholars' Committee, like the Emergency Committee in Aid of Displaced Foreign Physicians, was affiliated to the NCC/NRS. See Annual Reports of the Committee, NRS Papers. Yivo Archives, New York.
98. Duggan and Drury, *The Rescue of Science and Learning*, pp. 77–9.
99. Ibid., pp. 86, 87–8.
100. The Emergency Committee secured positions in 145 colleges and universities for 288 displaced scholars under its original program, and for forty-seven professionals under the Rosenwald plan. Duggan and Drury, *The Rescue of Science and Learning*, p.62. For the Rosenwald Plan, ibid., pp. 72–4, and for the complete list, pp. 204–8.
101. Duggan and Drury, *The Rescue of Science and Learning*, p. 192.
102. Joseph Chamberlain, 'Memorandum Regarding Emigration of Refugees from Germany and Austria', 20 July 1938. Chamberlain Papers, Box 4, Folder 96. Yivo Archives, New York.
103. Emanuel Libman, Chairman, Emergency Committee in Aid of Displaced Foreign Physicians, to Dr Charles J. Kaufman, Medical Director, National Jewish Hospital, Denver, Colorado, 10 August 1938. NCC Records, Folder 32, Yivo Archives, New York. See also Donald Fleming and Bernard Bailyn, *The Intellectual Migration – Europe and America, 1930–1960* (Cambridge, MA: Harvard University Press, 1969). For the full list of 288 scholars aided by the Emergency Committee and the forty-seven professionals under the Rosenwald Plan, see Appendix 1.

5 In Search of New Havens

Cecilia Razovsky worked on all fronts to fulfill what she considered 'a sacred mission' – to rescue as many Jewish refugees as possible from the Nazi inferno. In addition to her tremendous efforts inside the United States, she also tried to find new havens in Central and Latin American countries.[1] She negotiated with representatives of, among others, Cuba, Panama, Trinidad, the Dominican Republic, Costa Rica, Venezuela, British Honduras, Guatemala, Peru, Bolivia and Chile. Her primary objective was to persuade the governments of these countries to allow the entrance of Jewish refugees from Europe.

Also, since temporary refugees from Europe were already living in these countries, Razovsky was required to negotiate with the governments for the further temporary, if not permanent, stay of those émigrés, who were constantly under threat of deportation. In a memorandum to the Executive Committee, NRS, Razovsky reported a visit of Mr Julio Zadek, President of the *Sociedad Israellita de Guatemala City*, who stated that forty families in Guatemala were awaiting an American visa and that the President of Guatemala had granted them only temporary asylum. They were all registered with the American consuls abroad, 'but the American Consul in Guatemala City was apparently very rigid', and they were all about to be deported back to Germany. Moreover, there was the matter of 550 Jews in Guatemala, of whom 250 were recently arrived refugees and, although these were in no immediate danger of deportation, Razovsky knew that it would be safer for them if their stay were to be legalized.[2]

In order to facilitate the procedures as well as the negotiations with the authorities, and to improve conditions for the refugees, Razovsky strongly recommended organizing committees in many of the Central and South American countries to cope with housing, health, and other of the émigrés' adjustment problems. That matter, she emphasized, was 'of grave concern' and one, which called for an immediate solution.[3] Beginning in 1938, Razovsky recommended that the NCC Board of Directors and, later, the Board of NRS, organize committees or reinforce existing ones in those countries to continue with the work in order to achieve satisfactory results.[4] At the same time, she tried to arouse the interest of the authorities in those countries by making it known that the NRS was holding 'over four hundred thousand dollars and that the Committee in London was holding thousands of dollars for the people who were still in Germany'. In a letter to Morris Troper, the European representative of the JDC, Razovsky strongly suggested that, 'perhaps some new country of immigration could be found if they knew there was so much money available to be utilized for the benefit of these people'.[5] But the situation in Europe deteriorated in the late 1930s. The *Anschluss* (reunion with Vienna); the dismemberment of Czechoslovakia; *Kristallnacht* (the Night of Broken Glass) and the November pogroms that followed in Germany; the strengthening of the Italian role in the Axis, harassing Italians who happened to have Jewish blood in their veins, and Nazi Germany's filling of concentration camps with thousands of men and women all caused panic among the Jewish communities. Jews in their thousands sought to leave central Europe as quickly as possible and there was a huge rush to all consular officers of friendly countries to obtain immigration visas. Regrettably, governments in Europe and America preferred to close their eyes to Jewish misery.

The attitude of Latin American republics was particularly disappointing. Between 1933 and 1938 they had absorbed 47,300 German Jews; Argentina led with 18,000 immigrants and Brazil followed with 12,000. However, after 1938 the Argentine government placed obstacles in the path of the refugees by instructing its consuls to refer all visa applicants for the approval of an inter-ministerial board in Buenos Aires. The Argentine foreign minister was annoyed when, on 3 September 1938, the American ambassador to Argentina protested against this regulation, which threatened to leave 600 persons with now invalidated visas stranded in Berlin. Why had the US not doubled its German quota? he inquired. The implication was clear enough; his country would be guided by its own interests in devising immigration policies. Argentina had finally closed its doors to refugees and it was very difficult to secure admission; Argentina, the minister emphasized, needed farmers not 'artists and musicians'.[6] Only a foreigner who had very close relatives in Argentina with sufficient means to support him/her would have been afforded entry and, after September 1938, hardly anyone succeeded. In one instance Razovsky was driven to make an emotional appeal to Argentine officials and to the State Department when Jewish children, on their way to join their parents in Buenos Aires, were stranded in Bermuda as a result of a disaster on the high seas. Their ship had been lost at sea and they were among those rescued. At that time, however, direct passage from Bermuda to Buenos Aires was impossible and they could only proceed to Buenos Aires via the US. It was necessary, therefore, for these children to obtain US transit visas. Razovsky worked on all channels. She sent cables to Bermuda, to Buenos Aires and to London in the hope of obtaining more factual data. Unfortunately, she was unable to obtain any information about these children, except for their names. Her efforts, nonetheless, proved fruitful, helped, no doubt, by her personal connections in Washington. The Department of State issued the required transit visas and the government of Argentina eventually let the children join their parents in Buenos Aires.[7]

Brazil followed the example of its neighboring countries. Although it agreed to admit 9,000 refugees over three years, they would have to be proven agriculturists and possess the equivalent of $2,400 over and above traveling and settlement expenses. But still Razovsky persisted in trying to bring at least children of Jewish descent into Brazil. In December 1939 she began inquiring among the Jewish community as to the possibility of bringing in Polish children who were still in Vienna.[8] A report from Brazil in January 1940 indicated that

> there is a desire on the part of the local Jewish population to give hope to destitute and especially orphaned children from the war zone, especially from Poland ... There are many Jewish families here who wish to either take such children into their homes, or to contribute towards their maintenance.[9]

But with the situation in Brazil preventing the organization of such a project from their end, Mrs Lorch, of the Jewish community in Saõ Paulo, called for the cooperation of the JDC and the American Red Cross. The report assumed that 'the Brazilian government would be willing to give permission for the immigration of such children, but, naturally, not Jewish children exclusively would have to be given consideration'.[10] Although not yet in possession of approval by the Brazilian authorities, Razovsky's correspondence with the *Reichsvereinigung* revealed new hopes for the settlement of refugee children from the war zone: 'We hope that in view of the vast interest displayed in the Western Hemisphere for children at this time that you may be successful in working out a plan with Mrs. Lorch.'[11]

Throughout Latin America restriction was the rule, primarily in Chile, Ecuador, Paraguay, Peru and Columbia – all of which had been virtually closed to Jewish immigration since the end of the 1930s. Trinidad had closed its doors to additional immigration on 15 January 1939 and Razovsky enlisted the Council for German Jewry in an appeal to the authorities, until the government of Trinidad finally agreed to admit those refugees who had been on the high seas at the time the new law was passed. They also agreed to review each application from the holders of landing permits issued prior to the passage of the law, claiming that these permits had been issued by a subordinate official without proper authorization. At a February 1938 meeting of the NRS Board of Directors, Razovsky complained that Trinidad officials 'had been adamant in their determination to prevent any new-comers and it was only with great difficulty that the landing of several wives and children and parents of persons already in Trinidad was effected'.[12] To prevent further delays, Razovsky proposed sending out a social worker in order to set up suitable housing, to look into the health situation and to provide preventive health care for the refugees, so that 'the 400 refugees already there become an asset rather than a liability to Trinidad.'[13]

Given the tough anti-refugee policy of Central and Latin American countries, Razovsky decided to look for other places. The Philippines were considered as a haven and in 1940 Razovsky tried to interest the Jewish community in Manila to accept Jewish refugee children from central Europe. In a letter dated September 1940, offering cooperation to Mr Herbert S. Frieder of the Manila Jewish Refugee Committee, Razovsky suggested a plan similar to that already in practice in the US,[14] in which unaccompanied children would be brought to the Philippines for the duration of the war for education and training.[15]

This was not the first time Razovsky had approached the Jewish Refugee Committee in the Philippines. Indeed, her mail reveals daily correspondence with the agencies in Manila with regard to refugees sent to the Philippine Islands under the auspices of the Migration Division of the *Reichsvereinigung* of Germany and the Refugee Economic Corporation of the US. Already in 1939, the NRS, and Razovsky in particular, were considering the possibility of larger Jewish settlements in the Philippines. Answering inquiries concerning procedures for obtaining immigration visas to the Philippines, Razovsky listed the requirements, explaining that a list of all approved cases together with necessary data had to be furnished to the office of the US High Commissioner, who in turn would refer this list to the office of the president of the Philippines. The list had then to be returned to the US High Commissioner of the State Department in Washington with the request for correspondent visas from the American consuls in the applicants' various cities of residence.[16]

In an urgent and confidential letter, Razovsky appealed '[to] all Cooperating Agencies' affiliated with the NRS to find suitable applicants for settlement in the Philippine Islands. She explained that persons who were accepted for admission would be permitted to remain there permanently and would be privileged to engage in gainful occupations. Yet, in order to qualify, the newcomer was required to supply a guarantee from the Manila Committee or from a sponsoring agency that the immigrant had sufficient funds for his/her upkeep, or a minimum of $400. In addition, since the Philippines were a US protectorate, applicants who held a visitor visa in the United States could not apply.[17]

Cuba was another country where Razovsky hoped to find temporary, if not permanent shelter for Jewish refugees. The NCC arranged for over 5,000 German Jewish refugees to enter Havana and wait their turn in the quota. They arrived penniless and desperate and American Jewish organizations – NCC, HIAS, and JDC – formed a special committee to resolve their problems. After working for several months on a survey, Razovsky went to Cuba with a number of professional social workers, including nurses, to form 'an excellent center' – The Jewish Center for Cuba.[18] Many refugees who found the quota to the United States closed to them, or frustrated over the long wait for an American immigration visa, settled for permanent residence in Cuba. The Jewish residents of Havana, who, until the end of 1938 felt relatively at home, found themselves in 1939 facing increased antisemitic agitation in the press and radio urging the government to deny entrance to Jewish refugees. Already in autumn 1938, the NCC decided to suspend the dispatch of refugees to Cuba. In a letter to Mrs Alpert of Baltimore who inquired about the possibilities of immigration to Cuba, Razovsky explained that the NCC was waiting for the results of negotiations with the Cuban government. Razovsky doubled her efforts to persuade the Cubans to continue their former practice with regard to refugees, but the intransigent situation proved all her efforts to be futile:

We are doing our best with regard to the people who are held up pending their going to Cuba. This is a situation which is involving hundreds of people and since we have to negotiate with Cuba and the State Department about them, we are holding up sending people to Cuba until we reach a definite decision and agreement with the other officials.[19]

The tragic saga of the SS *St. Louis*, 'a poignant tragedy',[20] brought the issue of German Jewish refugees to a dramatic climax. On 27 May 1939, the *St. Louis*, a ship of the Hamburg-American Line (HAPAG) with a passenger list of 937 passengers who were mostly Jewish, docked at Havana harbor and were denied landing. Among the passengers, 743 had applied for American visas in Germany and preferred to wait their turn in Havana. Up till then the Cuban practice required a passport visa and the posting of a $500 bond per applicant for an immigration visa. For a tourist visa the applicant had to post an unofficial 'fee' of $160 to a private office, which was in fact maintained by Colonel Manuel Benitez Gonzales, the Cuban director-general of immigration. The 'visitor' accepted in return a letter authorizing entry into Cuba until the acceptance of an American immigration visa. Pressure of public opinion against Jewish refugees caused President Laredo Bru to issue a new decree on 5 May requiring a bond of 500 pesos from all aliens entering Cuba, except American citizens.

Although most of the passengers on board the *St. Louis* carried 'tourist letters', port authorities refused to allow them to leave the ship due to the new decree. Only twenty-two passengers, who had acquired immigration visas, were permitted to disembark. American Jewish organizations, Razovsky in particular, worked simultaneously on two fronts, conducting negotiations with the Cuban authorities using all kinds of personal connections and with the State Department in Washington and US Consul-General Coert du Bois and Ambassador J. Butler in Havana, who were officially instructed by the State Department not to interfere. In a telephone call from Avra Warren, the Consul-General was instructed 'not to intervene in the matter of the landing of the *Saint Louis* refugees', emphasizing 'that word had come from the White House'.[21] The NCC, nevertheless, refused to yield. In an urgent letter '[t]o Friends of the Committee', dated 15 June 1939, asking for support, Joseph Chamberlain reported that the committee had sent two representatives – Mr Lawrence Berenson, a New York attorney and President of the Cuban-American Chamber of Commerce in New York, representative of American Jewish Joint

Distribution Committee, and Miss Cecilia Razovsky – to Havana as
soon as it was informed that passengers were not permitted to land in
Cuba, to do everything possible to reverse the situation. Chamberlain
reported that they were authorized by the JDC to post a cash bond of
$500 per person, which was the sum formally required under the new
Cuban law to enter legally. Miss Razovsky undertook to keep in touch
with the passengers via the chairman of the shipboard Immigrant
Committee appointed by the passengers, 'so that every effort was
made to keep up the morale and the courage of the passengers'.[22] At
that stage Razovsky and Berenson were certain that if they were to
post even a temporary bond for each passenger admitted, the Cuban
authorities would permit the newcomers to settle in a location like the
Isle of Pines; Razovsky would stay and help with the resettlement. Past
experience and existing connections between the Cuban Jewish community and local officials, together with money guaranteed by
American Jewish organizations, promised good results. Enormous
fund-raising efforts were made by the NCC to cover the cost of bonds
for the passengers. One way was to contact relatives in the United
States. Razovsky started first with locating the relatives and then
appealing for their support. Often the relationship to the passenger
was not known but an appeal was made nonetheless. One example
among hundreds of appeals was her letter to a Mr Max Hirsch in
Portland, Oregon:

> The names of friends and relatives were given as possible
> resources in each case. We did make the request to you as a per-
> sonal one, not knowing whether or not you had any personal
> relationship with these people. We rather imagine that your
> name might have just been given because they had no one else
> to whom they could refer but since your name was given we
> referred the matter to you.[23]

But the situation in Cuba raised serious doubts. The Cuban government refused to recognize the validity of the Cuban visas held by most
of the stranded passengers. Razovsky recorded that she – and members
of the local staff, including journalists – invited the Cuban representatives to lunch, in an attempt to persuade them and other South
American countries to accept at least some of the refugees. Meanwhile,
negotiations with Secretary of State Hull and the senior officials of the
Department of State proved futile: 'Our State Department was un-sym-
pathetic and Franklin Delano was apathetic, although Eleanor did
every thing in her power to change their attitude', she lamented.[24]

The *St. Louis* had to leave Havana, no American port let the passengers disembark and, as Arthur Morse concluded, 'Within sight of freedom, 937 Jewish refugees from Hitler are turned back – then begin a harrowing voyage to doom.'[25] Negotiations continued, even after the boat set off on its long, sad journey back to Germany, but this time with European countries.[26] Morris Troper, the European director of JDC, eventually succeeded and England, France, Belgium and Holland agreed that each country would admit a percentage of the passengers.

Only one country proved to be an exception – the Dominican Republic. In fact, already during 1938 there had been a small influx of refugees into the Dominican Republic. In October 1938 Cecilia Razovsky received a report from one of the local Jewish merchants in San Domingo to the effect that he and his associates had been able to provide some half-dozen refugees with loans to help them establish small retail businesses. The loans had been arranged through the Refugee Economic Corporation of New York. By October, this report continued, every steamer was bringing in growing numbers of German refugees who were being admitted temporarily, until receiving the proper documents to enter another country for permanent residence.[27] By 1940, the island had a small Jewish community, including a score of prominent families proudly claiming descent from Sephardi Jews, who had migrated from Curaçao in the nineteenth century, a handful of Russian Jews, Cuban Jewish émigrés and a few German Jews who had migrated during the Hitler era.

While the American Jewish Joint Distribution Committee and the Refugee Economic Corporation were considering the needs of the refugees staying there, the government of the Dominican Republic invited officials of the US Immigration and Naturalization Service to send an expert to help them frame a new immigration law. The law was passed in January 1939, and included a provision for a $500 head tax on all refugees who could not show unrelinquished domicile. The ruling affected a number of persons on the high seas bound for San Domingo. After repeated appeals on their behalf to the Minister in Washington by newspaper publisher David Stern and others, who pleaded for their admission on the grounds that these persons had been on the high seas when the law was put into force, they were finally permitted to proceed to the Dominican Republic. However, sixteen refugees with visas for the Dominican Republic were kept in the United States. According to the Commissioner of Immigration these refugees had to leave shortly and make their way elsewhere. Razovsky appealed to the authorities both in the United States and in San Domingo, urging them to reach a definite understanding with regard to the admission and requirements for future admission of refugees.[28] Given these factors, it was indeed surprising that, in the summer of 1938, the Dominican Republic was the only country to offer shelter to Jewish refugees from Europe.[29]

The saga of Sosua, in the Dominican Republic, as an asylum for persecuted Jews began with the Evian refugee conference, convened on the French shore of Lake Geneva in July 1938. Earlier that year President Roosevelt had convened a thirty-two-nation conference at the fashionable French spa of Evian les Bains to discuss the resettlement of German and Austrian Jewish refugees in other lands. It was the first time the president had acknowledged that the question of Jewish refugees was a global issue. And yet, in order to ensure participation of as many countries as possible, two things had to be agreed upon. The first was to refrain from specifically mentioning 'Jews'; the second was to focus only on refugees from Germany and Austria. In other words, it was agreed to present the problem as a general refugee problem, and to limit the scope of the conference to Germany and Austria. In addition, participants were even loath to condemn Germany for its repression of Jews. They constantly spoke of the problem of political refugees, failing to draw attention to the fact that Jews were being persecuted for the very fact of their being Jews. Notwithstanding his sympathetic statement, Roosevelt instructed the US delegation to Evian to keep US Immigration Acts intact.[30] It was evident at the July 1938 conference, that the other representatives, following the US example, endorsed the idea of resettlement in general, but agreed that no nation should 'be expected or asked to receive a greater number of emigrants than is permitted by existing legislation'.[31] The chairman of the United States delegation to the conference, Myron C. Taylor, received clear instructions that '[n]o preferential treatment may be accorded to so-called political refugees as such, as distinguished from other immigrants'.[32] Such a resolution meant that in effect, no nation, including the United States, was expected to open its gates and rescue the mass of refugees. The conference resulted in much sympathy but no compassion. The delegates expressed high-sounding phrases and ideals, but concrete offers of help were another matter altogether. The sole achievement of the conference, which was eventually held on 6 July 1938, was the establishment of a permanent Inter-Governmental Committee on Refugees (IGCR), headed by Washington lawyer, George Rublee.

Although motivated by humanitarian considerations and good will, the committee took 'no effective action to evacuate refugees and probably did not have the necessary authority'.[33]

There was one notable exception to the overall negativism exhibited by the representatives at Evian.[34] The Dominican Republic, a small, undeveloped nation occupying the eastern two-thirds of the Caribbean island of Hispaniola, made a dramatic offer to accept German and Austrian refugees. Subsequently, Virgilio Molina, representative of the Dominican Republic, made a surprisingly generous and noble statement, declaring that the Dominican Republic would be prepared to make its contribution by granting special advantageous concessions to Austrian and German exiles. In addition, the newcomers could become Dominican citizens.

Given the general attitude at the Evian Conference, the Dominican Republic representative's statement was especially rewarding. Despite the financial difficulties involved in such a massive resettlement, the American Jewish Joint Distribution Committee (JDC) jumped at the offer, even though it would have to be financed entirely by private Jewish sources outside Germany, and mainly if not exclusively, by American Jewry. In spite of objections from a few American Jewish organizations, the JDC decided that the offer was too good to turn down.[35]

At a February 1939 meeting of the Inter-Governmental Refugee Committee in London, Dr Max Henriques-Urena, the Dominican delegate, announced that his country was willing to 'take immediately 50-100,000' refugees of the professional, business and laboring classes and 'to provide facilities for their settlement'.[36] This declaration was made after the disappointing failure of the Evian conference of July 1938 and after the fruitless attempts of the Inter-Governmental Committee, created in Evian, to locate some countries willing to accept a sizeable number of refugees. The many earlier projects for Jewish mass settlement anywhere else – in Kenya, Tanganyika, Guiana and Madagascar – all proved to be futile.

The San Domingo project was therefore greeted enthusiastically by those who believed in the possibility of mass Jewish colonization outside of Palestine as the quickest, cheapest and most efficient answer to the Jewish refugee problem. An expert commission was sent out in the spring of 1939 by the Refugee Economic Corporation, in collaboration with President Roosevelt's Advisory Committee on Refugees. The commission returned with a favorable report. The Agro-Joint[37] immediately took a lively interest in the Dominican project, and Mr

James Rosenberg, its chairman, became the leading figure in implementing the Dominican scheme.

After raising one million dollars to help finance the project,[38] the JDC began making the financial and administrative arrangements. On 1 December 1939, the American Jewish Joint Distribution Committee and the Dominican Republic founded the Dominican Republic Settlement Association (DORSA), with James N. Rosenberg of New York as president. On 30 January 1940, DORSA officials and representatives of the Dominican Republic signed the final agreement, guaranteeing

> To the settlers and their descendants full opportunity to continue their lives and occupations free from molestation, discrimination or persecution, with full freedom of religion and religious ceremonies with equality of opportunities and of civil, legal and economic rights, as well as other rights inherent to human beings.[39]

The contract also declared specifically that the executive power of the Republic would 'initiate a law to modify the Immigration Law now in force in order to exempt from all entry taxes, or similar taxes, present or future, the settlers covered by this agreement'.[40] The Association, for its part, was obliged 'to take care of and promote the economic life of the immigrants who enter the territory of the Republic for their enterprises'.[41] The agreement was to provide for the initial colonization of 500 families, with a gradual build-up to 100,000 people. The contract was signed in Ciudad Trujillo in the presence of General Rafael Leonidas Trujillo himself, president of the Dominican Republic, the vice-president of the Republic, leading cabinet dignitaries, laymen, clerics and chiefs of diplomatic missions. Representing DORSA were lawyer James Rosenberg, its president, and Joseph A. Rosen, vice-president. Both houses of the Dominican Congress unanimously ratified this contract at a special session on 21 February 1940. Moreover, General Trujillo donated a 26,000-acre estate, part of his personal property, for Jewish settlement; the land, located in Sosua, east of Puerto Plata on the island's north coast,[42] was the first site of the settlement.[43] Both DORSA officials and government representatives shared optimistic forecasts.

Dr J. A. Rosen, Vice-President of DORSA and the moving spirit behind its practical colonization activities, who enjoyed a considerable reputation as a colonization expert, expressed his conviction that the project had 'the best possibilities of success of any of the colonization schemes examined in recent years'.[44] At a President's Advisory Committee on Political Refugees meeting in New York in February 1940, James Rosenberg called the agreement with the Dominican Republic 'a unique document in modern history, whereby a government and a group of citizens engage mutually to foster a humanitarian project for the rehabilitation of stateless and homeless refugees'. James McDonald, also present at the meeting, stated 'the offer by the Dominican Republic, generous almost to the point of seeming to be unreal, was in such contrast to the cautious statements of the other governments as to stand out from the meeting as a whole'. Even President Roosevelt, in his letter to the President's Advisory Committee on Political Refugees on 12 December 1939, described the project as 'a turning point' in the refugee work.[45] Similar appraisals were heard from the Dominican Republic. At an April 1940 luncheon held in New York in honor of Minister Andres Pastoriza, Dominican Republic official representative in the United States, the guest of honor expressed his deepest hopes for a successful project:

> I can assure you that my government has done, and is willing to do, everything in its power to carry this plan through with success. My Government feels that the settlers who have arrived will become part of our life and development, and the new settlers will be welcomed, as heartily by my people as those who have come and I am sure that as soon as the war permits the settlers to come to our country in larger numbers, this plan will be carried successfully.[46]

At the same meeting the tasks of the Association and the necessary procedures were thoroughly discussed and special attention was paid to the problem of getting people to the Dominican Republic. George L. Warren, Secretary of the President's Advisory Committee on Political Refugees and a member of DORSA Board of Directors, advised the Board of the necessary changes due to war conditions, stating sadly that their tremendous efforts 'have for the moment seemingly gone to waste'.[47] However, in order to meet the situation it was agreed that in addition to the first 250 settlers scheduled to arrive at the Dominican Republic, a further 250 people would be selected for temporary refuge. As most of these people could not get out of Europe, efforts for a new selection of people from England and France was considered, since it was possible for refugees in those two countries to reach the Dominican Republic.

Representatives were sent to those European countries from which it was still possible to emigrate in order to select suitable settlers. Each settler had to pledge to become a Dominican citizen and to remain a permanent cultivator of the soil. With the assistance of Mr Trone and Mr Troper[48] in Amsterdam, Dr Bondy was able to select 250 new settlers. Dr Rosen, Vice-President of DORSA, agreed to substitute the original settlers, who had not been able to travel, with 213 others, as well as 500 young trainees and a further 500 children of both sexes aged under 16.[49] Razovsky prepared an additional program to bring older children into the Dominican Republic; in May 1940 she communicated with Kaete Rosenheim in Berlin asking her to locate suitable candidates for a trainee plan:

> If there are children you know between the ages of 16 and 20 who have relatives in the US who might be able to deposit money for their training in accordance with the statement prepared by us, will you please tell them to send their relatives to our office so that they might make application for them at once.[50]

Unfortunately, the plans for the children did not materialize.

Included in the numbers were refugees who desired to reside temporarily in the Dominican Republic and for whom, it was hoped, their relatives in the United States would be able to provided maintenance expenses. But the plan still involved raising the sum of $230,000 plus transportation costs. Notwithstanding the double problem of transporting the refugees to the Dominican Republic and raising almost a quarter of a million dollars, Warren sounded committed when he urged the Directors to 'share that problem with [him] so that [they] will all contribute to that effort is such ways as [they] can'. 'Here is a great opportunity not merely for temporary relief; but to rescue 1200 human beings, young people, children.'[51]

Most of the first settlers who came under the auspices of DORSA were young German and Austrian Jews. In theory, the recruits were supposed to have had previous agricultural experience. However, so desperate were they to escape Nazi persecution that many prospective colonists lied or exaggerated about their farming background. Among the Sosua refugees were carpenters, printers, construction workers, cobblers, engineers and at least one law student. Solomon Trone, a retired engineer, who screened the applicants, was in charge of determining their suitability for participation in the Dominican enterprise. A substantial number of the applicants had been living temporarily in Swiss refugee camps and, since there was no certainty that Switzerland would let them stay, departure to the New World seemed the best solution.[52]

But against the sympathetic attitude of the government of the Dominican Republic and the simplifying of visa procedures for the prospective settlers, the question of temporary refugees turned out to be more complicated, especially for the Association. In August 1940, Mrs Rebecca Hourwich Reyher, DORSA Executive Secretary, notified Razovsky and Warren that the government of the Dominican Republic had suspended the granting of visas to temporary refugees,[53] preferring settlers or specially equipped persons approved by DORSA. The onus, therefore, was on the Association to approve suitable individuals. Rosenberg explained to the Board that because of this responsibility, which the Dominican Government had settled on them, the Association had to select the applicants according to the agreed criteria. With the assistance of Razovsky, Director of Migration NRS, and the International Migration Service, he had to screen applications from over a thousand refugees, of which only 300 were approved after a careful study against 'even a single mistake being made or any improper person approved'.[54] Rosenberg explained to the Board that with regard to temporary refugees the Association required their relatives in the United States to furnish money in advance to assure the Dominican Government that such immigrants would not become public charges. The monies, he emphasized, would be returned to the American relatives if those refugees were unable to reach their destinations.[55] By November 1941, there were 413 settlers in Sosua.

Already in March 1940, Razovsky, with the assistance of George Warren, prepared a list of recommendations concerning the possibility of temporary refuge in the Dominican Republic. Included was a proposal dealing with arrangements in relation to relatives in the US. Every relative who was ready to sponsor a refugee should provide:

- A photostat copy of affidavit and supplementary documents submitted to the American consul abroad on behalf of the refugee.[56]
- A copy of a letter from the American consul giving the date of registration of the refugee.
- The sum of $1,500 or $2,000 to cover the cost of maintaining an individual or a couple for a period of three years, plus transportation costs and a fee of $100 for services to be rendered in connection with meeting the refugees and settling them in the Dominican Republic.

Radovsky urged Haber to accept responsibility for communicating with relatives and making the necessary arrangements for the deposit of funds, documents and other requirements: 'It would be of great assistance and give added prestige to the National Refugee Service, Inc., if we could serve these people in this capacity. The need is very great and grows greater daily.'[57] In a memorandum sent a few days later, Razovsky described the desperate situation in greater Germany and called for immediate efforts to find asylum for refugees awaiting their visas to the United States:

> Since there appears to be a lag of at least twenty months during which people who registered under the German quota must wait for their turns, and since it is essential that many of these people now in greater Germany leave Central Europe at once for asylum in some other country, it is exceedingly desirable that permission be secured from the government of the Dominican Republic to permit these people to await their visas in the Dominican Republic.[58]

In the meantime, Razovsky sought possible channels to ship people from Europe. As early as March 1940 she instructed all branches affiliated with the NRS to find suitable refugees for temporary refuge in the Dominican Republic. She reported that the steamship *Neptune* of the Italian Line was scheduled to sail from Genoa on 14 May 1940 directly for Santo Domingo. She urged Jewish women active in their communities to get sufficient funds together as soon as possible: 'If sufficient funds are available immediate arrangements to secure visas for a limited number of people can be made for temporary admission to Santo Domingo, where temporary asylum is desired.'[59] On the basis of these recommendations, George Warren sent to Razovsky '[a] Suggested Plan for Temporary Asylum in the Dominican Republic.' According to the Plan, refugees to be given consideration fell into five categories: settlers, trainees, refugees with capital, groups seeking temporary asylum or others desiring visitors' visas for the Dominican Republic, with the intention of remaining there for under three years while they awaited permanent admission into another country, particularly the US. The fifth and final category covered permanent entrants who desired to live in the Republic for the rest of their lives. This group consisted generally of older people whose relatives in other countries could provide funds to care for them indefinitely, if necessary. In addition to the previous recommendations the temporary asylum group had to present a statement from a recognized physician with regard to their health and an obligation from the supporting relative to pay $30 per month for each individual and $50 a month for a family of two, to cover maintenance until the refugee received a visa. The supporting relative had also to deposit an initial $1,500 for each individual or $2,500 for a couple to cover maintenance, plus transportation, with the understanding that the relatives would guarantee thereafter to continue to send monthly installments until the refugee obtained his visa. After the initial funds were exhausted the depositor would assume complete responsibility for the refugee, either while he\she was in the Dominican Republic or while he\she was in transit to some other country.[60] Additionally, Warren recommended placing the temporary asylum refugees 'as far as residence is concerned in various localities in order to avoid concentration and away from the permanent settlement project'.[61]

At the same time it was necessary to establish a compelling formula to protect the Jewish supporting agencies against commitments which might prove expensive, while assuring the Dominican Republic that, in admitting temporary residents, they would not be assuming unlimited burdens. On 11 April 1940, Warren clarified that only those whose chances of entering the US were appraised by the US Immigration procedures would be chosen for temporary refuge, in the hope that this would be strong enough protection against the group being a burden on either the Dominican Republic or the Jewish agencies involved.[62]

It was one thing to transfer the refugees to another part of the globe during wartime; but it was yet another problem integrating the European refugees in the Caribbean Dominican Republic – a mission which turned out to be no less of a difficulty. Physical conditions in Sosua were completely different from those the refugees had known in Vienna or Berlin before Hitler. In the expert opinion of Dr Atherton Lee, a Department of Agriculture expert on tropical agriculture,

> Santo Domingo is one of the most delightful of the West Indies countries; it has a very nice climate, particularly in the northern part of the island where the Sosua colony is; there are very pleasant breezes, and if there is any feeling that the colony is not a healthful situation, it should be dispelled.[63]

However, in spite of his assurance that 'the colony in Santo Domingo has remarkable good possibilities', the settlers faced tremendous difficulties.

The entire area consisted of bush. There was no grazing land and electricity was non-existent. Transportation was a problem and the only way to travel was on horseback.[64] Roads, where they existed at all, were generally poor and when it rained the road to Puerto Plata from Sosua was impassable. In addition, physical labor, a new occupation, an oppressive tropical climate, a different diet and a strange language required physical and psychological adjustment. Felix Koch, who arrived at Sosua by boat in 1941 after spending time in a French concentration camp at Bayonne, remembers that, upon arrival 'we slept in tents while the barracks were being built'. Nevertheless, he emphasizes, 'little by little, we made a community'.[65] The settlers did their best to improve their daily life; they held dances, arranged to see movies and even ran a Jewish theater. They built their own library and published a newspaper. In 1941, they founded a school, which offered the required Dominican curriculum as well as instruction in the Jewish religion and Jewish history, and a synagogue was erected.[66]

On paper, it looked as if Trujillo had offered a paradise to the devastated refugees. Unfortunately, the Dominican Republic never became a refugee haven of even modest proportions. In a 1942 study the Brookings Institute concluded that the country could 'never be more than a minor factor in refugee settlement'.[67] In fact, objective reasons had from the outset prevented the development of what was occasionally called 'the First Jewish Colony'. War in Europe, submarine warfare in the Atlantic and the need to use Allied ships for troops and supplies made it possible to relocate only a few refugees in the first year. In addition, most of those who eventually arrived were aged over fifty, which made it difficult for them to adjust to the hot and humid climate and to the need to start a new and unfamiliar career as farmers. Even so, James N. Rosenberg refused to let the experiment die. In his words: 'Half of the world lives now under the shadow of war, persecution, horror and death ... Now an open door of hope beckons ... We must carry this endeavor to accomplishment ... We dare not falter.'[68] And in a special meeting of the Board of Directors of DORSA on 12 June 1940, he vigorously stated: 'Despite the clouds, which overwhelm the world, we are proceeding with the utmost energy to make this ray of hope, this candle of light into a greater reality.'[69] Indeed, for most of the Jewish refugees who eventually settled in the Dominican Republic, President Trujillo remained a savior. After all, the alternative of remaining under Nazi rule was infinitely worse.

NOTES

1. See, for example, Razovsky's correspondence with the Humane Refugee Aid Society, Inc., New York, with regard to a group of people in Prague to be settled in agriculture in San Domingo. NCC Records, Folder 92. Yivo Archives, New York.
2. Razovsky, 'Memorandum to the Executive Committee, NRS', 30 October 1939. Razovsky Papers, Box 1, Folder 2: Refugee Relief Work USA 1938–1939, Including Reports of Countries of Possible Settlement. AJHS Archives, New York.
3. Razovsky, 'Report, Facts and Figures', 17 February 1939, p. 4. Chamberlain Papers, Box 4, Folder 97. Yivo Archives, New York.
4. Ibid.
5. Cecilia Razovsky to Morris Troper, American JDC, 15 November 1939. Razovsky Papers, Box 1, Folder 2: Refugee Relief Work USA 1938–1939, Including Reports of Countries of Possible Settlement. AJHS Archives, New York.
6. Cited in Tartakower Arie and Kurt R. Grossmann, *The Jewish Refugee* (New York: Institute of Jewish Affairs of the American Jewish Congress and World Jewish Congress, 1944), p. 316.
7. Razovsky, 'A List of Requirements from Other Countries', 10 March 1939. Razovsky Papers, Box 1, Folder 2: Refugee Relief Work 1938–1939, Including Reports of Countries of Possible Settlement. AJHS Archives, New York.
8. Razovsky to Mrs Luisa Klabin Lorch, Saõ Paulo, Brazil, Re: Admission of Polish Children. 7 December 1939. Razovsky Papers, Box 2, Folder: NRS, Relief Work, Sep. 1939–1940. AJHS Archives, New York.
9. Cited in Lotte Marcuse to Razovsky, 8 January 1940. Ibid.
10. Ibid.
11. Razovsky to *Reichsvereinigung* in Berlin, 22 July 1940. Ibid. See also Kaete Rosenheim, the *Reichsvereinigung*, to Mrs Luisa Klabin Lorch, Saõ Paulo, 1 July 1940. Ibid.
12. Razovsky, 'Report, Facts and Figures', 17 February 1939, p. 1. Chamberlain Papers, Box 4, Folder 97. Yivo Archives, New York.
13. Ibid. With regard to Panama, see Memorandum by Razovsky, 'Admission to Panama for Temporary Asylum', 13 March 1939. Razovsky Papers, Box 3: Folder: Refugee Relief Work, 1938–39. AJHS Archives, New York.
14. See Chapter 2: The German-Jewish Children's Aid Project.
15. Razovsky to Mr Herbert S. Frieder, Jewish Refugee Committee, Manila, Re: Children's Emigration to the Philippines, 10 September 1940. Razovsky Papers, Box 3, Folder: Refugee Relief Work, 1940–1941. AJHS Archives, New York.
16. Razovsky to Alex Frieder, President of the Jewish Refugee Committee, 23 May 1939. Razovsky Papers, Box 3. Folder: Refugee Relief Work, 1938–1939. AJHS Archives, New York.
17. According to US immigration laws, application for an immigration visa was possible only from outside the United States.
18. Cecilia Razovsky, 'Reminiscing,' November 1939 (day not given), p. 2. Razovsky Papers, Box 2: Folder: St. Louis Incident. AJHS Archives, New York.
19. Razovsky to Mrs. Louis A. Alpert, 15 November 1938; Razovsky to Dr Helen O. Curth, New York, 10 November 1938. Razovsky Papers, Box 2: Folder: NCC, Correspondence, November 1938. AJHS Archives, New York.
20. Razovsky, 'Reminiscing', November 1939 (day not given). Razovsky Papers, Box 3, Folder: St. Louis Incident. AJHS Archives, New York.
21. Cited in Richard Breitman and Alan M. Kraut, *American Refugee Policy and European Jewry, 1933–1945* (Bloomington and Indianapolis: Indiana University Press, 1987), p. 72.
22. Joseph Chamberlain, NCC, to 'Friends of the Committee', 15 June 1939. Razovsky Papers, Box 2: Folder: St. Louis Incident: (II): 'Even after the steamer left Cuba, telegrams were sent to the ship three times each day and the committee aboard the ship sent cables to Miss Razovsky three or four times daily.' p. 3. AJHS Archives, New York. See also Arthur D. Morse, *While Six Million Died. A Chronicle of American Apathy* (New York: Random House, 1967), p. 275.
23. Razovsky to Max Hirsch, Portland, Oregon with reference to Karmann, Richard Sidonie and Karl, on the SS *St. Louis*, 7 June 1939. Razovsky Papers, Box 3: Folder: St. Louis Incident (II). AJHS Archives, New York.

24. Razovsky, 'Reminiscing', November 1939. Razovsky Papers, Box 3: Folder: St. Louis Incident, p. 3. AJHS Archives, New York.
25. Arthur D. Morse, 'Voyage to Doom', *Look Magazine*, 28 November 1939.
26. Thelma K. Brown (Razovsky's secretary) to Emil Mayer, 5 June 1939. Razovsky Papers, Box 3, Folder: St. Louis Incident (II). AJHS Archives, New York.
27. Cited in Razovsky, 'Facts and Figures', 17 February 1939. Chamberlain Records, Box 4, Folder 97. Yivo Archives, New York.
28. Ibid., p. 2.
29. Trujillo's motivation has been the subject of much speculation over the years. Some have said that his generosity was a veiled attempt to win favor among international leaders, since he had massacred thousands of Haitians, mostly cane cutters who were working on the Dominican side of the island. Others claim his offer was really an effort to 'whiten' the population and develop the island. In his letter to James Rosenberg, the future president of DORSA, on 26 December 1940, Trujillo stated that he was doing it not only for humanitarian and moral reasons but because it was necessary 'to have robust, healthy, diligent immigrants who would constitute a valuable element in developing his country's resources'. Cited in Robert G. Weisbord and Thomas D. Morin, 'The Caribbean Refuge', *Congress Monthly*, 44, 2 (February 1977), p. 14.
30. S. Adler-Rudel, 'The Evian Conference on the Refugee Question', *Leo Baeck Institute Yearbook* 13 (1968), pp. 241–3.
31. 23 March 1938, Foreign Relations United States (FRUS), 1, 1938, pp. 740–1.
32. Myron C. Taylor to the Secretary of State, 'Statements on Immigration into the United States for Evian Conference', 29 June 1938. NA 840.48 Refugees/467.
33. The Morgenthau Diaries, VI, 'The Refugee Run-Around', *Collier's*, 1 November 1947, p. 23.
34. Freda Kirchwey, 'Caribbean Refuge', *The Nation*, 13 April 1940, pp. 466–8.
35. Not all the American Jewish organizations were ready to spend millions to build a Jewish colony for a few thousand refugees when the money could be better used to feed many tens of thousands of Jews starving across Europe. Eventually the American Jewish Joint Agricultural Corporation (Agro-Joint) agreed to finance the settlement project.
36. Cited in J. Schechtmann, 'Failure of the Dominican Scheme', *Congress Weekly*, 15 January 1943, pp. 8–9.
37. The American Jewish Joint Agricultural Corporation was an agency related to the American Jewish Joint Distribution Committee (JDC).
38. The Agro-Joint donated $200,000 to its capital.
39. Agreement between the Dominican Republic and Dominican Republic Settlement Association, Inc., in Razovsky Papers, Box 3: Folder: Dominican Republic, Settlement. AJHS Archives, New York.
40. Ibid.
41. Ibid.
42. In return Trujillo received shares in DORSA. Sosua had previously been developed as a banana plantation but was later abandoned by the United Fruit Company, and had been purchased by the Generalissimo from the company.
43. Robert G. Weisbord and Thomas D. Morin, 'The Caribbean Refuge', *Congress Monthly*, 44/2 (February 1977), p. 13. He later donated additional lands including a mountain area.
44. Cited in J. Schechtmann, 'Failure of the Dominican Scheme', *Congress Weekly*, 15 January 1943, p. 9.
45. President's Advisory Committee on Political Refugees, 'Concerning Refugee Settlement in the Dominican Republic', A meeting at the Town Hall Club, NYC, 12 February 1940. Razovsky Papers, Box 3: Folder: Dominican Republic, Settlement. AJHS Archives, New York.
46. Minister Pastoriza, 'Minutes of a Special Meeting of the Board of Directors, DORSA', 12 June 1940, p. 3. Chamberlain Papers, Folder 10. Yivo Archives, New York.
47. George Warren, 'Minutes of a Special Meeting of the Board of Directors, DORSA', 12 June 1940, pp. 11–12. Chamberlain Papers, Folder 10. Yivo Archives, New York.
48. Mr Troper was the European Head of the Joint Distribution Committee.
49. A cable from Generalissimo Trujillo to Minister Pastoriza and Mr Rosenberg, 17 June 1940, offered 'asylum to a number of children and young men and women coming from England and France who will settle in the settlement at Sosua as an extension of the

covenant cerebrated between the Dominican Government and the Association for the Establishment of Colonists in the Dominican Republic'. Chamberlain Papers, Folder 7. Yivo Archives, New York.

50. Razovsky, Director of Migration Department, NRS, to Kaete Rosenheim, *Reichsvereinigung*, Berlin, 13 May 1940. Razovsky Papers, Box 3: Folder: Dominican Republic. AJHS Archives, New York.

51. George Warren, 'Minutes of a Special Meeting of the Board of Directors, DORSA', 12 June 1940, p. 13. Chamberlain Papers, Folder 10. Yivo Archives, New York. See also Rosenberg's statement: 'this opportunity for 1200 people is a matter of vast importance. We are desperately in need of those $230,000.' Ibid., p. 13.

52. All of them preferred migration to the US but that was not possible because of restrictions on entry. See Bat-Ami Zucker, *In Search of Refuge, Jews and US Consuls in Nazi Germany, 1933–1941* (London and Portland, OR: Vallentine Mitchell, 2001)

53. Mrs Rebecca Hourwich Reyher to Miss Razovsky and Mr George Warren, citing a letter from Minister Pastoriza, on behalf of the Dominican Republic, 8 August 1940. Razovsky Papers, Box 3: Folder: Dominican Republic. AJHS Archives, New York.

54. Rosenberg, 'Minutes of a Special Meeting of the Board of Directors, DORSA', 12 June 1940, p. 15. Chamberlain Papers, Folder 10. Yivo Archives, New York.

55. Ibid., p. 15.

56. Cecilia Razovsky to Haber, Executive Director NRS, 19 March 1940. Razovsky Papers, Box 3: Folder: Dominican Republic, Settlement. AJHS Archives, New York.

57. Ibid.

58. Razovsky, 'Memorandum – Plan for Temporary Asylum in the Dominican Republic', 12 April 1940. Razovsky Papers, Box 3: Folder: Dominican Republic, Settlement. AJHS Archives, New York.

59. Razovsky to all Branches, 23 March 1940. Razovsky Papers, Box 3: Folder: Dominican Republic, Settlement. AJHS Archives, New York.

60. George Warren to Razovsky, 4 April 1940. Razovsky Papers, Box 3: Folder: Dominican Republic, Settlement. AJHS Archives, New York.

61. Ibid., p. 3.

62. George Warren, President, Advisory Committee for Political Refugees, to Irving Sartorious, DORSA, Miss Cecilia Razovsky, Mrs Rebecca H. Reyher, Executive Secretary of DORSA, 11 April 1940. Razovsky Papers, Box 3: Folder: Dominican Republic, Settlement. AJHS Archives, New York.

63. Dr Lee, Ibid., p. 11.

64. There were only two vehicles in all of Sosua in 1941, one an old bus. See Robert G. Weisbord and Thomas D. Morin, 'The Caribbean Refuge', *'Congress Monthly*, 44/2 (February 1977), p. 14.

65. Cited in Kimbelee Roth, 'Island Refuge', *Jewish Life*, 53, 43 (30 June 2000).

66. Lauren Levy, 'The Dominican Republic's Haven for Jewish Refugees', *Jerusalem Post*, 6 January 1995.

67. The Brookings Institution, *Refugee Settlement in the Dominican Republic* (Washington, DC: 1942), pp. 281–2, 284.

68. James Rosenberg, Razovsky Papers, Box 3: Folder: Dominican Republic, Settlement. AJHS Archives, New York.

69. Rosenberg, 'Minutes of a Special Meeting of the Board of Directors, DORSA', 12 June 1940. Chamberlain Papers, Folder 10. Yivo Archives, New York.

6   Internment Camps for Enemy Aliens

Among the numerous projects handled by Cecilia Razovsky were the cases of Jewish refugees who had reached the United States, Central and Latin American countries, and were subsequently classified as enemy aliens, 'dangerous to US national security' and were therefore detained in camps. This chapter deals with Razovsky's efforts to provide the legal aid necessary to facilitate their release and, at the same time, to improve internment camp conditions, supply the refugees' material needs and to provide spiritual assistance.

With the rapid advance of the Nazis across Europe during 1939/40, the issue of national security gained momentum in the United States and soon reached levels of hysteria. According to a Roper poll in a July 1940 edition of *Fortune*, 71 per cent of the respondents were convinced that Germany had 'already started to organize a fifth column in the [United States]'.[1] Since the majority of the newcomers at that time were refugees from Germany, they were the easiest target. Popular magazine articles and movies titillated suspicions. It should be emphasized that most of the media treatment of the subject was probably designed to exploit the perceived danger for its commercial value by capitalizing on the inherent drama of spies and espionage. In the summer of 1940 *The American Magazine* published six articles about 'fifth columnists'.[2] Though serious journals such as the *Nation* and *Fortune* tended to treat the issue with greater concern for accuracy and less for sensationalism, they still helped to exacerbate the fear. The movies, for obvious reasons, also exploited the intriguing theme. Far from providing a balanced portrayal of Germans in America, films fanned the flames of prejudice and xenophobia.[3] These movies eventually prompted the US Senate to convene a series of hearings between 9 and 26 September 1941 to assess the role of propaganda in American motion pictures. The hearings were also an effort to curb America's heightened anti-German feelings.[4] But, given the general anti-German atmosphere, there is no doubt that American pre-war and wartime films were influential in promoting concerns that a fifth column was operating in the United States.[5]

The president, as well as American officials, was neither immune to the rumors nor able to remain passive in face of such animosity. Experienced statesmen such as Under-Secretary of State Sumner Welles and Assistant Secretary of State Adolf Berle[6] made known their opinion that subversion by refugees constituted more than mere rumor.[7] George Messersmith, former Consul-General to Berlin and at that time ambassador to Cuba, took seriously reports from American sources in Europe and Cuba indicating that Jews remained loyal to Germany, and used them as cues to recommend tighter immigration restrictions.[8] William C. Bullitt, former ambassador to France, further fueled concern by telling a Philadelphia audience that 'more than one half the spies captured doing actual military spy work against the French army were refugees from Germany'.[9] Though Bullitt's contention was unconfirmed and even contradicted by experts, it nevertheless added to the general apprehension that had already reached as far as the White House.[10] In his fireside chat in May 1940, Roosevelt openly stated that,

> Today threat to our national security is not a matter of military weapons alone. We know of new methods of attack, the Trojan Horse, the fifth column that betrays a nation unprepared for treachery. Spies, saboteurs, and traitors are the actors in this new strategy. With all that we must and will deal vigorously.[11]

Moreover, the president did not hesitate to state publicly that he was haunted by the specter of a fifth column whose members included some of the refugees. Though referring with sympathy to the suffering refugees from Nazi Germany, Roosevelt added at a June press conference that:

> Now, of course, the refugees has [sic] got to be checked because unfortunately, among the refugees there are some spies, as has been found in other countries. And not all of them are voluntary spies – it is rather a horrible story but in some of the other countries that refugees out of Germany have gone to, especially Jewish refugees; they have found a number of definitely proven spies ... Though [such cases involved] a very, very small percentage of

refugees coming out of Germany ... it is something we have got to watch.[12]

The State Department showed little interest in evidence that refuted the spy stories concerning Jewish refugees. Karl Lowenstein, a well-known scholar, prepared a carefully reasoned memorandum, which pointed out that planting spies among Jewish refugees was by no means a simple task because of the unique ethnicity and cohesiveness of the refugees, 'conditioned by the requirements of mutual help', which would make agents relatively conspicuous. His conclusion: the most dangerous place for a spy to be was in the refugee stream.[13] According to Alfred Wagg III, a prominent refugee reporter and former State Department official, only a few government officials were able to see the refugee as a potentially good American. 'Refugee in Washington', he stated, 'means "alien" to the bureaucrat and "secret agent" to the military man.'[14] In June 1941, he challenged the security scare, declaring that '[the] motive comes not from any genuine concern about Nazi spies but from the same little nest of anti-Semites ... in the state Department'.[15] Yet, the 76th Congress that rapidly approved the measures designed to restrict the activities of aliens or the State Department affecting them, had hardly noticed such revelations.[16]

An offensive drive against the alleged 'fifth column' was soon underway in response to the alleged threat. A special defense unit was established to investigate persons suspected of being unfriendly to the US, or of being agents of foreign governments. So well did the Department operate that within less than a week after war was declared in Europe in September 1939, more that 1,000 Japanese and 3,000 Germans and Italians had been apprehended and held. Because of this advance preparation, on the very day of the attack on Pearl Harbor and shortly thereafter, the Attorney-General was able to submit to the President for his signature proclamations declaring Japanese, Germans and Italians to be aliens of enemy nationality.[17] The proclamations authorized the attorney general to intern anyone considered by him to be dangerous to internal security.[18] The Enemy Alien Act of 1798[19] was the basic law substantially unaltered in this respect, and was administered in consonance with public safety and according to the dictates of humanity and national hospitality. Strict rules that first required internment of all enemy aliens were later changed to grant them reasonable time to depart under threat of expulsion. Finally, the rule was modified to permit them to remain in liberty, conditional on good behavior, reserving always the right to intern military reservists or individual alien enemies thought to be dangerous, and even to expel all, or large groups of, enemy aliens. Authority was given to the secretary of war to deal with suspected aliens in the Panama Canal Zone, Hawaii and the Philippines. The Department of Justice established a rule to the effect that these new regulations would apply to every person aged 14 years or above, who was at that time a citizen or subject of Germany, Italy or Japan. Persons who regarded themselves as stateless – Jewish German refugees, for example – but whose last allegiance was to Germany, were also regarded as enemy aliens. Exceptions were made with respect to several groups, namely, Austrians who had registered as Austrians or Austro-Hungarians in 1940 when aliens of all nationalities were obliged to register under the Alien Registration Act,[20] as well as Koreans and natives of the Dodecanese Islands. These exceptions were based on the theory that enemy nationality had been imposed on these groups. However, the Department could and did apprehend any alien suspected of being dangerous, regardless of his or her nationality. A large number of these aliens were sent across the border to Canada and to Australia, where they were held in internment camps for several years. However, when public opinion favored the release of these refugees, the majority were freed after hearings were held and testimony given as to their loyalty. In fact, quite a few of them subsequently joined the armed forces.[21]

A division known as the Enemy Alien Control Unit was established by the Attorney-General immediately after the proclamations were issued. The Unit's mission was to set up procedures for hearings and review of the cases of the apprehended enemy aliens, and to put into effect regulations to control their travel and other conduct. This Unit also coordinated the activities of US attorneys, the FBI, hearing boards and the Immigration Service, the Departments of State and War, and other departments concerned with the issue.

Before an enemy alien could be apprehended, a presidential warrant of apprehension had to be issued. The FBI secured this after presenting its evidence to the US Attorney, who decided whether or not to apply for a warrant. If the warrant was issued, the FBI had the authority to arrest the alien. The conventions of international and national law did not require that an enemy alien be given any kind of trial before being interned for the duration of war. But as a means of providing a fair procedure in keeping with American tradition, every enemy alien who had been apprehended was given a hearing upon request.[22]

On 9 September 1939, the president created the Emergency Detention Program, instructing the Justice Department 'to arrest and detain those persons deemed dangerous in the event of war, invasion, or insurrection in and of a foreign enemy'.[23] Once arrested, each enemy alien's case would be evaluated by the Attorney-General's office, with the eventual result of (a) conditional or unconditional release, (b) parole, with or without bond, or (c) internment for the duration of the war. To prepare for the third possibility, the program called for the construction of detention camps to be located in the south-east, the mid-south, and the south-western parts of the United States. It was agreed that the army would maintain and transport arrested aliens as far as the camp, at which point they would be handed over to the Immigration and Naturalization Service, now under the authority of the Justice Department. Attorney-General Biddle appointed Edward J. Ennis, a respected attorney with the Immigration and Naturalization Service, to head the new Enemy Alien Control Unit. And, together with the Immigration and Naturalization Service, Chief Earl G. Harrison and Attorney-General Biddle worked to establish the internment process. Ennis created a network of small tribunals called Civilian Enemy Alien Hearing Boards to evaluate the cases. Their recommendation on each case was to be forwarded to the Attorney-General's office in Washington for final disposition. It was a tiring and time-consuming process. An arrested alien had to wait weeks and often months until the hearing board reviewed his or her case. On 27 August 1940, Congress passed the Alien Registration Act (Public Law Number 670), part of the larger Smith Act, which required all non-citizens to register at their local post office, to be fingerprinted and photographed. Another law was aimed to help aliens who wished to leave the country to obtain a permit. In October 1941 all aliens with assets over $1,000 were required to provide a detailed accounting of those assets to the Treasury Department. Aliens and enemy aliens' movement and employment were also bound by numerous state and local restrictions and there were businesses that would not hire foreigners, as well as landlords who refused to rent apartments to Germans.[24] All registration forms were sent directly to the Department of Justice headquarters in Washington, DC.

Following Presidential Proclamation 2525-2527 (December 1941) and 2537, dated 14 January 1942, the Attorney-General issued regulations requiring application for and issuance of certificates of identification to all 'enemy aliens' aged 14 and above, outlining restrictions on their movement and property ownership rights. These presidential proclamations authorized the Department of Justice to establish a series of restrictive regulations for the conduct of aliens of enemy nationalities residing in the United States. These regulations, in general, included:

a. Restrictions on travel.
b. Surrender of personal possessions such as hand cameras, radio transmitters and other articles and equipment, which may be used against US national defense.
c. Prohibited and Restricted areas. The control of the presence and conduct of such aliens in areas in military zones designated and controlled by the United States War Department.
d. Certificate of Identity, which each alien enemy was required to carry with him at all times and to show upon request to a police officer or authorized government agent.
e. Provisions for aliens notifying proper authorities immediately of change of places of residence and employment.

Alien Enemies were defined as follows:

a. All aliens aged 14 years or older on 7 December 1941, or were citizens or subjects of Germany or Japan, and,
b. All aliens aged 14 years or older who at present are stateless but who at the time they became stateless were citizens or subjects of Germany or Japan.

It should, however, be stressed that the Presidential Executive Order of 21 March 1942 exempted from the classification of alien enemy all applicants or American citizens whom the Attorney-General, after investigation, certified as loyal to the United States. Such investigation, however, would only be conducted when the applicant's final petition for naturalization was pending in court.

The effects of these regulations on Jewish immigrants were horrendous and, according to NRS estimates, about 200,000 Jewish refugees throughout the United States were affected. The majority of these Jews were pro-democratic refugees who had demonstrated their loyalty to the United States in many ways: by active participation in war, membership in American organizations and by investing capital and labor in American industry.

An April 1942 report on the west coast situation by Victory Garvey, NRS representative in the field, illustrates the gloomy atmosphere in Jewish circles and the confusion among Jewish leaders: 'Regulations for prohibited and restricted areas for enemy aliens hit the West Coast communities like a bombshell.'[25] Though unofficial sources indicated that soon civilian boards might be set up to give individual attention and change the category of individuals from 'enemy aliens' to 'friendly aliens from enemy lands', American Jewish leaders were confused with regard to a suitable response.

The NRS's first reaction was 'to allay the hysteria and to give the refugee group a feeling of confidence that everything was being done in their behalf'.[26] However, as time passed, the vast majority of Jewish leaders opposed taking collective action against the restrictions, 'fearing that it may be a reflection upon the Jews throughout the country for them to ask for special consideration for refugees'. A minority of leaders called for more decisive action though even they stressed, that 'it is an enemy alien problem and not a Jewish problem'.[27] A similar attitude was expressed in a memorandum prepared by Razovsky in February 1942, calling for cautious behavior on the part of the NRS:

> It has always been necessary for the NRS representatives when conferring with authorities ... on this subject, to bear in mind that no matter how passionately we felt on the status of refugees as enemy aliens, there were other groups that felt equally fervent concerning aliens who are not refugees but who, in their opinion, are just as loyal and just as entitled to consideration as are the refugees. To ask for special consideration for Jews, even though they have suffered and have been persecuted, would under the circumstances jeopardize our efforts and subject us to undue criticism.[28]

However, for the aliens who found themselves categorized as enemy aliens, it was not so much the loss of a camera or the inconveniences involved in traveling from city to city that caused grief, as it was the shocking realization that they were being classified as enemy aliens together with fascists and Nazis – the very people at whose hands they had suffered untold hardships, indignities and insult. Moreover, Attorney-General Biddle's announcement on 19 October 1942, of the removal of the 'alien enemy' stigma from aliens of Italian nationality only served to intensify the sense of betrayal among stateless Jewish aliens from Germany.[29] It was little wonder, therefore, that they found these regulations offensive and frustrating in their efforts to become Americans as quickly as possible and in their strong desire to build a permanent home in the United States.

Perhaps the most unusual case was that of internee Kurt Sanger. Born in Vienna in 1920, Sanger escaped Austria in May 1939 and, after spending a year in a transit camp for male Jewish refugees in England, he received a visa to the United States. Eventually he found employment as an elastics cutter at the Maidenform Brassier Company. On 3 January 1942, he was arrested without warning and accused of being a Nazi spy on the hearsay of a certain Smith who worked with him. In his 'Petition for Release' he stated that for him 'to arrive to America was ... like heaven'.[30] It took until the fall of 1942 for Sanger to gain his release.[31] Or the case of Eddie Friedman (pseudonym), who was born in Hamburg in 1892. Dr Friedman (as attorneys were known in Germany), practiced law until he was forbidden to do so by Nazi edicts. He and his wife were granted exit permits in 1938. However, before they could escape, he was arrested and imprisoned in Oranienberg-Sachsenhousen concentration camp outside Berlin. Relying upon his connections in the legal community, Friedman was able to secure his release from the camp, fled to America with his wife and settled in San Francisco. Since his English was not fluent, he was unable to pursue employment in his profession and found work delivering Viennese pastries door-to-door in German communities. To FBI agents, his connection to suspicious German Americans indicated that he was a dangerous Nazi. During the 8 December raids following Pearl Harbor, the FBI took him into custody. Eddie Friedman, a Jew who had narrowly escaped extermination in Germany, wound up behind barbed wire at Fort Lincoln Internment Camp, outside Bismarck, North Dakota. It was to be over six months before his protests of innocence were finally heard and he was released, marked for life by his internment experience.

Moreover, those regulations tended to exacerbate employers' suspicions toward aliens and contributed to discrimination against foreigners in employment.[32] But a note of hope for Jewish refugees could be found in Biddle's announcement: 'I wish to emphasize that in thus removing the label of alien enemy from Italians, we do not forget that there are other loyal persons now classed as enemy aliens. Their situation is being carefully and sympathetically studied by the Department of Justice.'[33] Approximately one million enemy aliens were registered, including 300,000 German-born aliens, who were not permitted to enter federally designated areas. If enemy aliens violated these or other applicable regulations, they were subject to arrest, detention and internment for the duration of the war.

Anti-Nazi refugees, Jews in particular, were not exempt from the Enemy Alien Program. For example, the case of a young Jewish boy, who became one of America's premier historians and a noted author on the Second World War, indicates the absurdity of including German Jewish refugees in the campaign. Gerhard Weinberg, who fled with his parents from Nazi Germany to the United States in 1940, found himself classified as an enemy alien. At 14 he joined the Albany New York High School debate team and was periodically humiliated because he had to register with the authorities to compete.[34] The treatment of Jewish refugees and their classification as enemy aliens is difficult to understand. However, given J. Edgar Hoover's suspicion of all foreigners, including Jews who fled Germany as 'Nazi plants', the spread of antisemitism in the United States during the 1930s, and its increase as the war wore on,[35] might explain that irrational phenomenon and its too ready acceptance by the American public.[36]

In the spring of 1941, once again citing the dangers of subversives among the refugees, the State Department instructed consuls to reject applicants 'if they had children, parents, spouse, brothers or sisters' still residing in the territories under Nazi domination.[37] And on 20 June 1941 the President signed the Bloom–Van Neuys legislation, which authorized American consuls to withhold any type of visa from an alien seeking admission to the United States 'if the official has reason to believe that the applicant might engage in activities that would "endanger the public safety"'.[38]

In addition to keeping its German inhabitants under strict surveillance, the United States and the State Department had long maintained a close watch on America's enemies in Latin American countries. In 1941, the Office of Strategic Services ordered its Latin America Section to investigate the extent and commitment of pro-Nazi sentiments in those regions. The reports confirmed that there was real reason for concern about the possibility of Axis sabotage in the western hemisphere.[39] The administration viewed the presence of over a million-and-a-half ethnic unassimilated Germans in Latin American countries as an immediate threat to US national security, and that a Nazi takeover of the continent by a 'fifth column' could be imminent. According to Professor Max Friedman, who had made a thorough study of the issue, 'FDR believed it, and his military prepared for it'.[40]

Such presumptions evolved into a program for the deportation and internment of thousands of people from Latin American countries. Officials in Washington were able to prevail upon their Latin American counterparts to collaborate in the program. Except for Argentina, Brazil, Chile, Venezuela and Mexico, all of whom refused to deliver German nationals for internment in the United States, fifteen smaller countries of the Caribbean basin, Central and South America were correspondingly more vulnerable to US pressure and cooperated with the deportation program.

The issue of hemispheric security aside, America's intention was to build up a reserve of internees to trade with the enemy. Latin America's Germans were meant to be exchanged for American citizens held in Nazi camps.[41] In addition, there was also the issue of commercial competition, to which Latin American governments responded gladly, using the detention of wealthy Germans as an excuse to seize their businesses and property, which ranged from huge plantations to successful manufacturing plants.[42] Given these reasons, the United States decided to apply pressure to Latin American countries for cooperation. At a meeting of Latin American ministers of foreign affairs in Rio de Janeiro in mid January 1942, the commitment of the governments concerned to cooperate with the United States was reaffirmed..

Following US direction, Latin American countries captured German Latin Americans, including German and Austrian Jews who had fled persecution. Under US guard, prisoners were shipped to the United States in the dark, damp holds of boats and were rarely permitted on deck. Open-bucket latrines were placed among the prisoners. No one told them what was going to happen to them. They were interned and about two thousand were later forcibly shipped back to Germany. On 12 December 1942, General George Marshall informed the Caribbean Defense command that these interned nationals are to be used for exchange with interned American civilian nationals being kept in Germany'.[43] However, the US administration made sure that its meddling in the internal affairs of the republics would not be known. In a memorandum to Special Division Department of State, Division of the American Republics, J. M. Cabot emphasized:

> I think it is undesirable for the written record to show that the initiative came from us ... I fear that in the post-war period, unfriendly leaders in the other republics may use incidents such as this to demonstrate that behind the façade of Good Neighborship the US was really interfering in the internal affairs of the other republics ... If we really must take the initiative and exert pressure in connection with deportation, it should at least be done with great discretion ...[44] Herewith the kind of thing which I have been fearing and which in my opinion may well

rise to damn us when the present crisis is over.[45]

Meanwhile, the construction of federal detention camps was under way. On 22 March 1942, the Army Provost Marshal General ordered the preparation of nine permanent alien enemy internment camps, plus a camp reserved only for families. Each camp had a distinct population, men only, single women and childless couples, or family groups including children. The following camps are relevant to our study:[46]

- Camp Kennedy, Texas, operated by the INS – included German and Japanese as well as a large contingent from Latin America.[47]
- Camp Seagoville, Texas, operated by the INS – included single women, South Americans and some German and Italian families.
- Crystal City, Texas, operated by INS – families, and consisted of Germans, Italians, Japanese, and aliens from Latin America.
- Camp Stringtown, Oklahoma – operated by the army, included Germans, Latin Americans, men only.
- Camp Fort Forrest, Tennessee – operated by the army, included Germans, Italians and Latin Americans.

Of all the camps, Camp Seagoville was the most civilized. It had been built to resemble a small college campus; but it was still a closed camp surrounded by high wire fences.

Jewish refugees who succeeded escaping from Germany and finding shelter in Central and South American countries soon found themselves interrogated by local authorities. A total of eighty-one Jews were among the 4,058 Germans shipped from Latin America to be interned in the United States.[48] These Jewish Germans included citizens and legal residents of Latin American countries and quite a few refugees from Hitler. Most Latin American countries did not detain Jews in particular, but they did not release them if they were in custody. Only Panama and British Honduras, governed by antisemitic officials, proved eager to include Jews in their selections. Those Jews who were refugees from Nazi Germany, or who seemed in any way suspicious, were sent to the Balboa Detention Center in the Canal Zone for several weeks of US army interrogation. Afterwards, they joined their fellow Jews and their families who were dispersed among the camps at Seagoville, Stringtown, Blanding, Florida, and Fort Oglethorpe, Georgia. The Blanding, Oglethorpe, Algiers and Louisiana camps,[49] which were maintained by the army for Axis prisoners of war and Nazi sympathizers, were the worst. The fact that these camps were most dangerous for Jews did not prevent the US authorities from locating them there. Moreover, a review of the lists of Latin American German internees shows that Jews were not placed in a separate category.[50] They were listed as Germans. Max Friedman states that Assistant Secretary of State Breckinridge Long, the most senior US official closely involved in the internment program, made sure that they would not receive hearings or be otherwise able to argue their case, even while knowing that the majority of them had survived Nazi concentration camps.[51] He resisted investigation of Jewish internees already in the camps on the grounds that 'we might be considerably embarrassed',[52] should they be proved innocent and released. In his diary he referred to Jewish refugees as 'lawless, scheming, defiant and in many ways unassimilable [sic].[53] Some [were] certainly German spies trying to enter the US.'[54] In a confidential letter to George Messersmith, American Ambassador to Mexico, he openly stated his understanding that 'here are a great many people trying to get into this country who have every indication of being of the intention to execute some kind of nefarious purpose once they get in. The intention is to weed out the dangerous element.'[55] As late as August 1942, Jews were still included on lists of future repatriation. Moreover, in September that year, Long refused to promise not to deport Jewish internees to Germany against their will.[56]

When it came to Jews, the camp authorities, whose job it was to keep the internees safe, especially from Nazi sympathizers, expressed a hostile attitude. One US official complained that one of the Jewish internees 'made a nuisance of himself for several years in an effort to get released from confinement'. Other officials rejected, as a matter of course, numerous appeals on behalf of the Jews. Rabbi S. B. Yampol of Nashville, who regularly drove to Camp Forrest, Tennessee, to visit the twenty Jewish internees from Panama and to hold religious services for them, appealed vigorously to the Department of State on their behalf, but his appeals fell on deaf ears.[57] In his answer to Rabbi Yampol's complaints, Albert E. Clattenburg of the Special Division presented a choice for the Jewish internees: to be repatriated or subject to internment. In other words, if they did not like the way they were being treated in the US, they were free to go back to Nazi Germany.[58]

German and Austrian refugees living in Panama who were classified and arrested as enemy aliens were obliged to undergo especially severe interrogations. The Panamanian government took a number of these refugees into custody at a time when all aliens of enemy nationality

(German, Austrians, Italians and Japanese) were arrested and interned. Rabbi Nathan Witkin, of the Jewish Welfare Board at Balboa, Canal Zone, brought the matter to the attention of the NRS when he came to the US in the spring of 1942. At that time he explained that when the Panamanian government took all aliens of enemy nationality into custody, no distinction was made between bona fide refugees who fled from Germany because of the Hitler regime, and other aliens of enemy nationalities. He stated that he knew many of the Jewish men and women in question through his work in the Canal Zone and because of the social service activities which he and his wife carried out on their behalf. He also advised that officers were fully aware of the entire situation and had dossiers on each individual concerned. According to his report, most of the persons interned were elderly people who had voluntarily agreed to accompany their interned sons. Most of the younger people were strong and active and, if they were released, could be useful in defense activities and in the war effort.[59]

The NRS started pulling strings in order to get news about the Jewish refugees who had found shelter from Nazi persecution in Latin American countries and were now being forcibly deported to detention camps in the United States as enemy aliens. In fact, the question of treatment of enemy aliens during wartime, with special reference to refugees, had been the subject of consideration by the NRS since the fall of 1940. When the Alien Registration Act was passed, immigration officials in Washington held several conferences to which representatives of the NRS were invited in order to draft the questionnaires and to discuss regulations. At that time the question of a clear definition of nationality, particularly as it affected stateless persons, was thoroughly discussed and the questions in the Alien Registration form were devised in such a way as to permit refugees to explain their position in the US. The subject came to the fore again at the time that refugees were sent from England to be interned in Canada and Australia and in connection with efforts to secure their release. It was not until after 1 July 1941, when the Department of Justice had established a bureau known as the special Defense Unit which dealt with problems affecting the treatment of alien enemies, that the NRS started negotiating with the administration. The issue began to receive proper attention with the help of prominent individuals such as Professor Chamberlain, Solicitor General and later Attorney-General Francis Biddle, Edward Ennis, Director, Enemy Alien Control Unit, L. M. C. Smith of the Special Defense Unit,

George Warren of the President's Advisory Committee, James C. McDonald and others. Professor Chamberlain and Cecilia Razovsky held several conferences in an attempt to deal specifically with the matter of stateless Jewish refugees.[60] At one conference in Washington in December 1941, Professor Chamberlain presented a brief, which was later sent to important government leaders, with the request to exempt certain categories from the Enemy Alien classification, such as stateless Austrian or Austro-Hungarian people, who had lost their enemy alien citizenship due to the 25 November 1941 decree issued by the German government. Further unofficial meetings took place, all to bring the matter to the government as well as to the public's attention.[61] Razovsky took upon herself to visit the internees as many times as she possibly could. Personal meetings with them served not only to acquaint her, first hand, with their problems, but, more importantly, to pacify their fears and assure them they were not alone and that Jewish organizations were taking care of their needs.

Cecilia Razovsky was in charge of negotiating with Mr Ennis, Chief of the Enemy Alien Control Unit, Department of Justice. Following her visit to the camps of Texas and Oklahoma on 30 November 1942, she arranged three important meetings in Washington. The first conference was with Ennis, with whom she discussed two problems; the steps to be taken to effect the release of Jewish men in the immigration camps, and also to have eight men who were at Camp McAlester and two men at Camp Forrest transferred to Camp Kennedy. Her objective was to keep all twenty-two Jewish refugees in a single camp in order to facilitate the arrangement of hearing boards or some other form of examination which would facilitate their release.[62] The meeting with Ennis was productive; he approved and promised to deal with the issue immediately. Razovsky suggested that NRS would take responsibility for collecting all available proof that these people were bona fide Jewish refugees and, so far as they knew, were not dangerous or subversive elements. Ennis confessed, in confidence, to Razovsky, that according to the State Department, the Panama government considered all persons, including Jewish refugees, brought up from Panama, to be dangerous and subversive. It would be necessary, suggested Ennis, to secure definite and convincing proof to counter these charges.[63]

The second meeting was with Ennis' assistant, Mr Gitlin, who was in charge of enabling the release of stateless internees. As a precedent that might prove decisive, Razovsky raised an episode from early September 1941 in which the steamer *American Legion* had brought to the United States 125 Jewish people of German nationality from the Canal Zone. The NRS had provided a guarantee to the authorities that these people would not become public charges; they all had hearings before the boards of special inquiry and practically all of them were admitted without any difficulty.[64] Gitlin, too, was cooperative and promised to act on her suggestion and prepare hearings for these refugees.

The third meeting was held at the British Embassy with Mr John Russell, who was in charge of the internees from British Honduras, held in Seagoville.[65] Razovsky raised the case of Mrs Leo Keiles, a British subject married to Leo Keiles, a German national. According to the authorities in British Honduras, Keiles had lost her British citizenship when she married the German. Razovsky, however, was able to prove that she was a legal British subject holding a valid passport. Razovsky complained that Mrs Keiles had been badly treated by the British authorities and was not given the chance of a hearing. Mr Russell promised to take care of the matter. Apologizing for Britain's handling of Mrs Keiles' case, which he described as 'a stink', he advised sending her back to British Honduras, where he guaranteed she would receive a fair hearing.[66]

The situation of the detainees from British Honduras was also discussed in a letter from Razovsky to Leo Gitlin dated 5 February 1943. According to Razovsky's letter, the NRS had, in a number of earlier instances, corresponded with agencies abroad long before the refugees left Germany. The correspondence indicated that they were at all times regarded as bona fide Jewish refugees attempting to free themselves from Nazi persecution. She also attached documents she had gathered on Dr Leo Friedmann, Dr Wilhelm Stein, and Mr Eric Joseph, all internees from British Honduras. Razovsky emphasized that the Jewish Refugee Committee of London, England, had known about Dr Leo Friedmann and Dr Wilhelm Stein even before they left Germany and had attempted to help them by securing permission from the British government to send them to British Honduras.[67] This notwithstanding, the Jewish refugees in British Honduras were rounded up on 22 June 1942, as part of the much-publicized capture of a Nazi spy ring operating from British Honduras and the Canal Zone.[68] The British colonial governor, Sir John Adams Hunter, a notorious antisemite, made sure that Jewish refugees were included in the round-up and, in fact, used the Nazi spy ring case as an opportunity to make the colony '*Judenrein*', or free of Jews.[69]

In order to speed up the procedure and ensure a rapid hearing,

Razovsky operated on two fronts. Recruiting volunteer women all around the United States, she undertook a general and thorough search for relatives or friends to persuade them to sign affidavits on behalf of the detainees. Simultaneously, she negotiated with Gitlin to make all the necessary arrangements for the hearings, since '[w] e are endeavoring to assemble at this time affidavits and statements from relatives, closer friends and acquaintances of the detainees and will forward them to you as fast as we receive them'.

The case of Tone Mucher, interned at the Seagoville camp, reflect-ed the general situation facing the refugees. With the help of *Juedischer Hilfsverein*, which 'gave us funds to emigrate', the Mucher family had emigrated to Bogotá, Columbia, and then to the Republic of Panama. According to Tone Mucher, in March 1942 she and her husband had 'asked to be interned voluntarily, so that we might come to the United States'. Based on her statement, the Panamanian government claimed a technical irregularity in their papers in order to encourage them to leave, 'due to antisemitism feelings on the part of the Panamanian gov-ernment'.[70] In April 1942, nineteen Jewish aliens were transferred to internment camps in the United States. Eventually the Mucher family was detained in Seagoville, Texas.[71]

The Muchers were but one family among eighty-one Jewish refugees who were, in fact, kidnapped and brought by force to deten-tion camps in the US. Appeals to the NRS from refugees at camps and relatives in the United States described the frustration of the Jewish refugees who found themselves held as prisoners. Most poignant was Eric Joseph's letter, in which he defined himself as:

> A poor stateless Jewish refugee, who would be very grateful to this country, if permitted to join their armed forces & to do my share for the victory of the United Nations. There is nothing what could prevent me to do my duty ... & my earnest decision to become a soldier of the US Army.[72]

One letter from Otto Manheimer, spokesman for the Jewish detainees at Camp Forest, Tennessee, to the Refugee Committee, NRS, at Chattanooga, Tennessee, described the hopeless situation in the camp, and urged for some action on the behalf of the inmates:

> We are deeply depressed ... It is terrible that we will have to wait probably several more months, far from our families. We realize that the government cannot be pushed by Miss Razovsky, but for God's sake what has been done during 8 months? We do know positively, that Rabbi Witkin of the J.W.B.[73] Balboa, Canal

Zone, as long as February reported our situation to New York. Suppose nothing could be done until our arrival in the US. But we are already 4 months here, isn't this time enough to get on at least one step forward? Very strange indeed.[74]

Or another letter from Walter Wolff, detained at Camp Algiers, Louisiana, pleading for Razovsky's help: 'The people are desperate since they know that their release won't happen in the near future ... We can take it and we will bear it as men, hoping that you now will double your efforts to get us out of this mess.'[75] It was the uncertainty about their future that seems to have most affected the detainees. In reponse to Wolff's cry for help,[76] Razovsky and the community in New Orleans did their utmost to comfort the detainees. In a letter to Rabbi S.B. Yampol, Razovsky described the activities in the camp:

> Local rabbis conduct a weekly afternoon religious service, a teacher in English goes out twice a week, a committee on Personal Service from the Council of Jewish Women visits twice a week and bring over sewing and knitting material for the women. The men have been supplied with needs and are planting a garden. The group has been provided with all kinds of games. Plans are being made for Passover observance. Canteen needs are being met and other incidental expenditures are being taken care of. Visits are often made to the detainees who are at present in the hospital.[77]

Another internee, Werner Kappel, actually joined the army after his release from the camp in 1943, fought bravely in the Philippines, was wounded and awarded the Purple Heart. He became an American citizen shortly after the war ended but was finally released from supervision by the government's Enemy Alien Control Unit only six months later. His story is typical of other young aliens who had escaped Germany with or without their parents, and a few years later were imprisoned as Nazi spies. After the Gestapo threatened him and his father, a Jewish leather-goods dealer in Berlin, the two escaped Germany in 1938 and found shelter in Panama. However, both were deported to the US after Pearl Harbor as 'dangerous aliens', and interned in Seagoville Camp, Texas.

Conditions at the station in Belize, British Honduras, were no easier to bear. Karl Lowenthal sent Razovsky a desperate letter, complaining of the terrible conditions and the harsh climate there.[78] Mr Dragten, an attorney in Belize, in a letter to Emery H. Komlos,

Assistant Secretary, Refugee Economic Corp, New York, which was transferred to Razovsky, stated that the Jewish refugees there were unjustly detained by the US government and sent to the US 'at the special request of that Government'. He suggested approaching the State Department in Washington since 'there seems no reason why these unfortunate people could not be released'.[79]

Conditions at Seagoville camp were a little better but the morale was extremely low. According to a report from supervisor Jack Gershtenson, sent by the Jewish Welfare Federation in February 1943, the 'group that was originally in British Honduras ... seems terribly upset about their own position'. A representative of the State Department visited Seagoville and told the group that his department had nothing to do with the detainees from British Honduras and that 'they will not be released either now or after the War'. These aliens, concluded Gershtenson, had lost all hope of being released soon and were sinking into a deep depression.[80] Rabbi Israel Gerstein of Chattanooga, Tennessee, coming to Sabbath services for the Jewish internees in Fort Oglethorpe, Georgia, described the atmosphere among the Jewish internees 'as a Tsha B'Av mood ... It was like Yom Kippur because of the tears and outcries.'[81] Or as Irene Wolff, separated from her husband, wrote to Cecilia Razovsky, 'We are the loneliest Jewish people who are in the USA.'[82]

In addition, Gershtenson complained of hostility between the different groups among the forty-five Jewish detainees in Seagoville. The refugees were divided into three different factions. They labeled themselves the 'German Group', the 'Austrian Group' and the group from British Honduras. Internal squabbling developed because of the frustration of prolonged confinement. Gershtenson urged them to recognize the need for better relations.[83] Eventually, the three factions established a committee to resolve disputes among the detainees. A rabbi from Dallas who served as a visiting chaplain to the detainees mediated any conflicts that the committee could not resolve.[84]

As Head of Migration Department of the NRS, Razovsky was in charge of all contacts with the Enemy Alien Control Unit. She not only appealed for rapid hearings for the detainees but corresponded almost daily with Leo Gitlen, assistant to Edward J. Ennis, Director, Enemy Alien Control Unit, furnishing affidavits from relatives in the United States. She also sent the required documents which established the detainees' Jewish ethnicity and their involvement in Jewish organizations – all this to prove that the refugees were anti-Nazis, and therefore certainly offered no security threat to the US. A letter from Edward Ennis to Razovsky in April 1943 specified all the required information for scheduling a hearing: 'All possible affidavits and testimony on behalf of these detainees [in Algiers] should be obtained in order that their files may reflect your representations that they were improperly apprehended and transferred to the US.' He also suggested that a member of the NRS should personally contact these aliens to ascertain the full details of their behavior and conduct in Panama, their history prior to their arrival in Panama and any other material as was determinative of their loyalties in the present conflict.[85] Razovsky instructed her staff, which was helping the refugees to fill the petitions, to pay especial attention to the following requirements: (a) To secure a full biographical statement from the detainee in person. This statement should contain full particulars regarding the detainee's parents – their occupation, their affiliations with Jewish organizations, synagogues, etc. (b) Full biographical data regarding the detainee – place of birth, the schools attended, skills and trades, or professions learned, colleges, other education and institutions attended. (c) Full history of occupations, places of employment, names of employers, particularly if such employers were already in the United States. (d) Affiliations with Jewish institutions, synagogues, etc. (d) Names and addresses of friends, schoolmates, *Landsleute*, close relatives and distant relatives, particularly if these were in the US or in neutral countries outside the US. (e) Names and addresses of friends living in the country from which the detainee was brought to the US who might be willing to vouch for the detainee. As soon as the information was received at the Central Office, the representative of the NRS would send copies to the Migration Department. The Migration Department would then clear the names and, where there was no record, would make up a case record on each detainee for immediate approach to the persons listed, who might be able to provide affidavits of character and loyalty regarding the detainee, or other necessary information. In addition, birth certificates, past and present letters of reference, which could help in obtaining a positive response from the authorities, were also required. Razovsky emphasized the importance of securing documentary proof of the detainee's loyalty from Central and South American countries and of the fact that the person was connected with Jewish organizations abroad and was in no way involved politically with the Nazis. As soon as all the documents were assembled they were mailed to Mr Ennis, Director, Enemy Alien Control Unit, Washington. However, the Department of Justice was entirely responsible for whether or not hearings would be held, and their dates.[86]

Razovsky was especially concerned with the women and children in the camps because they had chosen voluntarily to accompany the male member of their family. Again and again she pleaded with Leo Gitlin and Edward Ennis to speed up their release:

> It seems to me that in view of the labor shortage, it is a pity to waste the skills of these young persons against whom there is no charge whatsoever. They chose to come up with their relatives from Central and South America in order not to be separated from them ... I feel certain that it would raise the morale of the entire group if we succeed in getting these women, all of whom are able to work in the community [released], instead of remaining at the camp.[87]

It took tremendous efforts by the American Jewish Joint Distribution Committee, the National Refugee Service, Catholic groups, the American Civil Liberties Union, the Jewish communities of Dallas, New Orleans, Chattanooga and Nashville to untangle the bureaucratic red tape and combat the antisemitism that caused the incarceration of eighty-one Jews from Latin America in hostile enemy internment camps in the United States. Eventually, Razovsky's efforts to secure hearings were successful. The majority were paroled in mid-February 1943 and allowed to resettle wherever they could find sponsors. Those who chose to serve in the US military could, after a while, get their status changed.[88] The rest were liable for deportation at the end of the war. On 29 November 1943, the Justice Department lifted parole supervision over the Jews, and they were released on a case-by-case basis. However, the process was enduring and the 'Enemy Alien' label was still hanging over them as late as December 1945. In a long and moving letter, Ann P. Petluck, who replaced Razovsky as the Director of Migration Department, NRS, pleaded with the Department of Justice, Immigration and Naturalization Service, to lift that shameful label and enable those Jewish refugees to apply for American citizenship. She attached a list of persons 'who are meritorious factors', asking for them the 'privilege of pre-examination'.

Elaborating on each case, she stated that they were all Jewish refugees who had been brought to the US as part of the 'Latin-American Internee' program. Most of the women in the group were voluntary internees, who had chosen to accompany or join their husbands and fathers in detention camps in the southern US. She emphasized that in 1942, the Enemy Alien Control Unit of the Department of Justice examined their records in Latin America and they were '*found not to be security problems*' (original emphasis). In cooperation with the Department of Justice, the then NRS (changed later to United Service for New Americans) secured sponsors and helped to resettle them in various large cities in the US, as close as possible to their American relatives. She explained that the Department of State subsequently found them to be free of suspicion and posing no security problems and they were released from the Enemy Alien Program on the basis of their good records. Since their adjustment in their communities had been uniformly excellent both economically and socially and the war had been terminated, there was no further need to keep them under the stigma of the category of 'Enemy Aliens'. Moreover, since their closest ties were in the US, and 'they are very eager to be permitted to remain in the US', they should be given the privilege of pre-examination or suspension of deportation, based on the special facts of their respective cases.[89]

Although the NRS efforts – and those of Cecilia Razovsky in particular – to obtain the release of internees were generally productive, the case of internees from British Honduras raised particular difficulties. The State Department argued that since the British government was responsible for their confinement, only the British government could release them. Yet, even if the British authorities were ready to release them they would have to remain in the United States until after the war, a fact which was not well received by the US. Eventually the British government agreed to change the internees' status to internees-at-large as long as they remained in the US. The NRS accepted responsibility for the refugees and sponsors were found for them, with the help of the Jewish communities in Dallas and Houston, Texas. Since the status of internee-at-large given to people with limited parole required a well-known and established American citizen to guarantee the refugee's good behavior, therefore the task of finding the right sponsors preoccupied Razovsky and her team. The NRS launched a project in the mid-west and south and, with the help of local Jewish communities, it was able to find volunteers to act as sponsors.[90]

Edward Ennis, Director of the Enemy Alien Control Unit, and his assistant Leo Gitlin were sympathetic and cooperated over many cases with the NRS, and especially with Razovsky, to help bring forward hearings and release of refugees from Central and South America. In the case of four of the internees from British Honduras – Friedmann, Stein, Keiles and Eric Joseph – Ennis asked Razovsky early in March 1943 to start looking for sponsors, in the event of parole being granted. He reminded her that she had earlier mentioned that the NRS local committee in Dallas, Texas was in the position to insure proper parole supervision over some of these persons, or to grant a modified internment, permitting their release from actual detention quarters. He therefore urged her to forward to his office the names of such responsible citizens so 'that action on the report may be facilitated by establishing the proper parole sponsorship'.[91] Two weeks later, the names of the sponsors had already been forwarded to Ennis. The final stage required the consent of the Attorney General in Dallas in order to arrange the dispatch of refugees to communities chosen by the NRS.[92] By the end of that month British Honduras internees were released to parole sponsors in Dallas.

Dr Friedmann was given modified parole,[93] which meant that he would be free to live in the interior of the country but would not be permitted to reside in either the east or west coast.[94] As for financing the care of the refugee families, in a meeting at Razovsky's office the same day it was decided that Dallas should be asked to make funds available until such time as their own funds were released, when they would repay the Dallas Committee directly or through the NRS. Mr Resnik in Dallas agreed to advance funds for the care of these families, promising also to secure housing and provide other services until permanent resettlement plans could be drafted.[95] Every one of the former internees had to register as aliens with the Alien Registration Division. They also had to secure certificates of identification as aliens of enemy nationality, and, since they were of military age, they were also obliged to register with the draft board. In Razovsky's words, 'they should act exactly as if they had entered the country in a routine fashion'.[96]

The situation was similar for the Jewish detainees at Camp Algiers, Louisiana. By 6 May Razovsky had gathered full details about their stay in Panama, the circumstances of their arrests, whether they had been granted hearings and the names and addresses of Panama residents who could vouch for them. In addition, she sent the Enemy Alien Control Unit complete biographical material concerning their life in Germany or Austria. Things seemed to move. On 1 May 1943, Razovsky was advised by the Department of Justice that one of their men was being sent to Panama to read the records on these detainees and to get as much information as possible about them and their activities in Panama. Hearings were to take place on his return,[97] which Razovsky was requested to attend in person.[98] A week later, Gitlin informed Razovsky that he expected to start hearings on 29 June and again asked her to attend those in New Orleans. As with the internees from British Honduras, Gitlin urged her to obtain sponsors for these internees in the cities in which they were to be settled. Razovsky asked Mr Beck, the representative in New Orleans, to quickly find sponsors to enable the internees' release when approved by the Attorney-General.[99]

'Thank you' letters from former internees expressing their gratitude and appreciation for Razovsky's help reveal a little of her doings. Leo Friedmann's sentimental letter is just one example:

> We don't know how to thank you for helping us when in distress. We feel that we were still forgotten ... without your assistance. It was a great comfort in our misery to know that there was at least one who believed our version of the story. We find it hard to get used to liberty after ten months behind iron bars.[100]

The efforts of Razovsky and her team with regard to enemy aliens in general and the internees from British Honduras in particular, reflect what a strong-willed person, who spared no effort to release the unjustly accused refugees in the face of an antisemitic conspiracy, could achieve.[101]

By the middle of 1943, the federal government reclassified most of the Jews as 'internees-at-large', and eligible to live outside the camps for the duration. The last Jews in internment were set free in early 1946. Of the eighty-one Jewish internees from Latin America, two voluntarily returned to Latin America, four died before they were released,[102] and seventy-five chose to remain in the United States.[103] But it was only the enactment of the 1953 Refugee Relief Act,[104] which permitted any alien brought to the US from Latin America before 1 July 1953 to request a change of status, that finally brought the sad experience of the Jewish internees to an end.

NOTES

1. *Fortune*, July 1940, in Hadley Cantril, (ed.), *Public Opinion: 1935–1946* (Princeton, NJ: Princeton University Press, 1951), p. 809.
2. Sensational titles included: 'Hitler's Slave Spies in America', 'Enemies Within the Gates'.
3. See, for example, *Confessions of a Nazi Spy* (1939); *Keeper of the Flame* (1942); *Home on 92nd Street* (1945).
4. U.S. House of Congress: 'Propaganda in Motion Pictures', *Hearings before a Subcommittee of the Committee on Interstate Commerce: United States Senate*, Resolution 152, 77 Cong. 1 sess., 9–26 September 1941.

5. Arnold Krammer, *Undue Process. The Untold Story of America's German Alien Internees* (New York: Rowman and Littlefield, 1997), pp. 6–9.
6. It should be emphasized that Assistant Secretary Adolf Berle was the main force behind the initiation of the deportation program. See Jordan A. Schwarz, *Liberal: Adolf A. Berle and the Vision of an American Era* (New York: The Free Press, 1987), pp. 20–2.
7. Adolf Berle Papers, Diary, 8 May 1940, cited in Richard Breitman and Alan M. Kraut, *American Refuge Policy and European Jewry, 1933–1945* (Bloomington and Indianapolis: Indiana University Press, 1987), p. 121.
8. For example, he cited rumors that some Jewish refugees in Havana allegedly celebrated the fall of Paris to the German Army. See Messersmith to Secretary of State, 21 June 1940, NA, RG 59, 150.626 J/798. See also Messersmith to Long, 31 May 1940, Long Papers, File 211, 1940. Manuscript Division, Library of Congress, Washington, DC.
9. *New York Times*, 2, 19 August 1940.
10. See Samuel Lubelle, 'War by Refugees', *Saturday Evening Post*, CCXIII, 29 March 1941, claiming that the Nazis were using the refugee stream to plant their agents 'all over the world' and had established a special school in Prague where Gestapo agents learned to pass as Jews; and Heinz Pol, a refugee correspondent, 'An Open Letter to Ambassador Bullitt', *The Nation*, 31 May 1940, pp. 167–8, repudiating the accusations.
11. *New York Times*, 26 May 1940, p. 1.
12. Presidential Press Conferences, 5 June 1940, *Complete Presidential Press Conferences of Franklin D. Roosevelt* (New York: De Capo Press, 1972), vol. 15, pp. 495–9.
13. 'Lowenstein Memorandum', 5 October 1942, cited by Henry Feingold, *Politics of Rescue. The Roosevelt Administration and the Holocaust 1938–1945* (New Brunswick, NJ: Rutgers University Press), p. 131.
14. Alfred Wagg III, 'Washington Step-Child, the Refugee', *The New Republic*, 28 April 1941, pp. 594–5.
15. Alfred Wagg III, *The New Republic*, 30 June 1941, p. 873.
16. See, for example, Senator Lewis B. Schwellenback referring to the suggested restrictive measures, as quoted in *Contemporary Jewish Records*, May–June 1940, p.24.
17. The status of enemy aliens in wartime may be regulated by presidential proclamation under Section 2 of Title 50 of the United States Code, (Sec. 4067 Revised Statutes). That Section authorizes the president to direct the conduct to be observed on the part of the United States towards 'all natives, citizens, denizens, or subjects of the hostile nation of government, being of the age of 14 years or upward who shall be within the United States and not actually naturalized'. With regard to the Proclamations applying to Germans and Austro-Hungarians, see 40 Stat. 1650 and 1716.
18. Internment is a well respected and long established component of international law. It permits a country to intern those aliens residing in its territory who are subjects or nationals of any country with which the former is at war. Internment is part of US law (6 July, c. 66, I Stat; R. S. 4067; 50 US Code 21), and is based on the 'Enemy Alien Act of 1798'. The constitutionality of internment was twice reaffirmed by the Supreme Court shortly after the end of World War II in 'Ludecke v. Watkins' (335 U.S. 160, 171 n18–1948) and 'Johnson v. Eisentrager' (339 U.S. 763–1950).
19. The Enemy Alien Act, 1789.
20. Known also as the Smith Act, 1940. Cecilia Razovsky, a member of the Advisory Committee, to Mr Earl Harrison, Administrator of the Alien Registration Act. See Arthur D. Greenleigh, NRS, to Department Heads, 'Meeting re Alien Registration', 30 August 1940. NRS Papers, Folder 150. Yivo Archives, New York.
21. See, for example, the story of Werner Kappel, below pp. 171, 188.
22. Razovsky, 'Treatment of Enemy Aliens in War Time', Razovsky Records, Box 3, Folder: Treatment of Enemy Aliens in War Time. AJHS Archives, New York.
23. Cited in Athan Theoharis, *Spying on Americans: Political Surveillance from Hoover to the Houston Plan* (Philadelphia: Temple University Press, 1973), p 40.
24. All this notwithstanding, it should be stressed that aliens and enemy aliens still had access to the judicial system.
25. Victory Garvey, field representative, to Joseph Galkin, NRS, 'Confidential Field Report on West Coast Situation', 20 April 1942. NRS Papers, Folder 99, p. 1. Yivo Archives, New York.
26. Ibid.

27. Ibid., pp. 2–3.
28. Razovsky, 'Treatment of Enemy Aliens in War Time', 19 February 1942. Razovsky Papers, Box 3, Folder: NRS: Jews Interned at Detention Centers in Southwest US, 1941–1943. AJHS Archives, New York.
29. The removal of Italians from the alien enemy class was announced on Columbus Day 1942, at a celebration in Carnegie Hall, New York in the presence of thousands of wildly cheering Italians. 'Migration and Alien Status Committee of the National Refugee Service for Subcommittee on Alien Enemy Status and Reclassification', 17 March 1943. Chamberlain Papers, Folder 24. Yivo Archives, New York.
30. 'Petition for Re-classification as a Non-Enemy Alien and for Release from Internment of Kurt Sanger', 8 August 8, 1942, cited in 'Enemies are Humane', a paper presented to The Dayton Christian-Jewish Dialogue on 10 May 1998, by John A. Heitmann, Professor of History, University of Dayton.
31. Harvey Strum, 'Jewish Internees in the American South, 1942–1945', *American Jewish Archives*, XLII, 1 (Spring/Summer 1990), pp. 27–48.
32. 'Migration and Alien Status Committee on the NRS for Subcommittee on Alien Enemy Status and Reclassification', 17 March 1943. Chamberlain Papers, Folder 24. Yivo Archives, New York.
33. Cited in 'Migration and Alien Status Committee of the National Refugee Service for Subcommittee on Alien Enemy Status and Reclassification', 17 March 1943. Chamberlain Papers. Yivo Archives, New York.
34. Weinberg's important studies include: *The Foreign Policy of Hitler's Germany 1937–1942* (Chicago: Chicago University Press, 1970); *Germany, Hitler, and World War II* (New York: Cambridge University Press, 1995); *The World at Arms: A Global History of World War II* (Cambridge: Cambridge University Press, 2005).
35. Bat-Ami Zucker, *In Search of Refuge: Jews and U.S. Consuls in Nazi Germany 1933–1941* (London and Portland, OR: Vallentine Mitchell, 2001), pp. 18–27.
36. Geoffrey Perrett, *Days of Sadness, Years of Triumph: the American People 1939–1945* (New York: Coward, McCann and Geoghegan, 1973).
37. 'Circular Telegram to Certain Diplomatic Missions and to All consular Offices except those in France, Belgium, the Netherlands, Germany and Italy', 5 June 1941, NA, RG 59, 811.111 W.R./ 359 1/2.
38. US Statutes 252, Public Law 113, 77th Congress.
39. Arnold Krammer, *Undue Process*, pp. 88–100.
40. See the excellent and well-documented study by Paul Max Friedman, *Nazis and Good Neighbors: the United States Campaign against the Germans of Latin America in World War II* (Cambridge, MA: Cambridge University Press, 2003), p. 2. And Stephen Fox, 'The Deportation of Latin American Germans, 1941–1947: Fresh Legs for Mr. Monroe's, Doctrine', *Yearbook of German-American Studies*, 32 (1997), pp. 117–42, who argues that officially the US involved itself for reasons of national security, but the deportation program was actually an elaborate plan connected with historic US objectives in the western hemisphere: the purpose was to replace German interests in the region with those of the US and cooperative republics. Policymakers in the State Department who had been concerned for years about German economic and political influence in the western hemisphere jumped at the opportunity created by wartime security fears to carry out the scheme.
41. 'Memo,' Cordell Hull to Roosevelt, 27 August 1942, and 'Memo', Department of State, 3 November and 30 December 1942, NA. RG 59 (records of the Department of State); 'Memo – Regarding the Activities of the United States Government in Removing from the Other American Republics Dangerous Subversive Aliens', 3 November 1942, 3 RG 59, Subject Files, Box 180, Records of the Special War Problems Division. And Leslie B. Rout Jr and John F. Bratzel, *The Shadow War; German Espionage and United States Counterespionage in Latin America during World War II* (Lanham, MD: University Publications of America, 1986).
42. Fox, 'The Deportation of Latin American Germans, 1941–1947, pp. 117–18.
43. Ibid., pp. 117–42.
44. Memorandum from J. M. Cabot, Department of State, Division of the American Republics to Special Division Department of State, Division of the American Republics, 24 November 1943, RG 59: Special War Problems Division, Department of State. Cited in Arthur D. Jacobs and Joseph E. Fallan, (eds), *German-Americans in the World Wars*. Vol. IV: *The World War II*

Experience (München, New Providence, London, Paris: K.G. Saur, 1995), p. 1674.

45. J. M. Cabot, Department of State, Division of the American Republics to Messrs. Wright and Bonsal, 15 November 1943, RG 59: Special War Problems Division, Department of State. Cited in ibid., p. 1671.

46. This chapter deals with Jewish refugees, especially from Latin American countries, who were interned in enemy alien camps.

47. Latin American countries' refers here to internees from South America, Central America and the Caribbean.

48. White to Bingham, 'Statistics', 28 January 1946, NA, RG 59 Subject Files 1939–54, Box 70, Special War Problem Division. Joseph E. Fallan estimates that the number of Latin Americans of German descent interned in the US was over 5,000. See Joseph E. Fallan, 'The Censored History of Internment, *Chronicles: a Magazine of American Culture*, Rockford, IL: The Rockford Institution (February 1998). Andy Lindstrom argues, 'In a hasty move made in the name of national security, FDR needlessly swept some 4,000 civilians from their homes in Latin America.' Lindstrom 'Roosevelt's Wrong Enemies', in Friedman, *Nazis and Good Neighbors*, pp. 28–9.

49. The Algiers camp was the INS quarantine station where internees were held pending their trans-shipment to other camps.

50. Franz G. Wirz, chief spokesman, Seagoville Internment Camp. Cited in *German-Americans in the World Wars*, Don Heinrich Tolzmann (ed.), Vol. IV: *The World War II Experience, the Internment of German-Americans*, Jacobs and Fallan, p. 1678.

51. Fallan, 'The Censored History of Internment', *Cross Ideas: A Magazine of American Culture The Monthly Magazine of the Rockford Institute*, February 1998.

52. Friedman, *Nazis and Good Neighbors*, pp. 156–7.

53. Fallan, 'The Censored History of Internment', who argues that the available evidence strongly suggests that the US government knowingly shipped German Jewish Latin Americans to the Nazis as part of the program. However, Cecilia Razovsky's article, 'Deportation of Aliens, Past and Present', *Jewish Social Service Quarterly*, 20, 1 (September 1949), states that 'for the two years period of 1941 and 1942, the 79 Jewish aliens were deported – 64 were sent to Canada, 8 to Europe, 5 to Great Britain and 7 to Central and South America ... No Jewish aliens were deported to Axis or Axis occupied countries', pp. 22–3. This does not rule out the possibility, still to be verified, that Jewish internees were later sent back to Germany.

54. *The War Diary of Breckenridge Long. Selection from the Years 1939–1944*, selected and edited by Fred L. Israel (Lincoln, NE: University of Nebraska Press, 1966), p. 281.

55. Long to Messersmith, American Ambassador to Mexico, 28 September 1942. Long Papers, File 199: Messersmith, October–December 1942. Manuscript Division, Library of Congress, Washington, DC.

56. Long to Mohler, 24 September 1942, Folder 'W', Names Files of Internment enemy aliens from Latin America, 1942–8, NA, RG Box 35.

57. Rabbi S. B. Yampol to Razovsky, 5 April 1943, NRS Records, Folder 537: Internees from Latin America. Yivo Archives, New York. See also Otto Manheimer, for the Jewish internees at Camp Forrest to George Blike, Razovsky Papers, Box 3, Folder: NRS, Internees. AJHS Archives, New York.

58. Yampol to Hull, 10 August 1942 and Clattenburg to Yampol, 24 October 1942. NA, RG 59, 740.00114 EW 1939/4823.

59. Cited in Razovsky, Assistant to the Executive Director NRS, to Leo Gitlin, Enemy Alien Control Unit, Department of Justice, 5 February 1943. NRS Records, Folder 537. Yivo Archives, New York. In another letter to Gitlin, 9 February 1943, Razovsky informed him that she was sending additional testimonials prepared by friends regarding Dr Stein of Seagoville 'in connection with the possible hearing to take place soon' (ibid.). In fact the young aliens eligible for military service were recruited and even awarded medals. See the career of Werner Kappel and Eric Joseph, below, pp. 177, 181

60. Razovsky, 'Treatment of Enemy Aliens in War Time', 19 February 1942. Razovsky Papers, Box 3, Folder: NRS, Jews Interned at Detention Centers in Southwest US, 1941–1943. AJHS Archives, New York.

61. Ibid., p. 3.

62. There were already twelve Jewish internees at Camp Kennedy. With the addition of ten transferred from other camps, the final number would be twenty-two.

63. Cited in Razovsky to Albert Abrahamson, Executive Directive NRS, 'Report on Visit to Washington and Philadelphia', 30 November 1942. NRS Records, Folder 537. Yivo Archives, New York.

64. Ibid., p. 2.

65. The situation of this group differed from that of refugees from Panama and other Central American countries since they were under the jurisdiction of the British government.

66. Razovsky to Albert Abrahamson, Executive Director NRS, 'Report on Visit to Washington and Philadelphia', 30 November 1942. NRS Records, Folder 537. Yivo Archives, New York. Ibid., p. 3.

67. Razovsky to Leo Gitlin, 5 February 1943. Razovsky Papers, Box 3, Folder: NRS: Jews Interned at Detention Centers in southwest US, 1941–1945. AJHS Archives, New York.

68. *New York Times*, 26 June, 3, 4, 12 July 1942.

69. Strum, 'Jewish Internees in the American South, 1942–1945', *American Jewish Archives*, pp. 34–5.

70. Professor Richard Behrendt, University of New Mexico to Dr Ernst Fraenkel, American Federation of Jews from Central Europe, 23 November 1942: 'I can say already now that the atmosphere which prevailed in Panama at that time with regard to refugees from Europe, especially Jewish ones, was by no means conductive to a detached and objective appraisal of those people, their background and activities. This holds particularly good for the period of the dictatorship of Arnolfo Arias, October 1940 and September 1941. Under him pro-fascist and anti-Semitic elements became very powerful and some of them have remained in office after he was ousted.' Attached letter from Fraenkel to Razovsky, 27 November 1942. Razovsky Papers, Box 3, Folder: NRS: Jews Interned at Detention Centers in Southwest US, 1941-1943. AJHS Archives, New York. See the statements of Gerhard and Charlotte Schlesinger, 30 November 1942 and of Fred Kappel, 12 December 1942. Ibid. And Fred Kappel to the Joint Distribution Committee (JDC), 12, 28 April 1942, File 411. JDC Archives, New York.

71. Cited in Report of Razovsky to Abrahamson, 11 November 1942. NRS Records, Folder 537. Yivo Archives, New York.

72. Eric Joseph, Camp Forest, Tenn., to Razovsky, 9 November 1942. NRS Records, Folder 537. Yivo Archives, New York.

73. Rabbi Nathan Witkin was the representative of the Jewish Welfare Board and American Jewish Joint Distribution Committee who lived in Balboa, Panama.

74. Otto Manheimer to George Berke, Chairman, Refugee Committee, Chattanooga, Tenn., 5 August 1943. Razovsky Papers, Box 3: Folder: NRS: Jews Interned at Detention Centers in Southwest US, 1941–1943. AJHS Archives, New York.

75. Walter Wolff, Camp Algiers, Louisiana, to Razovsky, 17 April 1943. NRS Records, Folder: Jews Interned at Detention Centers in Southwest US, 1941–1943. Yivo Archives, New York. See also Kurt Mucha, Detention Station Algiers, to Razovsky, 17 April 1943: 'In our opinion, the present status of our cases is quite hopeless. Some way out will be found.' Ibid.

76. See his wife Irene's letter to Razovsky, 5 June 1942. Chamberlain Papers, Folder 49. Yivo Archives, New York.

77. Razovsky to Rabbi S. B. Yampol, 12 April 1943. NRS Records, Folder 537. Yivo Archives, New York.

78. Karl Lowenthal, Belize, to Razovsky, 24 January 1943 (in German). NRS Records, Folder 537. Yivo Archives, New York.

79. Cited in a letter from Razovsky to Dorothy Kahn and Augusta Mayerson, 4 February 1943. NRS Records, Folder: Jews Interned at Detention Centers in Southwest US, 1941–1943. Yivo Archives, New York.

80. Jack Gershtenson, Supervisor, Case Work Department, Jewish Welfare Federation, formerly known as Jewish Federation for Social Service, to Razovsky, 4 February 1943. NRS Records, Folder 538. Yivo Archives, New York.

81. Cited in Strum, 'Jewish Internees in the American South, 1942–1945', *American Jewish Archives*, p. 27.

82. Irene Wolff to Cecilia Razovsky, 5 June 1942, Chamberlain Papers, Folder 49. Yivo Archives, New York.

83. In her letter to Gershtenson, Razovsky thanked him for his efforts to encourage them 'to carry on in a more amicable spirit in the future and not bring to the attention of the outside agencies the fact they are not getting along with each other'. Razovsky to Gershtenson, 10 February 1943. NRS Records, Folder 538. Yivo Archives, New York.

84. *National Refugee Service News*, 4 September 1942. Razovsky Papers, Box 3, Folder: AJHS Archives, New York; Razovsky to Reuben Resnick, 21 January 1943, Jack Gershtenson to Razovsky, 19 January, 1, 2 February 1943, NRS Records, Folder 538: Treatment of Enemy Aliens in Wartime. Yivo Archives, New York.

85. Edward J. Ennis, Director, Enemy Alien Control Unit to Razovsky, Assistant Executive Director, NRS, 19 April 1943. Razovsky to Leo Gitlin, 28 April 1943. Razovsky Papers, Box 3, Folder: Treatment of Enemy Aliens in Wartime, n.d. AJHS Archives, New York.

86. Razovsky to Staff, 'Material to be Secured on Behalf of Detainees Prior to Hearings to be Held by the Department of Justice', 11 June 1943. NRS Records, Folder 537. Yivo Archives, New York.

87. Razovsky to Leo Gitlin, Enemy Alien Control Unit, 28 April 1943. NRS Records, Folder: Jews Interned at Detention Centers in Southwest US, 1941–1943. Yivo Archives, New York.

88. The process was not an easy one, as the case of Werner Kappel, a Jewish refugee from Germany and a resident of Panama shows. He was classified 'an enemy alien' and against his will was shipped to a camp in the US. He was paroled in late 1943, joined the US army, was wounded in the Philippines, and awarded a Purple Heart decoration. His first application for citizenship was denied on the grounds that he had entered the US illegally – not taking into account that he was forced into the country. Only by the end of June 1945 was he able to obtain his citizenship, and it took a further six months to be released from the supervision of the government's Enemy Alien Control Unit. For his story see Friedman, *Nazis and Good Neighbors*, 'Introduction'.

89. Ann P. Petluck, Director of Migration Department, NRS, to Commissioner of Immigration and Naturalization Service, 21 December 1945. NRS Records, Folder 537, p. 2. Yivo Archives, New York.

90. The former detainees were settled in Denver, Chicago, Detroit, St. Paul/Minneapolis, Memphis, Cleveland, Cincinnati, Milwaukee, Pittsburgh, Kansas City, St. Louis and Youngstown. Relatives could be sponsors provided they were safe and responsible citizens. See Razovsky to Mrs Marmell, 5 April 1943. NRS Records, Folder 537. Yivo Archives, New York.

91. Edward J. Ennis to Razovsky, 10 March 1943. NRS Records, Folder 537. Yivo Archives, New York.

92. Razovsky to Evelyn W. Hersay, Immigration and Naturalization Service, 24 March 1943.

93. No reason was given for Dr Friedmann's limited parole. Perhaps it was because he was, in Razovsky's words, 'a trouble maker', or the fact that he was spokesman for the internees. Razovsky to Mrs Marmell, 5 April 1943. NRS Records, Folder 537. Yivo Archives, New York.

94. Jules Seitz, Representing the Community Relations Department, NRS, British Honduras Internees in Seagoville, to Ephraim Gomberg, 30 March 1943, citing a letter Razovsky received from Gitlin on 29 March 1943. NRS Records, Folder 537. Yivo Archives, New York.

95. Ibid., p. 2.

96. Razovsky to Mrs Marmell, 5 April 1943. NRS Records, Folder 537. Yivo Archives, New York.

97. The NRS and the Jewish communities concerned negotiated the settlement details for the released internees. Razovsky to Jules Seitz, NRS, 2 April 1943. NRS Records, Folder 537. Yivo Archives, New York.

98. Razovsky to Joseph Beck, 6 May 1943. NRS Records, Folder 384. Yivo Archives, New York.

99. Razovsky to Beck, 17 May 1943. Ibid. It should, however, be remembered that with regard to the sixty internees from Panama whose status was 'internee-at-large', the Department of Justice preferred that they were settled in the south-west and be scattered. Ibid.

100. Grete and Leo Friedmann to Razovsky, 11 April 1943. Razovsky Papers, Box 3, Folder: Detainees in Internment Camps in the South, AJHS Archives, New York. See also Dr Stein to Razovsky, 8 April 1943. NRS Records, Folder 537. Yivo Archives, New York.

101. 'We are doing everything in our power to expedite action by the Department of Justice in arranging for hearings for these people so that they may eventually be free ... I have been in touch with the Department of Justice at least once a week on their situation'. Razovsky to Rabbi S. B. Yampol, 12 April 1943, with regard to the Panamanian internees in Algiers, Louisiana. NRS Records, Folder 538. Yivo Archives, New York.

102. Razovsky maintained personal relations with the internees, sharing their griefs and worries. See Razovsky's letter of condolence to Mrs Lucy Kallman, who lost her husband. NRS Records, Folder 537. Yivo Archives, New York. Also Razovsky to Mr Leo Keiles, 1 April 1943, one of the internees released from British Honduras, who was worried about the outcome: 'I am quite sure that you will all be treated fairly and equally.' NRS Records, Folder 538. Yivo Archives, New York.

103. Strum, 'Jewish Internees in the American South, 1942–1945', *American Jewish Archives*, pp. 24–48.

104. Refugee Relief Act, 1953. US Statutes at Large, Public Law 203, Ch. 336, pp. 200–407.

7 Cecilia Razovsky: A Woman Who Made A Difference

On 28 January 1934, 13-year-old Erich Oppenheim faced the congregation of his synagogue in the German town of Neutershausen on the day of his bar mitzva and, for the first time in his life, publicly read from the Torah. The following day, he and his younger brother boarded a ship for America to escape Nazi persecution. The two boys were never to see their parents and two brothers again. Sixty-four years later he remembered tearfully how '[his] father settled [them] in [their] cabin, blessed [them] for the last time and left'.[1]

Many such stories have been told by other children, all aged under 16 at the time, all taken, unaccompanied by their parents, on the road to America in an attempt to escape the Nazi menace. Werner Michel was 12 years old when his mother accompanied him to the train in Mannheim. He remembers that the day was bitterly cold and that his mother had made certain he wore his heavy overcoat and wool cap. She sat close to him and held his hand to encourage him. Werner's mother broke down at the station in Mannheim. They tried to smile for each other; surely they would meet again soon. Alone on the train to Hamburg, he waved to his mother for as long as he could, until he could no longer see her. Then, one of fifty confused children who were separated from their parents on their way to the unknown, Werner boarded the SS *New York*, bound for America.[2]

It is impossible to express the agony, the pain, the longing and yearning for their parents and the emptiness these children underwent. A prayer written for New Year's Eve, 1934, by Hans J., one of the refugee children, reflects their complicated condition:

Dear God
In this New Year,
Enter into all people's hearts,
Join all countries in peace,
Bless each good person and mankind's holy righteousness,
Bless goodwill,
But vanquish evil,
Take away the hate from people's hearts,
And dear God take away all pain.
Continue giving strength to the weak,
And have patience with us.
These are my wishes for the New Year.[3]

About one thousand Jewish children were smuggled clandestinely out of Europe – mainly from Germany and Austria – between 1934 and 1945 and taken to live with Jewish foster-families in America. Although their stories vary, most of the children found themselves in warm and supportive homes and took very well to their new families. Some children, however, were subject to miserable experiences, when their foster-parents forced them to act as the family's servants and chambermaids; these had to be placed in several homes, until the social services found suitable environments for them.[4] But, thankfully, they were spared the terrible fate of the million and a half children, who perished in Nazi Europe.

'In retrospect', concludes Iris Posner, who undertook the mission of bringing their stories to the public eye and giving their rescuers the credit they deserved,[5] 'these children were able to lead their lives in safety, to raise families of their own, and to achieve success and even fame'.[6] The children were brought into the United States through an 'underground railroad' operation, in a rescue project that was legal though secretive.[7] At a time of tight immigration quotas and widespread antisemitism, Jewish organizers in the United States feared a backlash and did their best to keep the operation quiet. To this very day, only a few scores of American Jews have heard about it.

The child-rescue project was one of many rescue projects undertaken by American Jewish women under the organization and supervision of Cecilia Razovsky, before and during World War II. Miss Razovsky, as she was called, was born in St. Louis, Missouri in 1886 to poor immigrants, Minna and Jonas Razovsky. As an adult she became an immigration and refugee relief worker and literally dedicated her life to the cause of Jewish refugees, eventually becoming the acknowledged authority on immigration, refugees, Jewish refugee children and displaced persons. She was highly efficient in her numerous projects, assisting and finding shelter for Jewish refugees,[8] obtaining the necessary visas, affidavits and information for entry into the United States. After their arrival, she helped the refugees to locate relatives, and found them jobs and cities in which to settle permanently. Most important, she initiated and administrated a successful program that brought over 1,000 Jewish refugee children to the US and saw to their placement with Jewish foster-families. She created and administrated a network in over one hundred cities all around the country with the aid of the professional and non-professional women she recruited – all working long hours for what Razovsky considered 'a sacred mission' – of rescuing Jewish refugees from Europe. Razovsky's tireless work on behalf of her people and her devotion to the refugees present a unique person who literally dedicated herself to the lives of others. She stimulated and inspired hundreds of American Jewish women, and initiated, organized and administered a national network for the rescue of refugees. Razovsky was always in the forefront of rescue operations, carrying the torch for those officials – federal and Jewish – working tirelessly for the relief of Jewish fugitives. She was an extraordinary woman, who succeeded in achieving the near impossible during the worst crisis that befell the Jewish people. It is worth mentioning one of the many letters of appreciation that she received. This letter, sent by Mildred A. Gutwillig, Chairman, Conference Committee, Arden, New York on 23 June 1939 and referring to Razovsky's address at the Refugee Session, is one of many sent by institutions and refugees documenting her personality and her tireless efforts: 'The simplicity and sincerity with which you spoke, cuts straight through all possible mental reservations. One feels the personality behind everything you say.'[9]

In the course of her work Razovsky often interacted with policymakers in the Jewish community, as well as the Roosevelt administration. She was in regular and direct contact with the federal officials in charge of immigration in the Departments of State and Labor, with the General Commissioner of Immigration, Col. Daniel MacCormack, and the American consuls in Europe.[10] The latter were legally responsible for granting or denying immigration visas and Razovsky's efforts focused mainly on enabling the full use of the quota accorded by law – 25,557 for Germany, 1,413 for Austria. It was, however, tragic that the horrendous events in Germany coincided with a difficult and unprecedented economic situation in the United

States, which exacerbated anti-immigrant feelings. Moreover, antisemitic, patriotic groups launched overt anti-Jewish propaganda, which
made it most difficult for the administration and Congress to even
consider opening the gates to Jewish refugees. Leonard Dinnerstein
has concluded that after 1933, the United States experienced 'an
explosion of unprecedented anti-Semitic fervor'. Jews were blamed
for the worldwide economic crisis and accused of exercising undue
influence on the Roosevelt administration. Employment and housing
discrimination against Jews were commonplace, and quotas limited
the number of Jews permitted to attend many colleges and universities. In 1939, 20 percent of Americans believed there was likely to be
a widespread campaign against Jews in the United States, and 12 per
cent said that they would actively support such a campaign.[11]

Given the general anti-immigrant climate and particularly the strict
and uncompromising attitudes of the Department of State and the US
consuls, who were consistently and systematically employing various
means to deny immigration visas,[12] Jewish leaders decided to seek
assistance from the secretary of labor, with whom Razovsky had
personal relations, and who appeared more sympathetic to Jewish
misery.[13] Already in late 1933, it was agreed that the rescue of German
Jewish children should be the first priority.[14] Jewish leaders made use
of an overlooked provision of the Immigration Act 1917, the legality
of which was later confirmed by the attorney general. This provision
enabled the secretary of labor, Frances Perkins, to authorize the
entrance of unaccompanied children under the age of sixteen.[15] Since
the secretary of labor also had the statutory right to accept bonds for
unaccompanied children,[16] the attorney general's decision opened a
promising avenue for bringing to the United States unaccompanied
German Jewish children, without invoking the public charge clause.

A new organization, the German-Jewish Children's Aid, Inc.,
which Razovsky was instrumental in establishing, becoming its executive director, was put in charge of bringing Jewish children into the
United States. In order to guarantee that the children would not
become a public charge, the GJCA opened a bank account of
$27,000.[17] Razovsky was encouraged by earlier discussions with
Secretary Perkins and Immigration Commissioner MacCormack,
who impressed her as being sympathetic to the plan.[18] Perkins did
indeed agree later that year to bring over 250 unaccompanied Jewish
children from Germany, as the first stage of the plan.[19] The first ten
German children arrived in New York on 9 November 1934 and
were greeted at the port by Razovsky.[20]

It was a massive and complicated operation that Razovsky directed on two fronts simultaneously. She established contact with the
Hilfsverein der Deutschen Juden, the Berlin-based Jewish organization in charge of locating and choosing the children, as well as delivering the relevant documents to the main office in New York.[21] At the
same time, Razovsky made all the necessary arrangements to receive
the children in the United States. This entailed locating appropriate
foster-homes, making provision for the children's maintenance after
arrival, and training qualified social workers to handle the special
problems of the children who were separated from their families.[22]

As the children's files reflect, Razovsky's concern for them went
far beyond the call of duty. She extended personal attention to each
child, seeing to his/her medical and behavioral problems as well as to
lesser issues. Notwithstanding certain difficulties, most of the children adjusted well and were happy with their foster-families. In
1941, Razovsky reported to the GJCA Board of Directors: 'They live
a happy, normal life in 103 American communities. Several of the
children have reached the age of 21 and are naturalized American citizens. Many of them are already self-supporting and a few others are
contributing toward their own support. Nine have married and 105
are reunited with their own parents.'[23] Under Razovsky's management, the GJCA brought over one thousand unaccompanied children
ranging in age from 2 to 16, in the period between 1934 and 1943.
This task was made all the more complicated by the fact that it was
carried out as a clandestine operation, *'without any form of publicity in the newspapers or any other public method of advertising'*
(emphasis in the original),[24] most likely out of fear of interference by
antisemitic organizations, which warned against 'a flood of Jews to
America'.[25]

Another issue that Razovsky tackled was that of affidavits. In order
to receive a visa, the applicant had to secure an affidavit from American
relatives guaranteeing that s/he would not become a public charge.
However, most applicants were unable to obtain such affidavits and
this was when Razovsky made yet another difference. Appealing to
American Jews, especially Jewish women, she succeeded in obtaining
hundreds of affidavits for Jewish refugees not only from relatives but
also from strangers, against promises that the NCC would guarantee
their well-being.

There were also the cases of Jews who were detained in concentration camps. Among these were applicants who held American visas but
who had been arrested before they could leave. Razovsky negotiated

with the State Department in Washington and demanded immediate action by the American consul-general in Berlin to help them out. In one case the husband was already in the United States, but his wife – who was in possession of a visa – and their son, were deported to Poland. In this case Razovsky exerted pressure on the State Department to cable the consul in Warsaw. Mercifully, this worked: the family was located and released, safe and sound, from their deadly fate.

In her discussions with the Immigration and Naturalization Services, Razovsky also dealt with hundreds of cases concerning persons staying in the United States on expired visitors' visas, and who were hence threatened with deportation. She gave each such case her full attention, applying personally to the commissioner. She pleaded every individual case, providing evidence why the person could not leave right away – be it for health or personal reasons – and guaranteed that these people would be available for questioning when required. Most cases had indeed been cleared as a result of her intense and energetic interventions.[26]

Both the Departments of State and Labor often acknowledged Razovsky's efficient work. One such expression came in the form of a letter from the commissioner of immigration in the fall of 1937: 'The Immigration and Naturalization Service is in hearty sympathy with your efforts to facilitate the better preparation for naturalization of the foreign born, and appreciates the value of your work, which has for its purpose arousing the interest of the principal civic, education and philanthropic agencies in that connection.'[27]

The rescue and immigration of German Jewish physicians, scholars, scientists and professors was another issue which engaged Cecilia Razovsky's attention. Many refugee physicians arrived in the United States having left well-established careers, but in order to be permitted to practice, they had to pass local examinations that differed from state to state. Razovsky established an information network that listed the different requirements according to state. Moreover, she organized classes for the study of English, and administered a national center for available job openings. She acted as a mediator between refugees and potential employers. Further, since receiving an American license to practice was a lengthy process, she arranged for temporary employment in paramedical fields, where licensing was either not necessary nor easier to acquire.[28]

While Razovsky was not terribly successful in pressuring the federal government to allow more refugees into the country, her achievements were far more substantial in regard to her work with refugees already in America. But this also was not an easy achievement. In her long days of hard work she handled over a hundred requests per day, assisting in such diverse matters as finding jobs and housing, securing medical care and schooling for the children, and even helping with financial matters, such as arranging loans.

When the possibilities of bringing refugees into the United States dwindled toward the late 1930s and early 1940s, she embarked on yet another mission, that of finding safe havens for refugees in Central and South America. In one such project, which came to be known as 'the First Jewish Colony', 2,000 Austrian Jews found refuge in the Dominican Republic.[29] A newly formed Dominican Republic Settlement Association (DORSA) was incorporated in New York State in December 1939. In actuality, the difficult conditions and the harsh tropical climate discouraged many who still hoped to enter the United States from coming to what was considered a wasteland. Razovsky was a key figure in this operation and negotiated with both the Dominican authorities and with DORSA president, James Rosenberg.[30]

Despite the increased number of requests for and toward the end of the 1930s – in 1939 she reported 1,300 incoming calls for help, 1,000 letters, and hundreds of individuals coming to her office every day[31] – Razovsky found the time to listen and to act on behalf of these despondent people. She often traveled to Washington DC for meetings with officials and to Jewish communities all around the country to encourage volunteers and to create more branches.[32]

Her deep concern for the refugees and her solidarity with their misery were also evident in her dealings with refugees who were classified as enemy aliens. These were detained at internment camps mostly in the south-west regions of the United States with the intention of being repatriated at a later date. The Department of Justice created a special Enemy Alien Control Unit to handle cases of enemy aliens who remained in the custody of the government. The directive provided for the establishment of an orderly procedure for disposing of these cases on an individual basis in accordance with standards to be approved by the secretary. In order to gain a hearing and possibly a discharge, the refugee had to supply a full and complete biographical dossier concerning his or her life in Germany or Austria. This was a most detailed report, and had to include complete occupational history, names of employers, particularly if such employers were already in the United States, as well as affiliations with Jewish institutions, synagogues,

names and addresses of friends, schoolmates and both close and distant relatives, particularly if they were in the US or in neutral countries outside the US. The detainee had to provide names and addresses of friends now living in the country who would be willing to vouch
for his or her loyalty to America.

Razovsky, in her capacity as Head of the Migration Department of
the NRS, was responsible for helping the detainees meet these
requirements. As soon as the information was received at the NRS
central office, its representatives would forward copies to the
Migration Department who would check the forms before sending
them on to the Justice Department.[33] In the meantime, Razovsky took
care of the detainees' needs, doing 'all in her power' to improve their
conditions. In view of the fact that there were about a thousand
American and Latin American detainees, Razovsky's efforts were
indeed extraordinary. A report from the summer of 1944 shows that
9,389 cases were reviewed by the Unit; of these, 50 percent were
denied, 35 percent were paroled and only 15 percent were released.[34]
Razovsky's correspondence with the Justice Department indicates
her personal involvement. Hundreds of letters of thanks from
detainees praised her 'great human understanding, which gave us
help, encouragement and also hope in a new life'.[35]

Her efforts on behalf of the refugees did not end after the war.
Following Germany's defeat, Razovsky traveled to concentration
camps to find surviving children, as a representative of the AJDC,
and as the Director of Emigration for Germany and Specialist for
Displaced Persons for UNRRA. She was there to bring the children
out of Buchenwald, Dachau and other camps. She accompanied con-
voys of children on their way from Germany to temporary places in
Switzerland and France, from which they were later sent to Palestine
and the United States. She visited a number of assembly centers in
France where thousands of Jewish survivors from eastern Europe
were sheltered, and cooperated in planning assistance measures for
them.[36] As director of immigration operations in Germany and
Austria, Razovsky also assisted in implementing President Truman's
directive of 22 December 1945, which authorized the admission to
the United States of displaced persons living in the American zones in
Germany and Austria. Her work took her to every single displaced
persons' camp and enabled her to obtain first-hand knowledge of the
abilities and skills of the people waiting to be resettled.[37]

As a specialist for displaced persons on the staff of UNRRA,
Razovsky spent her years in Europe for the most part dealing with

the core refugees who could not be repatriated by UNRRA, and had to be settled in other countries. But perhaps her most important project at that time consisted of preparing the Central File and Card Index of Displaced Persons. This record was invaluable to the many displaced persons who were trying anxiously to find surviving relatives. She recalled one such incident as follows:

> A little boy about ten years old had been in a concentration camp and did not know where his father was or whether he was alive. We included the child's name in our cable to Palestine and received a cable from his father from Palestine saying how happy he was to learn his child was alive, when we told the boy the news he gasped: you heard from my father ... my father is alive ... trembling from head to foot he took the cablegram and showed it to the other children.[38]

While working for the JDC in Paris from February until the end of June 1945 she organized a Personal Service division for emergency relief, arranged the reunion of fifty displaced children with their relatives in Britain, supervised casework for groups of displaced persons in various French camps, and arranged transit visas for children traveling through France to embarkation ports in Portugal and Spain. She was among the relief workers who accompanied the first contingent of children released from Buchenwald into temporary care in France and Switzerland.

In 1947, feeling that there was still much to be done, Razovsky began working as a consultant for the Citizens' Committee on Displaced Persons, an organization that was formed specifically in order to pass bills liberalizing immigration for displaced persons. She traveled to various communities throughout the United States, addressing the public and meeting with state and federal representatives to lobby for the proposed bill, which Congress did not pass. However, the Displaced Persons Act of 1948, though it prolonged the process and increased the red tape, provided instead a new and more liberal approach to immigration.

In the early 1950s Razovsky traveled to South America where she established a network to help newcomers from Europe. In 1957 she was again assigned to assist in the resettlement and integration of refugees in Latin America, this time by the United HIAS Service, which had become the International Jewish Migration Agency. And in 1963, she was called upon again by some of the Brazilian Jewish men and women with whom she had worked during the preceding years. She spent six months in Brazil, and a further month in Peru and the Argentine, contributing to the building of a united Jewish community in those countries.[39]

Her books, articles and speeches on immigration, refugees and children were well known among the thousands she rescued and the many organizations in which she was active.[40] She was praised as a person of 'competence and spirit' and played a major role in the rescue of Jewish refugees.[41] Given Razovsky's successful operations during the period between 1933 and 1945, one wonders how she accomplished what her male Jewish counterparts were less successful in achieving. The main reason was most probably Razovsky's keen intelligence and strong-willed personality, the fact that she never took 'no' for an answer; and her ability to focus her expertise on the issue of immigration.

Razovsky's absolute devotion to the rescue of Jewish refugees went back to her youth; growing up as she did in a poor immigrant neighborhood, she obtained first-hand knowledge of the immigrants' problems. Moreover, the fact that she spoke several European languages – including Yiddish – enabled her to converse freely with the immigrants. Having developed a sense of solidarity with the immigrants' misery and aspirations, it was quite natural for her to pursue a career as a social worker. Her activities were motivated above all by her very human compassion, which is so evident in her personal relations with the refugees or their relatives and in her heartfelt applications to the US administration, when she always emphasized the immorality and injustice of the Nazi regime. Nor was she loath to urge government officials to live up to America's traditional commitment and provide a 'haven for the oppressed'.

She adopted a grass-roots approach to her work, recruiting housewives, delivering speeches all around the country, creating volunteer centers and never allowing high politics to sway her from her cause. With much dedication and resolution, Razovsky set up an active national network of Jewish women based on the Jewish tradition of communal solidarity. Razovsky and these anonymous Jewish women charted the course, laid the groundwork, and institutionalized what turned out to be a major undertaking. In the long run, their deeds bore an ideological and moral message for their own community and society as a whole.

No doubt her single-minded focus on one objective – the rescue of refugees – was the major contributor to her success. High politics was never on her agenda. Even the emergence of antisemitism in the

United States and the anti-immigrant climate in Congress did not deter her from her enterprise. Unlike other American Jewish leaders, who were hindered by such considerations when attending to rescue issues, Razovsky refused to succumb to political interest and pressures. Despite the fact that Jews in America enjoyed civil and political rights, they were well aware that they were suspected of having a dual loyalty. They knew, too, that a national crisis could shake their political and civil status by arousing this suspicion. Memories of European pogroms were fresh in their minds and their sense of vulnerability kept them eager to prove their patriotism to America at every opportunity.[42] This was especially true at times of social and economic unrest of the kind that prevailed during the 1930s and 1940s.[43] This insecurity undoubtedly made American Jewish leaders reluctant to exert pressure on the administration to open the quotas for more Jewish refugees.[44] There can be little doubt that American Jews felt deep sympathy for their counterparts in Nazi Germany; their priority, however, was to look out for their own safety. They feared that any effort to bring Jewish refugees into America at the time of the Depression would provoke antisemitism and jeopardize their well-being. This resulted in behavior that was cautious, and which, in contrast to Razovsky's heroic persistance, proved lacking.[45]

Until her death at the age of 81, on 27 September 1968, Cecilia Razovsky remained active in Jewish community affairs, tirelessly searching for new avenues through which to help Jewish relief organizations. In a poignant obituary, Ralph Segalman from Austin, Texas wrote:

> Cecilia's death is a loss to all of us, not because of her Jewishness, which was positive; not because of any extraordinary behavioral science knowledge or social work skill, but because of her heart and her concern for people, which unfortunately are all too hard to find among the professional colleagues ... She was one of the last disappearing breed – namely those who are sincere in their concern for others – not just those in their clinic but those who are 'out there' and need to be helped, and even those who don't know that they can be helped.[46]

NOTES

1. 'Jewish Children Shipped to Safety', John Rivera, *Baltimore Sun*, 20 April 2001.
2. Between 1934 and 1945 about one thousand unaccompanied Jewish children arrived in the United States: 590 from central Europe, Belgium and the Netherlands; over 350 from France, Spain and Portugal, and several dozen from England. From 1934 to 1940 most of the children arrived directly from Germany and Austria. From 1941 onward the children had to reach Portugal to escape, after crossing several countries and undergoing unimaginable

difficulties. Some of their stories are told in *Don't Wave Goodbye*, Philip K Jason and Iris Posner (eds) (Westport, CT: Praeger Publishers, 2004).

3. 'Final Thoughts', *Don't Wave Goodbye*, Jason and Posner (eds.), p. 272. Hans J. became a teacher and poet.

4. See W. W.'s reflections on her foster-parents in Illinois: 'Foster care was the most miserable period of my life. No one understood me. My foster parents lived in their dream world and thought that by giving me a home they had done their bit for the struggle against Hitler. Once I arrived, they hardly paid any attention to me, leaving all my problems to the local caseworker in charge of me.' Cited in Judith Tydor Baumel, *Unfulfilled Promise. Rescue and Settlement of Jewish Refugee Children in the United States* (Juneau, Alaska: The Denali Press, 1990), p. 89.

5. Iris Posner recounts that after watching *Into the Arms of Strangers. Stories of the Kindertransport*, a documentary film recounting the emigration of 10,000 unaccompanied children to Great Britain from 1938 to 1940, her life changed. Together with a long-time friend, Leonore Moskowitz, the two retired Jewish researchers decided to find out whether Jewish children were also brought into the United States. Their discoveries led them in December 2000 to found 'One Thousand Children (OTC), Inc.' a non-profit research and education corporation located in Silver Spring, Maryland. After long months and much expensive research, they have identified 1,154 unaccompanied Jewish children who were brought to the United States between 1934 and 1945 and placed in foster-homes.

6. Among the more famous are: Jack Steinberger, 1988 Nobel Prize winner in Physics, for discovering with his colleagues Leon Lederer and Melvin Schwartz a new type of neutrino. Their work included the creation of a basic research tool that made possible the study of one of the four fundamental forces in nature; Herbert Freudenberger, psychologist, who was granted the Gold Medal Award for life achievement in the Practice of Psychology in 1999 from the American Psychological Foundation; Richard Schifter, former US Ambassador to Austria; Manfred Steinfeld, who translated the surrender documents of the German forces east of the Elbe. His 82nd American Airborne Division liberated the survivors of the concentration camp at Wobbelin. Steinfeld's military service earned him a Bronze Star and Purple Heart. In 1981 he received the Horatio Alger Award from the Horatio Alger Association of Distinguished Americans. Finally, Bill Graham, concert promoter and artist manager who in the words of the 'Rock and Roll Hall of Fame and Museum', 'forever changed the way rock and roll is presented'.

7. See Chapter 2.

8. To mention only few of her senior positions in major rescue Jewish organizations: National Council of Jewish Women (NCJW), American Jewish Joint Distribution Committee (DJC), National Coordinating Committee for Aid to Refugees and Emigrants Coming from Germany (NCC), German-Jewish Children's Aid (GJCA), National Refuge Service (NRS), United Nation Relief and Rehabilitation Administration (UNRRA). She was also active in non-Jewish Committees: National Council, US Committee for Refugees, American Council for Nationalities and the General Committee of Immigrant Aid at Ellis Island. Razovsky married Dr Morris Davidson in 1927. Dr Davidson was a certified ophthalmologist. He accompanied her on later trips to South America, assisting her with her work, and became an expert in Brazilian culture and history.

9. Mildred A. Gutwillig to Razovsky, 23 June 1939. CNN Records, Folder 89. Yivo Archives, New York.

10. On 10 September 1933 the Bureau of Immigration and Naturalization was reorganized as the Immigration and Naturalization Service (INS). In 1940 the INS was transferred to the Justice Department.

11. Leonard Dinnerstein, *Antisemitism in America* (Oxford and New York: Oxford University Press, 1994), pp. 105–27; Rita James Simon, *Public Opinion in America: 1936–1970* (New York: Oxford University Press, 1994), pp. 82–3.

12. Bat-Ami Zucker, *In Search of Refuge: Jews and U.S. Consuls in Nazi Germany, 1933–1941* (London and Portland, OR: Vallentine Mitchell, 2001). See also D. MacCormack to Dr Isador Lubin, Chief, Bureau of Labor Statistics, Department of Labor, 23 August 1933. File 5581/273: 'It appears to me that the situation is not one depending on new legislation but on the degree of rigidity in the enforcement of the consular regulations.'

13. Bat-Ami Zucker, 'Frances Perkins and the German-Jewish Refugees, 1933–1940,' *American Jewish History*, 89, 1 (March 2001), pp. 35–59.

14. See Chapter 2.
15. Attorney-General Commings to Secretary of Labor, 26 December 1933. Kohler Papers, Box 2. AJHS Archives, New York.
16. Section 3 of the Immigration Act, 1917, U.S. Code, Title 8, Sec. 13, Sub. M., pursuant to Sec. 21 of the same Act.
17. Mr Paul Felix Warburg opened a bank account and Mr Stephen Koshland was appointed as agent for the donors, responsible for purchasing the steamship tickets for the children. Solomon Lowenstein to Kohler, 2 May 1934; Kohler to Lowenstein, 3 May 1934, Folder 490; Lowenstein to Razovsky, 12 June 1934, Folder 621; Razovsky to Simmons, 7 November 1934, Folder 631; Chamberlain to Razovsky, 10 November 1934, Folder 490. GJCA Papers. Yivo Archives, New York. See also Razovsky Report to Colonel MacCormack, January 1935, Folder 29, ibid.
18. Razovsky, 'Memorandum', 12 April 1934, GJCA Papers, Folder 265. Yivo Archives, New York. See also Razovsky to Dr Solomon Lowenstein, 12 April 1934: 'I want to say that the plan ... was received with much sympathy by all the officials who feel that it is conservative and at the same time constructive, and that it will appeal to many Americans as a fine gesture of friendship'. GJCA Papers, Folder 490. Yivo Archives, New York. G. Messersmith, Consul-General in Berlin, also found the plan acceptable and promised full cooperation with the organization. G. Messersmith to Mr Baerwald, 3 May 1934. Ibid., Folder 316.
19. Max Kohler to Secretary Perkins, 6 April 1934. GJCA Papers, Folder 21. Yivo Archives, New York. Also in Warburg Papers, Box 269/8. American Jewish Archives. (hereafter AJA). See also MacCormack to Professor Chamberlain, 28 August 1934. Folder 16: Correspondence 1934. Chamberlain Papers, Yivo Archives, New York.
20. Undated letter to Commissioner MacCormack from Dr Lowenstein, Chairman of GJCA. Folder 6: Correspondence 1934. GJCA Papers. Yivo Archives, New York.
21. See correspondence between Razovsky and the organization, 1934–1936, GJCA Papers, Folders 63, 64. Yivo Archives, New York.
22. See Chapter 2.
23. Razovsky, 'Report', 16 June 1941. GJCA Papers, Folder 29. Yivo Archives, New York. Also J. C. Hyman to Arthur D. Greenleigh, National Refugee Service, Inc., 16 July 1941. Ibid.
24. Razovsky to NCJW Branches, 18 April 1934; Dr Lowenstein to Mrs Brin, 24 April 1934. GJCA, Folder 21. See also, identical letter to Max Kohler, Committee on German-Jewish Immigration Policy, 24 April 1934. GJCA, Folder 3. Yivo Archives, New York.
25. However, when news about the children's arrival spread, the American Coalition of Patriotic, Civil and Fraternal Societies blasted the Department of Labor for the 'systematic importation of indigent alien children'. Its spokesman, Captain John B. Trevor, called for a congressional investigation into what he considered a violation of the immigration laws.
26. Razovsky, Director of Migration, NRS (the NRS was founded in 1939 as a continuation of the National Coordinating Committee) to Commissioner of Immigration, 21 August 1939. NRS Records, Folder 523: Appeals for Exclusion, File of Cecilia Razovsky, Director of Immigration, December 1939–1940. Yivo Archives, New York. See also Razovsky's letters to the general commissioner, 24 March 1939, 6 March 1940, 19 March 1940, and many more, in File 524: Appeals for Extension of Visitors' Visas, File of Cecilia Razovsky, 1939–1940. Ibid. See Chapter 3.
27. James L. Houghteling to Razovsky, 23 September 1937. Razovsky Papers, Box 6, Folder: Published Works about Immigration, 1929–1939. AJHS Archives, New York.
28. See Chapter 4.
29. See Chapter 5.
30. For details, DORSA file, Razovsky Papers, Box 4, AJHS, New York; Freda Kirchwey, 'Caribbean Refuge', *The Nation*, 13 April 1940, pp. 466–8; J. Schechtmann, 'Failure of the Dominican Scheme', *Congress Weekly*, 15 January 1943, pp. 8–9.
31. Razovsky, 'Report Migration Department, October 1939'. Razovsky Papers, Box 3, Folder: NRS Relief Work. AJHS Archives, New York.
32. Grete and Leo Friedmann to Razovsky, 11 April 1943, Razovsky Papers, Box 3, Folder: NRS: Jews Interned at Detention Centers in Southwest US, 1941–1943. AJHS Archives, New York.

33. See Chapter 6.
34. Monthly Review, INS, June 1944. Department of Justice, Box 6, Folder: Foreign Experience. AJHS Archives, New York.
35. Razovsky Papers, Box 4, Folder: Jews Interned at Detention Centers in Southwest US, 1941–1943. Ibid.
36. See Razovsky's letters to her husband, Razovsky Papers, Box 6, Folder: Personal Correspondence 1945–1946. AJHS, New York.
37. She was also actively associated with the Citizens Committee on Displaced Persons in the United States, functioning in the capacity of liaison representative with national organizations to secure congressional legislation for the admission of displaced persons.
38. Cited in 'Collected Notes on Lecture by Cecilia Razovsky taken by Sylvia Milred', 25 July 1945. Razovsky Papers, Box 4, Folder: UNRRA Displaced Persons, 1944–1946. AJHS Archives, New York.
39. Ibid., Folder: Personal Documents, 1953–57, 1960, 1961–1967. AJHS, New York.
40. To mention only few: 'The Jew Re-Discovers America', *Jewish Social Service Quarterly* (March 1929), pp. 2–4; 'Deportation of Alien Jews', ibid., December 1931, pp. 76–7; 'The Problem of German Refugees', *The Reform Advocate*, 7 December 1934, pp. 329–30; *Making Americans, Guide for New Immigrants* (New York: National Council for Jewish Women, 1938); 'How the Refugee Reaches this Country', *Social Work Today*, Special Issue (December 1939), pp. 15–18.
41. Fred K. Hoehler, Director, Division on Displaced Persons, UNRRA, to Razovsky, 28 September 1945. Razovsky Papers, Box 4, Folder: UNRRA Specialist, Displaced Persons, 1944–1946. AJHS Archives, New York; Arthur D. Morse, *While Six Million Died. A Chronicle of American Apathy* (New York: Random House, 1967, 1968), pp. 160–6.
42. 'American Jewish Congress in Rosh Hashonah Message: Answer Charles A. Lindberg', For Release Monday, 22 September 1941. Stephen Wise Papers, Box 54. AJHS Archives, New York: 'Surely it is needless to state that we [Jews] are of and for America as truly as any other group within the nation.'
43. Gulie Ne'eman Arad, *America, Its Jews, and the Rise of Nazism* (Bloomington, IN: Indiana University Press, 2000), pp. 209–24.
44. Efraim Zuroff, 'Rescue Priority and Fund Raising as Issues during the Holocaust: A Case Study of the Relations between the Vaad HA-Hatzala and the Joint, 1939–1941', *American Jewish History*, 68, 3 (March 1979), pp. 312–13.
45. See Rabbi Stephen Wise's letter to Professor Otto Nathan in September 1940, with regard to Roosevelt's re-election: 'With regard to the political refugees … [Roosevelt's] re-election is much more important for everything that is worthwhile and that counts more than the admission of a few people, however imminent be their peril.' Cited in Gulie Ne'eman Arad, *America, Its Jews*, pp. 211–12.
46. Ralph Segalman, 'Fact and Opinion,' undated, Razovsky Papers, Box 1, Folder 2. AJHS Archives, New York.

Appendix I

The 288 Displaced Scholars assisted through the Emergency Committee, and their Fields of Study[*]

Hanokh Albeck, Talmudic Studies

Berthold Altmann, History

Eugen Altschul, Economics

Valentin Bargmann, Physics

David Baumgardt, Philosophy

Guido Beck (a), Physics

Maximilian Beck, Philosophy

Walter Beck (a), Psychology

Richard Behrendt, International Affairs

Adolf Berger, Law

Gustav Bergmann, Mathematics

Ernst Berl, Chemistry

Felix Bernstein, Mathematics

Hans Beutler (b), Physics

Margarete Bieber, Archaeology

Erwin Reinhold Biel, Meteorology

Justus Bier, History of Art

Felix Bloch, Physics

Erwin Bodky, Music

Werner A. Bohnstedt, Sociology

Enzo Joseph Bonaventura, Psychology

Curt Bondy, Education

Theodor von Brand, Biology

Alfred T. Brauer, Mathematics

Richard Brauer, Mathematics

Theodor Brauer (b), Economics

Kurt Braun, Economics

Otto Brendel, Archaeology

Warner F. Brook (b), Economics

Eberhard Friedrich Bruck, Law

Martin Buber, Philosophy

Manfred Bukofzer, Musicology

Walter V. Burg, Chemistry

Hans Cassel, Chemistry

Umberto Moshe David Cassuto, Philology

Gustave Cohen (a), Literature

Sigmund Cohn, Law

Ernst Cohn-Wiener (b), History of Art

Victor Conrad, Meteorology

Richard Courant, Mathematics

Heinz Dallmann, Law

Max Dehn, Mathematics

Max Delbrück, Physics

Leonid Doljanski, Pathology

Adolph B. Drucker, Economics

Ludwig Edelstein, Philology

Tilly Edinger, Paleontology

Maximilian Ehrenstein, Chemistry

Friedrich Engel-Janosi, History

Fritz Epstein, History

*In these lists a parenthetic a signifies: Returned to Europe; b, Deceased; c, Nobel Prize winner; d. Served in US Army; e, Served at Biarritx (France) American University, 1946; f, Formerly a grantee of the Committee; g, Subsequently a grantee of the Committee.

Richard Ettinghausen, History of Art

Ladislaus Farkas, Chemistry

Bruno Fels, Statistics

William Fiedler, Music

Eva Fiesel *(b)*, Linguistics

Ossip K. Flechtheim, Political Science

Max Förster *(a)*, Philology

Abraham Adolf Fraenkel, Mathematics

Hermann Fraenkel, Classics

James Franck *(c)*, Physics

Louis R. Franck, Economics

Erich Frank, Philosophy

Philipp Frank, Physics

Oskar Frankl, Education

Paul Frankl, History of Art

Erich Franzen, Letters

Aron Freimann, Bibliography

Rudolf Freund, Economics

Hans Fried, Law

Hans Fried *(b)*, Mathematics

Paul Friedlaender, Classical Philology

Walter Friedlaender, History of Art

Kurt Friedrichs, Mathematics

Walter Fuchs, Chemistry

William R. Gaede, Education

Felix M. Gatz *(b)*, Musicology

Bernhard Geiger, Oriental Philology

Moritz Geiger *(b)*, Philosophy

Hilda Geiringer, Mathematics

Karl Geiringer, Musicology

Melitta Gerhard, Literature

Felix Gilbert, History

Rudolf Glanz, Law

Kurt Gödel, Mathematics

Franz Goldmann, Public Health

G. E. von Grünebaum, Oriental Philology

Gotthard Günther, Philosophy

Wolfgang Guenther, Law

Emil J. Gumbel, Statistics

Herman S. Gundersheimer, History of Art

Julius Guttmann, Philosophy

Fritz Haas, Zoology

Otto H. Haas, Paleontology

William S. Haas, Sociology and Anthropology

Jacques Hadamard *(a)*, Mathematics

Ludwig Halberstaedter, Radiology

Wolfgang Hallgarten *(d)*, History

Ludwig Hamburger, Economics

Viktor Hamburger, Zoology

Joseph Hanè, Government Service

Willy Hartner *(a)*, Astronomy

Werner Hegemann *(b)*, Architecture and City Planning

Robert von Heine-Geldern, Ethnology

Ernst Hellinger, Mathematics

John L. Herma *(d)*, Psychology

Léon Hermann *(a)*, Classical Literature

Gerhard Herz, Musicology

John H. Herz, Law

Ernst Emil Herzfeld, Archaeology

Artur von Hippel, Physics

Rudolf Höber, Physiology

Heinrich Hoeniger, Law

Oscar Hoffman, Engineering

Hajo Holborn, History

Richard Martin Honig, History and Philosophy of Law

Erich Hula, Law

Hugo Iltis, Biology
Luigi Jacchia, Astronomy
Ernest Jack, International
  Relations
Fritz Jahoda, Music
Roman Jakobson, Philology
Fritz John, Mathematics
Victor Jollos (b), Zoology
Oswald Jonas, Musicology
Henry R. Kahane, Linguistics
Alfred Kähler, Economics
Richard A. Kahn, Economics
  and Public Administration
Franz Kallmann, Psychiatry
Ernst Kanitz, Music
Ernst Kantorowicz, History
Ernst Kapp, Classical Philology
Fritz Karsen, Education
Adolf Katzenellenbogen,
  History of Art
Felix Kaufmann, Philosophy
Fritz Kaufmann, Philosophy
Stephen S. Kayser, History of Art
Robert M. W. Kempner, Police
  Administration
Friedrich Kessler, Law
Hans Kirchberger, Law
Otto Kirchheimer, Law
Guido Kisch, Law
Jacob Klatzkin, Philosophy
Jacob Klein, History of Mathem-
  atics and Mathematical Physics
Richard Koebner, History
Zdenek Kopal, Astronomy
Siegfried Kraus, Sociology
Richard Krautheimer, History
  of Art
Manfred Kridl, Literature
Heinrich Kronstein, Law
Helmut Kuhn, Philosophy
Gustav Land, Astronomy

Carl Landauer, Economics
Oscar Lassner, Music
Rudolf von Laun (a), Law
Albert Lauterbach, Economics
Max Lederer, Language and
  Literature
Fritz Lehmann (b), Economics
Karl Lehmann, (Lehmann-
  Hartleeben), Archaeology
Frederick Lehner, Language and
  Literature
Arthur Lenhoff, Law
Friedrich Lenz, Classical
  Language and Literature
Wolf Leslau, Languages
Kurt Lewin (b), Psychology
Hans Lewy, Mathematics
Julius Lewy, Philology
Wolfgang Liepe, Language and
  Literature
Julius Lips, Anthropology
Karl Loewenstein, Law
Karl Loewner, Mathematics
Moritz Löwi (b), Psychology
Edward Lowinsky, Musicology
Erna Magnus, Sociology
Nicolai Malko, Music
Alfred Manes, Insurance and
  Economics
Ernst Manheim, Sociology
Fritz Karl Mann, Economics
Thomas Mann (c), Letters
Siegfried Marck, Philosophy
Herbert Marcuse, Philosophy
Jacques Maritain (a), Philosophy
Carl Mayer, Sociology
Karl W. Meissner, Physics
Kaethe Mengelberg, Economics
Julie Meyer, Sociology
Kathi Meyer-Baer, Musicology
Franz Michael, Chinese History

and Far Eastern Affairs
Rudolf Minkowski, Physics
Hans Morgenthau, Law
Otto Nathan, Economics
Alfons Nehring, Philology
Hans Neisser, Economics
Paul Nettl, Musicology
Otto Neugebauer, Mathematics
Franz Neumann, Economics
Sigmund Neumann, Sociology
Robert Neuner, Law
Emmy Noether *(b)*, Mathematics
Lothar Wolfgang Nordheim,
    Physics
Arthur Nussbaum, Law
Leonardo Olschki, Philology
Oskar Oppenheimer,
    Psychology
Melchior Palyi, Economics
Wolfgang Paulsen, Language
    and Literature
Alexander H. Pekelis *(b)*, Law
Nicolás Percas, Languages
Georg Petschek *(b)*, Law
Kurt Pinthus, History of
    Literature and of the Theater
Willibald Ploechl, Law
Ernst Posner, Archives
    Administration
Richard Prager *(b)*, Astronomy
Karl Pribram, Economics
Peter Pringsheim, Physics
Luis Quintanilla, Painting
Ernst Rabel, Law
Giulio Racah, Physics
Hans Rademacher, Mathematics
Hermann Ranke *(a)*, Archaeology
Egon Ranshofen-Wertheimer,
    Political Science
Franz J. Rapp, History of
    Theater Art

Anton Raubitschek, Archaeology
Victor Regener, Physics
Fritz Reiche, Physics
Max Rheinstein, Law
Werner Richter, Language and
    Literature
Fernando de los Rios, Political
    Science
Arthur Rosenberg *(b)*, History
Hans Rosenberg, History
Hans Rosenberg *(a, b)*,
    Astronomy
Arthur Rosenthal, Mathematics
Herbert Rosinski, Military and
    Naval Theory
Bruno Rossi, Physics
Curt Sachs, Musicology
Alfred Salmony, History of Art
Richard Salomon, History
Arthur Salz, Economics
Martin Scheerer, Psychology
Guido Schoenberger, History of
    Art
Alfred Schuhmann, Philosophy
Heinrich Schwarz, History of Art
Rudolf Schwenger, Economics
Anna Selig, Education
Friedrich Sell, Language and
    Literature
Carl L. Siegel, Mathematics
Rolf Singer, Mycology
Sigmund Skard *(a)*, Literature
Karl Sollner, Chemistry
Friedrich Solmsen, Classics
Clemens Sommer, History of Art
Martin Sommerfeld *(b)*,
    Language and Literature
Alexander Sperber, Philology
Friedrich Spiegelberg, Philosophy
Herbert Spiegelberg, Philosophy

Diether von den Steinen, Languages
Hugo Steiner-Prag *(b)*, Graphic Arts
William Stern *(b)*, Psychology
Richard Stoehr, Music
Walter Sulzbach, Economics
Otto Szasz, Mathematics
Gabor Szegö *(e)*, Mathematics
Alfred Tarski, Mathematics and Logic
Paul Tedesco, Philology
Paul Tillich, Philosophy
Dinko Tomasic, Sociology
Harry Torczyner, Philology
Otto Treitel, Botany
Curt Victorius, Economics
Werner F. Vogel, Engineering
Leo Waibel, Geography
Gotthold Weil, Philology
Martin Weinbaum, History
Martin Weinberger, History of Art

Sucher B. Weinryb, Talmudic Studies
Herbert Weinschel, Political Science
Richard Weissenberg, Zoology
Heinz Werner, Psychology
Ernst Wertheimer, Physiology
Helene Wieruszowski, History
Ernst Karl Winter, Government Service
Rachel Wischnitzer-Bernstein, History of Art
Kaarl A. Wittfogel, History of Chinese Institutions and Society
Hans Julius Wolff, Law
Werner Wolff, Psychology
Leo Wollemborg, History
Sergius Yakobson, Philology
Edgar Zilsel *(b)*, Philosophy
Heinrich Zimmer *(b)*, Philosophy
Bernard Zondek, Gynecology
Antoni Zygmund, Mathematics

THE 47 ROSENWALD FELLOWS OF THE EMERGENCY COMMITTEE AND THEIR FIELDS OF SPECIALIZATION AT TIME OF ARRIVAL IN UNITED STATES

Marc Abramowitsch, Sociology
Hans Baron, History
Klaus Berger *(e)*, History of Art
Josef Berolzheimer, Economics
Beate Berwin, Language and Literature
Egon Vitalis Biel, Painting
Ferdinand Bruckner, Play Writing
Renata Calabresi, Psychology
Adolf Caspary, Political Science
Ladislas Czettel *(f)*, Costume Design
Albert Ehrenstein, Letters
Susanne Engelmann, Education

Walter Fales, Philosophy
Ilse Falk, History of Art
Julius Fischer *(b)*, Law
Ruth Fischer, Sociology
Joseph Floch, Painting
Bernhard Ganzel, Geography
Judith Grunfeld, Economics
Eugen Guerster-Steinhausen, Letters
Ivan Heilbut, Letters
Hans Heymann *(f)*, Economics
Emil Kaufmann, History of Art
Simon Lissim, Decorative Arts
Raphael Mahler, History

Hugo Marx, Law
Paul W. Massing, Economics
Artur Michel, History of the Dance
Kurt Nadeenann, Law
Toni Oelsner, Sociology
Adolf Leo Oppenheim *(f)*, Oriental Philology
Karl Otto Paetel, Letters
Robert Pick, Letters
Victor Polzer, Letters
Rudolf Ray, Painting
Bernard Reder, Sculpture

Hans Sahl, Letters
Berta Segall *(f)*, History of Art
Alfred Sendrey, Musicology
George Stefansky, Philosophy
Victor Tischler, Painting
Ludwig Ullmann, History of the Theater
Veil Valentin *(b, f)*, History
Dario Viterbo, Sculpture
Hedwig Wachenheim, Social Work
Karl Weigl *(g)*, Music
Friederick Welt, Law

Source: Stephen Duggan and Betty Drury, *The Rescue of Science and Learning, The Story of the Emergency Committee In Aid of Displaced Foreign Scholars* (New York: The Macmillan Company, 1948), pp. 204–8.

Appendix II

Chronology

4 May 1886	Born in St. Louis, Missouri to Minna (Meyerson) and Jonas.
1904–17	Volunteered as a teacher and a club leader for the Jewish Educational Alliance, St. Louis, MO.
1909–17	Taught evening classes to foreigners in public school for the St. Louis Board of Education.
1911–18	Handled cases of delinquent children as an employment attendance and probation officer for the St. Louis Board of Education.
April 1918–20	Enforced the child labor law as an inspector for the Child Labor Division of the US Children's Bureau in Washington DC.
1921–32	Hired as Executive Secretary of the National Council of Jewish Women (NCJW), Department of Immigrant Aid.
1921–30	Edited NCJW's *The Immigrant*.
1923	Surveyed conditions for Jewish refugees in European ports.
September 1923	Appointed as one of NCJW delegated to the First World Congress of Jewish Women in Austria, and chaired its Session on migration.
1924	Visited Cuba to study refugee conditions and plan a community center. Her report helped the NCJW obtain funding to create a model refugee program in Havana.
1925–35	Secretary, Jewish Committee for Cuba. Published *What Women Should Know About Citizenship*.

1926–29	Served in different capacities for the National Conference of Social Work: 1926: Vice chairman of Division X 1927: Chair of Division X 1928: Chair of Conference on Immigration Policy. Reported on Jewish refugees in ports in Juarez, Mexico and Canada.
1927	Weds Dr Morris Davidson. Served as an official delegate to the International Association for Protection of Migrants, an advisory committee to the League of Nations in Geneva, Switzerland. Reported on Jewish refugee conditions in ports of Tia Juana, Mexico.
1930–37	NCJW representative for the Joint Legislation Committee of National Organizations interested in immigrant legislation. Visited Soviet Russia to study social services. Chairman of committee to study effect of increased fees, National Council on Naturalization and Citizenship; author of *Handicaps in Naturalization* (Congressional Record 1932), published by National Council on naturalization and Citizenship that caused Congress to reduce naturalization fees. Represented NCJW at the World Conference of Jewish Women (Vienna, Austria); member of committee on contact with Jewish communal Agencies and Committee for Social Work for Aliens at the International Conference on Social Work (Frankfurt am Main, Germany), appointed by John Addams.
1932–34	Appointed Associate Director of NCJW. Published *What Every Emigrant Should Know*.
1933	Chaired committee of twelve specialists appointed by Secretary of Labor Perkins to advise Committee of Forty-Eight on Ellis Island and other port conditions.
1933–36	Served as chair on General Committee of Immigrant Aid at Ellis Island and NY harbor.
January 1934	Created a document at NCJW citing the need

for a coordinating agency. This agency becomes the National Coordinating Committee. Razovsky served as Secretary and Executive Director, NCC.

Loaned to National Coordinating Committee by NCJW. Served as Executive Secretary and Director of the German-Jewish Children's Aid.

1937
Accompanied by her husband on trip to various Latin American countries to study immigration possibilities. Reported on port conditions in Brazil and Argentina.

Served as Secretary for the General Committee of Immigrant Aid at Ellis Island and NY harbor.

Making Americans, published by NCJW.

1938
National Refugee Service (NRS) created, Razovsky served as Director of the Migration Department.

1939
Participated in establishment of a refugee haven in Sosua, Dominican Republic.

June 1939
Witnessed the debarking of SS *St. Louis*, a ship holding 937 Jewish refugees that was denied access to Cuba. Tried to maintain the refugees' morale and prevent suicide attempts.

September 1940
Negotiated, with the help of Evelyn Hersey (Executive Director American Committee for Christian Refugees), the admission of SS *Quanza* into the United States, after being denied landing rights in Mexico.

15 June 1943
Resigned from NRS following a change in board leadership.

September 1943–
October 1944
Worked as Chief of Special Services and Editor of Interpreter Releases, Common Council for American Unity, New York.

October 1944–
July 1945
Appointed as a Displaced Person Specialist for the United Nation Relief and Rehabilitation Administration (UNRRA).

Loaned by UNRRA to the Paris headquarters of the American Jewish Joint Distribution Committee (JDC).

July–September
Returned to New York and worked as a

1945	Consultant for UNRRA, Public Information Division. Addressed various groups on behalf of UNRRA.
October 1945–	Arranged leave without pay. Resigned from
February 1946–	UNRRA on 14 February 1946.
September 1946	Worked as Director of Emigration Operations for Germany and Austria for the JDC.
October–December 1946	Visited Brazil, Argentina and other South American countries on behalf of JDC.
March 1947–48	Worked as a consultant for the Citizens Committee on Displaced Persons. Retired to join husband in Jackson, Massachusetts, where Dr Davidson worked as an ophthalmologist at the Veteran Hospital. Spoke on behalf of AJDC annual campaign in the South, worked temporarily at the Family Service Association and volunteered for local civic agencies such as Community Chest, Jackson Juvenile Council, Veterans Hospital (American Red Cross), and others.
March–November 1950	Came out of retirement to work as a field representative for the United Service for New Americans. Visits six southern states to encourage Jewish communities to accept family refugee quotas and to assist with problem cases.
1954	Visited Israel and Brazil.
February 1957– June 1958	Worked as an Assistant Editor for Hadassah Newsletter in New York.
	Moved to Austin, Texas. Worked as a South American Resettlement Supervisor for the United Hebrew Immigrant Aid Society Service. Visited Brazil, Chile, Columbia, Ecuador, Mexico, Panama, Paraguay and Peru.
December 1960	Studied Cuban refugees fleeing Castro in Tampa, Florida, for The United States Committee for Refugees.
January 1961	Attended the conference called by US government to plan a resettlement program for Cuban refugees fleeing Castro that was held in Miami Beach, Florida. Among those refugees she found several families whom she had assisted

	in Cuba in 1924.
Fall 1961	Moved to El Paso, Texas, where Dr Davidson resumed his practice. Volunteered for Social Service Department of Jewish Community Council.
1963	Revisited Latin America, at invitation of friends she had worked with during her previous visits. Led training courses in Social Service for volunteers, and addressed faculty members and graduate students at various schools of Social Work. Moved to San Diego, California.
27 September 1968	Passed away at age 81.

MEMBERSHIPS

American Association of Social Workers
Charter member, Academy of Social Workers
American Council for Nationalities Service
American Immigration and Naturalization Conference
International Conference of Social Work
El Paso County National Association of Social Workers
National Council, US Committee for Refugees
National Council of Jewish Women
Board of National Council on Naturalization and Citizenship
Steering Committee of Overseas Committee of National Council of Jewish Women
National Committee of American Joint Distribution Committee
Chairman, Conference on Immigration Policy (1925–29?)
Vice President, Capitol B & PW, Jackson, Massachusetts
First Vice President, Hadassah, Jackson, Massachusetts
President, Hadassah, Austin, Texas
Coordinate Women's Organization for Civil Defense, Jackson, Massachusetts

Bibliography

Archives

National Archives, Washington, DC, Suitland, Maryland
United States Department of State, Central Decimal Files, Record Group 59
United States, Department of Labor

Manuscript Division, Library of Congress, Washington, DC
Felix Frankfurter Papers (microfilm)
Emanuel Celler Papers

American Jewish Archives (AJA), Hebrew Union College, Cincinnati, Ohio
Jacob Billikopf Papers, 1900–1951
Samuel Dickstein Papers
Morris L. Waldman Papers, 1912–1963
Felix M. Warburg Papers, 1895–1937
World Jewish Congress Collection, 1918–1982:
    Series C: Institute of Jewish Affairs, 1925–1979
    Sub-series 1: Executive Files and Correspondence, 1926–1979

American Jewish Committee Archives (AJCA), Historical Documents Section, Blaustein Library, New York
Cyrus Adler, Chronological File
Jewish Telegraphy Agency
Minutes of Executive Committee
Selected Correspondence

American Jewish Historical Society (AJHS) New York
Max Kohler Papers
Cecilia Razovsky Papers

Stephen S. Wise Papers, 1893–1969

American Jewish Joint Distribution Committee Archives, New York
Refugees, 1933–1944
Immigration, 1933–1944
Emigration
Germany
Austria

Organizations
YIVO Institute for Jewish Research, New York:
American Jewish Committee (AJC) Records
German Jewish Children's Aid (GJCA)
Morris Waldman Papers/Records
National Community Relations Advisory Council Files (NCRAC)
National Coordinating Committee for Aid to Refugees and
    Emigrants Coming from Germany (NCC)
National Council of Jewish Women (NCJW)
National Refugee Service Records (NRS) (microfilm)
Joseph Chamberlain Papers
Hebrew Sheltering and Immigration Aid Society (HIAS-ICA)

Public Documents
Annual Reports of the Immigration and Naturalization Service
    (Philadelphia, 1943).
Joseph Chamberlain, Chairman NCC, *Statement Issued to Press
    Representative* (2 September 1938).
Harry Greenstein, *Reorganization Study of the NCC and Its Affiliated
    Agencies* (New York, 1939).
James G. McDonald, *High Commissioner for Refugees*, Press Release
    (7 July 1934).
Minutes of a Special Meeting of the Board of Directors, DORSA (12
    June 1940).
William Rosenwald, *Report of the Activities of NCC* (14 May 1937).
*Report of the Emergency Committee in Aid of Displaced German
    Scholars* (December 1938, January 1942).
'Rescue of the Jewish and Other People in Nazi-occupied Territory',
    *Extracts from Hearings before the Committee on Foreign Affairs,
    House of Representatives*. 78th Cong., 1st sess. (26 November 1943).
*Review of Refusals of Visas by Consular Officers, Hearings, House of
    Representatives, Committee on Immigration and Naturalization*.
    73rd Cong., 1st sess. (18 May 1933).

Simmons, John Farr, *The Issuance of Visas by American Consuls Abroad*, Press Release 17 (18 December 1937): 483–90.

Twenty-Seventh Annual Report of the Secretary of Labor for the Fiscal Year Ended 30 June 1939 (Washington, DC, 1939).

Twenty-Eighth Annual Report of the Secretary of Labor for the Fiscal Year Ended 30 June 1939 (Washington, DC, 1940).

US Congress, *Admission of German Refugee Children, Joint Hearings before a Subcommittee of the Committee on Immigration, United States Senate and a Subcommittee of the Committee on Immigration and Naturalization, House of Representatives*. 76th Cong., 1st sess. (1939).

US Congressional Record, Vols LXXVII–LXXXV

US Department of State, *The Immigration Work of the Department of State and its Consular Offices*. Washington, DC: Government Printing Office, 1935.

Unpublished Dissertations

Hurwitz, Ariel, 'American Jewry, the American Government and Society and the Destruction of European Jewry, 1942–1944' (in Hebrew). Unpublished PhD diss., Hebrew University, Jerusalem, 1990.

Ne'eman-Arad, Guile, 'The American Jewish Leadership's Response to the Rise of the Nazi Menace. A Reflection of Their American Experience'. Unpublished PhD diss., Tel-Aviv University, 1994.

Neuringer, Sheldon M., 'American Jewry and United States Immigration Policy, 1881–1953'. Unpublished PhD diss., University of Wisconsin, 1969.

Smith, Sharon Kay, 'Elbert D. Thomas and America's Response to the Holocaust'. Unpublished PhD diss., Brigham Young University, 1992.

Taylor, Melissa Jane, 'Experts in Misery? American Consuls in Austria, Jewish Refugees and Restrictionist Immigration Policy, 1938–1941'. Unpublished PhD diss., University of South Carolina, 2006.

Serial Publications

American Jewish Year Book, 1933–1942
Contemporary Jewish Records, 1938–1942
The Nation, 1936–1945
The New Republic, 1939–1945

Books

Adler, Cyrus, *I Have Considered the Days*. Philadelphia, PA: Jewish Publication Society of America, 1941.

Adler, Cyrus and Aaron M. Margalith, *With Firmness in the Right: American Diplomatic Action Affecting Jews, 1840–1945*. New York: American Jewish Committee, 1946.

Baumel, Judith T., *Unfulfilled Promises: Rescue and Resettlement of Jewish Refugee Children in the United States*. Juneau, Alaska: The Denali Press, 1990

Bauer, Yehuda, *American Jewry and the Holocaust: The American Jewish Joint Distribution Committee, 1939–1945*. Detroit, MI: Wayne State University Press, 1981.

Bennett, Marion T. *American Immigration Policies*. Washington, DC: Public Affairs Press, 1963.

Bentwich, Norman, *The Rescue and Achievements of Refugee Scholars: The Story of Displaced Scholars and Scientists, 1933–1952*. The Hague: Martinus Nijhoff, 1953.

Berenbaum, Michael, *The World Must Know*. Boston, MA: Little, Brown, 1993.

Breitman, Richard and Alan M. Kraut, *American Refugee Policy and European Jewry, 1933–1945*. Bloomington, IN: Indiana University Press, 1987.

Cantril, Hadley (ed.), *Public Opinion: 1935–1946*. Princeton, NJ: Princeton University Press, 1951.

Celler, Emanuel, *You Never Leave Brooklyn*. New York: John Day, 1952.

Close, Kathryn, *Transplanted Children, a History*. New York: The United States Committee for the Care of European Children, Inc., 1953.

Cohen, Naomi, *Not Free to Desist: The American Jewish Committee, 1906–1966*. Philadelphia: Jewish Publication Society of America, 1972.

Coser, Lewis A., *Refugee Scholars in America: their Impact and Experiences*. New Haven, CT: Yale University Press, 1984.

Dallek, Robert, *Franklin Roosevelt and American Foreign Policy, 1932–1945*. Oxford and New York: Oxford University Press, 1979.

Daniel, Jonathan, *White House Witness, 1942–1945*. Garden City, NY: Doubleday, 1975.

Davie, Maurice R., *Refugees in America: the Report of the Committee for the Study of Recent Immigration from Europe*. New York: Harpers, 1947.

Dinnerstein, Leonard, *Anti-Semitism in America*. Oxford and New York: Oxford University Press, 1994.

Dinnerstein, Leonard and David M. Reimers (eds), *Ethnic Americans: A History of Immigration and Assimilation*. New York: Dodd, Mead, 1975.

Divine, Robert A., *American Immigration Policy, 1924–1952*. New Haven, CT: Yale University Press, 1957.

Dobkowski, Michael N. (ed.), *The Politics of Indifference: A Documentary History of Holocaust Victims in America*. Washington, DC: University Press of America, 1982.

Dobkowski, Michael N. (ed.), *The Tarnished Dream: The Basis of American Anti-Semitism*. Westport, CT: Greenwood Press, 1983.

Dodd, Martha, *Through Embassy Eyes*. New York: Harcourt, Brace, 1939.

Dodd, William E., *Ambassador Dodd's Diary, 1933–1938*. New York: Harcourt, Brace, 1941.

Duggan, Stephen and Betty Drury, *The Rescue of Science and Learning. The Story of the Emergency Committee in Aid of Displaced Foreign Scholars*. New York: Macmillan, 1948.

Elbogen, Ismar, *A Century of Jewish Life*. Philadelphia, PA: Jewish Publication Society of America, 1944.

Feingold, Henry L., *The Politics of Rescue: The Roosevelt Administration and the Holocaust*. New York: Walden Press, 1970.

Feingold, Henry L., *A Time for Searching: Entering the Mainstream, 1920–1945*. Baltimore, MD: Johns Hopkins University Press, 1992.

Feingold, Henry L., *Bearing Witness: How America and Its Jews Responded to the Holocaust*. Syracuse, NY: Syracuse University Press, 1995.

Feldman, Egal, *Dual Destinies: The Jewish Encounter with Protestant America, 1920–1945*. Baltimore, MD: Johns Hopkins University Press, 1992.

Finger, Seymour Maxwell (ed.), *American Jewry during the Holocaust*. New York: American Jewish Commission on the Holocaust, 1984.

Friedman, Max (ed.), *Roosevelt and Frankfurter: Their Correspondence 1928–1945*. Boston, MA: Little, Brown, 1967.

Friedlander, Saul, *Nazi Germany and the Jews*. Vol. 1: *The Years of Persecution, 1933–1939*. New York: HarperCollins, 1997.

Friedman, Max P., *Nazis and Good Neighbors: The United States Campaign against the Germans of Latin America in World War II*. Cambridge, MA: Cambridge University Press, 2003.

Friedman, Saul S., *No Haven for the Oppressed: United States Policy toward Jewish Refugees, 1938–1945*. Detroit, MI: Wayne State University Press, 1973.

Fry, Varian, *Surrender on Demand*. New York: Random House, 1945.

Genizi, Haim, *American Apathy: the Plight of Christian Refugees from Nazism*. Ramat-Gan, Israel: Bar-Ilan University Press, 1983.

Genizi, Haim, *America's Fair Share*. Detroit, MI: Wayne State University Press, 1993.

Gerber David A. (ed.), *Anti-Semitism in American History*. Urbana, IL: University of Illinois Press, 1987.

Gottlieb, Moshe R., *American Anti-Nazi Resistance, 1933–1941: An Historical Analysis*. New York: KTAV Publishing, 1982.

Graeber, Isaque (ed.), *Jews in a Gentile World*. New York: Macmillan, 1942.

Hacker, Louis M. and Mark D. Hirsch, *Proskauer: His Life and Times*. Tuscaloosa, AL: University of Alabama Press, 1978.

Handlin, Oscar, *Adventures in Freedom: Three Hundred Years of Jewish Life in America*. Port Washington, NY: Kennikat Press, 1971.

Harris, Jonathan and Deborah Oppenheimer, *Into the Arms of Strangers: Stories of the Kindertransport*. New York: Bloomsbury, 2000.

Hecht, Ben, *A Child of the Century*. New York: Simon and Schuster, 1955.

Hertzberg, Arthur, *The Jews in America, Four Centuries of an Uneasy Encounter: A History*. New York: Simon and Schuster, 1988.

Higham, John, *Send These to Me: Jews and other Immigrants in Urban America* (revised edn). Baltimore, MD: Johns Hopkins University Press, 1984.

Hilberg, Paul, *The Destruction of the European Jews*. Chicago: Quadrangle Books, 1961; New York: Holmes and Mier, 1985.

Hilberg, Paul, *Perpetrators, Victims, Bystanders: The Jewish Catastrophe, 1933–1945*. New York: HarperCollins, 1992.

Hirshler, Eric E. (ed.), *Jews from Germany in the United States*. New York: Farrar, Straus and Cudahy, 1955.

Hull, Cordell, *The Memoirs of Cordell Hull*. New York: Macmillan, 1948.

Israel, Fred L. (ed.), *The War Diary of Breckenridge Long*. Lincoln, NE: University of Nebraska Press, 1966.

Jacobs, Arthur D. and Joseph E. Fallan (eds), *German-Americans in the World Wars*, Vol. IV: *The World War II Experience*. Munich/München, New Providence, London, Paris: K. G. Saur, 1995.

Jason, Philip and Iris Posner (eds), *Don't Wave Goodbye*. Westport, CT: Praeger Publishers, 2004.

Karp, Abraham J., *Haven and Home: A History of the Jews in America*. New York: Schocken Books, 1985.

Kohler, Max J., *Immigration and Aliens in the United States: Studies of American Immigration Laws and Legal Status of Aliens in the United States*. New York: Block Publishing, 1936.

Krammer, Arnold, *Undue Process. The Untold Story of America's German Alien Internees*. New York: Rowman and Littlefield Publishers, 1997.

Kranzler, David, *Thy Brother's Blood: The Orthodox Jewish Response during the Holocaust*. New York: Menorah Publications, 1987.

Learsi, Rufus, *The Jews in America: A History*. Cleveland, OH: World Publishing Company, 1954.

Lipstadt, Deborah E., *Beyond Belief: The American Press and the Coming of the Holocaust, 1933–1945*. New York: Free Press, 1986.

Lookstein, Haskel, *Were We Our Brothers' Keepers? The Public Response of American Jews in the Holocaust, 1938–1944*. New York: Vintage, 1988.

Martin, George, *Madam Secretary, Francis Perkins*. Boston, MA: Houghton Mifflin, 1976.

Medoff, Rafael, *The Deafening Silence. American Jewish Leaders and the Holocaust, 1933–1945*. New York: Shapolsky Publishers, 1987.

Morrison, David, *Heroes, Antiheroes and the Holocaust: American Jewry and Historical Choice*. Jerusalem and London: Milah Press, 1995.

Morse, Arthur D., *While Six Million Died: A Chronicle of American Apathy*. New York: Random House, 1967.

Novick, Peter, *The Holocaust in American Life*. New York: Houghton Mifflin, 1999.

Nurenberger, M. J., *The Scared and the Doomed: The Jewish Establishment vs. the Six Million*. Oakville, NY: Mosaic Press, 1985.

Perkins, Frances, *The Roosevelt I Knew*. New York: Viking Press, 1946.

Perrett, Geoffrey, *Days of Sadness, Years of Triumph: the American People 1939–1945*. New York: Coward, McCann and Geoghegan, 1973.

Peters, Clarence A., *The Immigration Problem*. New York: The H. W. Wilson Company, 1948.

Porter, David L., *The Seventy-Sixth Congress and World War II*. Columbia and London: University of Missouri Press, 1979.

Read, Anthony and David Fisher, *Kristallnacht: Unleashing the Holocaust*. New York: Papermac, 1991.

Rischin, Moses (ed.), *Immigration and the American Tradition*. Indianapolis, IN: Bobbs-Merrill, 1976.

Rout, Leslie B. Jr. and John F. Bratzel, *The Shadow War: German Espionage and United States Counterespionage in Latin America during World War II*. Lanham, MD: University Press Of America, 1986.

Rubinstein, William D., *The Myth of Rescue: Why the Democracies Could Not Have Saved More Jews from the Nazis*. London: Routledge, 1997.

Sanders, Roland, *Shores of Refuge: A Hundred Years of Jewish Emigration*. New York: Schocken Books, 1988.

Sarna, Jonathan D., *The American Jewish Experience*. New York: Holmes and Meier, 1986.

Sarna, Jonathan D., *American Judaism: A History*. New Haven, CT and London: Yale University Press, 2004.

Schwarz, Jordan A., *Liberal: Adolf A. Berle and the Vision of an American Era*. New York: The Free Press, 1987.

Shandler, Jeffrey, *While America Watches: Televising the Holocaust*. New York: Oxford University Press, 1999

Sherman, Bezalel C., *The Jews within American Society*. Detroit, MI: Wayne State University Press, 1965.

Sklare, Marshall (ed.), *The Jews: Social Patterns of an American Group*. New York: Free Press, 1958.

Stemberg, Charles Herbert et al., *Jews in the Mind of Americans*. New York: Basic Books, 1966.

Stewart, Barbara McDonald, *United States Government Policy on Refugees from Nazism, 1933–1940*. New York and London: Garland Publishing, 1982.

Strong, Donald S., *Organized Anti-Semitism in America: The Rise of Group Prejudice during the Decade 1930–1940*. Washington, DC: American Council on Public Affairs, 1941.

Tartakower, Arieh and Kurt R. Grossmann, *The Jewish Refugee*. New York: Institute of Jewish Affairs of the American Jewish Congress and World Jewish Congress, 1944.

Theoharis, Atham, *Spying on America: Political Surveillance from Hoover to the Houston Plan*. Philadelphia, PA: Temple University Press, 1973.

Thompson, Dorothy, *Refugees: Anarchy or Organization?* New York: Random House, 1938.

Urofsky, Melvin I., *A Voice that Spoke for Justice: The Life and Times of Stephen S. Wise*. Albany, NY: State University of New York Press, 1982.

Voss, Carl. H. (ed.), *Stephen S. Wise, Servant of the People: Selected Letters*. Philadelphia, PA: Jewish Publication Society of America, 1970.

Wells, Leon Weliczker, *Who Speaks for the Vanquished? American Jewish Leaders and the Holocaust*. New York: Peter Lang, 1987.

Wirtz, William, *The First Fifty Years: A History of the National Council of Jewish Women*. New York: n.p., 1943.

Wischnitzer, Mark, *To Dwell in Safety: The Story of Jewish Migration since 1800*. Philadelphia, PA: Jewish Publication Society of America, 1948.

Wise, Stephen S. *As I See It*. New York: Jewish Opinion Publishing Corporation, 1944.

Wyman, David S., *Paper Walls: America and the Refugee Crisis, 1938–1941*. New York: Pantheon Books, 1968.

Wyman, David S., *The Abandonment of the Jews: America and the Holocaust, 1941–1945*. New York: Pantheon Books, 1984.

Wyman, David S., (ed.), *America and the Holocaust*. Vol. 4: *Barring the Gates to America*. New York: Garland Publishing, 1990.

Wyman, David and Rafael Medoff, *A Race against Death*. New York: The New Press, 2002.

Zucker, Bat-Ami. *In Search of Refuge: Jews and US Consuls in Nazi Germany, 1933–1941*. London and Portland, OR: Vallentine Mitchell, 2001.

Articles and Chapters in Books

Adamic, Louis, 'Shall we send them back?' *The Nation* (25 March 1936): 377–78.

Adler-Rudel, S., 'Anti-Semitism is Here', Editorial, *The Nation* (20 August 1938): 767.

Belth, Norton, 'Problems of Anti-Semitism in the United States', *Contemporary Jewish Records*, II (May–June 1939): 6–19.

Bliven, Bruce, 'Where Can the Refugees Go?', *New Republic* (10 November 1937): 11, 12.

Breitman, Richard, 'American Inaction during the Holocaust', *Dimensions*, 8/2 (1994): 3–8.

Britt, George, 'Poison in the Melting Pot: Jew Baiting in the United States', *The Nation* (1 April 1939): 374–76.

Brody, David, 'American Jewry: the Refugees and Immigration

Restriction, 1932–1942', *Publications of the American Jewish Historical Society*, 45 (1955–1956): 20–47.

Daniels, Roger, 'American Refugee Policy in Historical Perspective', in Jarrell C. Jackman and Carla M. Borden (eds), *The Muses Flee Hitler: Cultural Transfer and Adaption, 1930–1945*. Washington, DC: Smithsonian Institution Press, 1983: 61–77.

Daniels, Roger, 'Changes in Immigration Law and Nativism since 1924', *American Jewish History*, 76 (December 1986): 159–72.

Diamond, Sander A., 'The *Kristallnacht* and the Reaction in America', *YIVO Annual of Jewish Social Science*, 14 (1969). Cited in Peter Novick, *The Holocaust in America*. Boston, MA and New York: Houghton Mifflin Books, 2000: 215–19.

Duggan, Stephen and Betty Drury, 'The Problem of the Refugee Physician', *Journal of the American Medical Association*, 112/8, Editorial, (25 February 1939): 735.

Edsall, D., 'The Émigré Physician', *Journal of the American Medical Association*, 117 (29 November 1941): 1881–82.

Fairchild, Henry P., 'Should the Jews Come In?', *New Republic* (25 January 1939): 344.

Fallan, Joseph E., 'The Censored History of Internment', *Cross Ideas: A Magazine of American Culture* (February 1998): 156–57.

Feingold, Henry L., 'Who Shall Bear the Guilt for the Holocaust?: the Human Dilemma', *American Jewish History*, 68/3 (March 1979): 261–82.

Feingold, Henry L., 'Did American Jewry Do Enough during the Holocaust?' B.G. Rudolph Lecture. (Pamphlet). Syracuse University, April 1984.

Feingold, Henry L., 'Roosevelt and Europe's Jews: Deceit and Indifference, or Politics and Powerlessness?', *Dimensions*, 8/2 (2000): 9–14.

Fields, Harold, 'Closing Immigration throughout the World', *American Journal of International Law*, 26/4 (October 1932): 671–99.

Fox, Stephen, 'The Deportation of Latin American Germans 1941–1947. Fresh Legs for Mr. Monroe's Doctrine', *Yearbook of German-American Studies*, 32 (1997): 117–42.

Gellman, Irwin F., 'The *St. Louis* Tragedy', *American Jewish Historical Quarterly*, 61 (December 1971): 5–38.

Gottschalk, Alfred, 'The German Pogrom of November 1938 and the Reaction of American Jewry', The Leo Baeck Memorial Lecture. Leo Baeck Institute, New York, 1988.

Gottschalk, Max, 'The Jewish Emigrant – 1941', *Contemporary Jewish Records*, IV/3 (June 1941): 261–68.

Haber, William, 'The Refugees in America', *Menorah Journal*, 28 (Summer 1940): 205–14.

Kichefsky, Gertrude, 'Quota Immigration, 1925–1944'. *Monthly Review*, 11/12 (June 1945): 156–59.

Kirchwey, Freda, 'Jews and Refugees', *The Nation* (20 May 1939): 577.

Kirchwey, Freda, 'State Department versus Political Refugees', *The Nation* (19 July 1941): 45.

Kirchwey, Freda, 'A Scandal in the State Department', *The Nation* (28 December 1940): 648–49.

Kraut, Alan M., Richard Breitman and Thomas W. Imhoof, 'The State Department, the Labor Department, and German Jewish Immigration, 1930–1940', *Journal of American Ethnic History*, 3/2 (Spring 1984): 5–38.

Kraut, Alan and Richard Breitman, 'Anti-Semitism in the State Department, 1933–44: Four Case Studies', in David A. Gerber (ed.), *Anti-Semitism in American History*. Urbana, IL: University of Illinois Press, 1986: 167–200.

Layen, Frederick A., 'The Response of the American Jewish Committee to the Crisis of German Jewry, 1933–1939 in America and the Holocaust', *American Jewish Historical Quarterly*, 58/3 (March 1979): 283–304.

Lewis, Read and Marian Schibsby, 'Status of the Refugee under American Immigration Laws', *The Annals of the American Academy of Political and Social Science*, 203 (May 1939): 74–79.

Lubelle, Samuel, 'War by Refugees', *Saturday Evening Post* (29 March 1941): 12–13.

Mann, Thomas, 'America and the Refugee', *New Republic* (8 November 1939): 38–9.

Medoff, Rafael, 'New Biography Handles FDR with Kid Gloves on Holocaust', *New Jersey Jewish News*, LVIII/1 (8 January 2004): 7.

Medoff, Rafael and Benyamin Korn, 'Another Side of Zora. A Voice for Rescuing Jews from the Holocaust', *Orlando Sentinel* (13 January 2005): A21.

Meyer, Michael, 'The Refugee Scholars Project of the Hebrew Union College', in Bertram Wallace Koren (ed.), *A Bicentennial Festschrift for Jacob Rader Marcus*. New York: KTAV Publishing House, 1976: 359–75.

Mims, Edwin Jr., 'German Refugees and American Bureaucrats', *Today* (20 January 1943): 3–4.

Morgenthau, Henry Jr., 'The Morgenthau Diaries, IV, The Refugee Run Around', *Colliers* (1 November 1947): 22–3, 62–5.

Pol, Heinz, 'An Open Letter to Ambassador Bullitt', *The Nation* (31 August 1940): 167–8.

Razovsky, Cecilia, 'The Problem of the German Refugees', *The Reform Advocate* (7 December 1934): 329–30.

Razovsky, Cecilia, 'Immigration and the Alien in 1936', *Better Times*, (1 June 1936). Offprint, Razovsky Papers, Box 6, File: Published Works about Immigration 1929–1939. American Jewish Historical Society, New York.

Razovsky, Cecilia, 'The Migration of Jews from Germany', *The Form*, 20 (December 1937): 214.

Razovsky, Cecilia, 'Deportation of Aliens, Past and Present', *Jewish Social Service Quarterly*, 20/1 (September 1949): 22–3.

Rosenstock, Werner, 'Exodus 1933–1939. A Survey of Jewish Emigration from Germany', *Leo Baeck Yearbook*, 1 (1956): 373–90.

Selver, Henry I., 'Problems in Placement of Refugee Children', *Jewish Social Service Quarterly*, 15/2 (December 1939): 214–21.

Strum, Harvey, 'Jewish Internees in the American South', *American Jewish Archive*, XLII (Spring, Summer 1990): 27–48.

Stuart, Graham H., 'Wartime Visa-Control Procedure', *Department of State Bulletin* (10 September 1944): 271–8.

Wagg, Alfred, 3rd, 'Washington's Stepchild: The Refugee', *New Republic* (28 April 1941): 592–94.

Wischnitzer, Mark, 'Jewish Immigration from Germany, 1933–1938', *Jewish Social Studies*, II (January 1940): 23–44.

Index

ORT, the Second World War and the Rehabilitation of Holocaust Survivors

Sarah Kavanaugh,

Royal Holloway, University of London

This book centres on the role played by ORT in the rehabilitation of Holocaust survivors inside the Displaced Persons camps after the Second World War. A brief history of the ORT organisation is followed by the author highlighting ORT's work during the 1920s and 1930s, using Berlin as a case study. The important and often life-saving work carried out by ORT workers inside the ghettos of Eastern Europe, primarily in Warsaw and Kovno is then examined. The book then focuses on the liberation of the concentration camps, the set-up of the post-war allied zones of occupation, the establishment of the DP camps and ORT's arrival within them. The mature period of ORT's work in the DP camps is then covered, looking at Belsen in the British zone of occupation and Landsberg in the American zone. The book also explores ORT's work in Austria and Italy. The final chapter highlights the closure of the DP camps, the subsequent immigration of the DPs and the creation of the State of Israel.

2008   176 pages   2x8 page plate sections
978 0 85303 806 1   cloth   £29.95/$49.95

We are Strangers Here

An Enemy Alien in Prison in 1940

Ruth Borchard

Introduction by Professor Charmian Brinson,
Imperial College London

Ruth Borchard's *We Are Strangers Here*, now published here with an introduction by Charmian Brinson, was written but not completed in 1943, and only came to light after the author's recent death. The novel vividly describes the plight of a young German refugee, Anna Silver, as an 'enemy alien' in Britain on the outbreak of war, and her subsequent detention in Holmdale Prison, a situation made more complex by her young child.

The novel finishes as Anna Silver arrives at the Internment Camp on the Isle of Man; the second part of the novel, dealing with events on the Isle of Man, was planned but appears never to have been written. This book highlights the plight of German anti-Nazis and Jews in British exile and has a distinct air of tragicomedy about it.

Little has been written on the internment of women during the Second World War, and this book will appeal to readers interested in modern history, social history and women's studies.

2008   160 pages
978 0 85303 753 8   paper   £15.00/$25.00

Cartoons and Extremism
Israel and the Jews in Arab and Western Media

Joel Kotek

Foreword by **Alan Dershowitz,** Harvard Law School
Introduction by **Abraham H. Foxman,** National Director,
Anti-Defamation League

The outrage sparked by the Danish cartoon affair – the publication of images of the Prophet Muhammad in the European press – was a sharp reminder of the potency of the cartoon in the modern media. It is one of the most popular and effective means of communication. By exaggerating and exasperating, cartoons by their very nature lack neutrality, and the cartoon is an important weapon in the Middle Eastern crisis. In response to the Danish cartoon affair, an Iranian newspaper announced a competition for cartoons about the Holocaust, even though it had had nothing to do with Israel or the Jewish people.

Antisemitic cartoons have long been rife in the Arab-Muslim media. The September 2001 Durban Conference against Racism, intended to denounce and combat racism in all its forms, also featured the distribution of antisemitic cartoons by an Arab organisation, yet this elicited no reaction from Western NGOs at the conference. This event set the author on a trail that revealed thousands of such drawings. In the name of anti-Zionism, Jews are depicted as sadistic and bloodthirsty monsters, solely interested in money and power. This return to anti-Jewish hatred is of a new order, in line with current trends – an Arab-Muslim form unexpectedly metamorphosed from the antisemitism traditionally linked with the Christian West. By reproducing more than 400 of these cartoons, taken from both Arab and Western media, this book denounces the use of hatred in the media and hopes to raise the alarm.

2008   259 colour / 178 black and white illus   224 pages
978 0 85303 752 1   paper   £15.00/$29.50

Israeli Society, the Holocaust and its Survivors

Dina Porat, Tel Aviv University

This collection of twenty essays analyses the encounters of the Yishuv (the Hebrew community in pre-state Israel) and Israeli society with the Holocaust while it occurred, and with its survivors. Sixty years after the end of the Second World War this is still a painful topic, very much at the centre of the agendas of both Israel and the Jewish communities worldwide, focusing on a soul-searching issue: was the tragedy unfolding in Europe part and parcel of public life in the Yishuv, its priorities and anxieties, and did Israeli society embrace the survivors as they deserved? Based on a wide scope of primary sources and on many years of research, the essays deal with a variety of poignant sub-issues, such as the attitudes of David Ben-Gurion, Martin Buber and other leaders, the understanding of the information about the 'Final Solution', relations and tensions between the Yishuv and the Jewish communities and youth movements in Nazi-occupied Europe, rescue plans and their failure, decisions regarding rescue made during a global war, and parallel changes in the attitude to the survivors and in Israeli and Jewish identity. The balanced answers provided in this collection take into consideration the limited resources of a small community under a mandate and of a young, post-war country flooded by immigration, and the many dominant factors present during a world war and in its aftermath on which the Yishuv and Israel could have no impact, yet could not avoid criticism and pin-pointing of failures and deficiencies.

2007   464 pages

978 0 85303 741 5   cloth   £49.50/$75.00
978 0 85303 742 2   paper   £20.00/$35.00

Genocide, the World Wars and the Unweaving of Europe

Donald Bloxham, Edinburgh University

The murder of at least one million Armenian Christians in 1915-16 and of some six million Jews from 1939-45 were the most extreme instances of mass murder in the First and Second World Wars respectively. This book examines the development and dynamics of both genocides. While bringing out the many differences in the origins, course and nature of the crimes, it argues that both need to be placed into the context of the wider violent agendas and demographic schemes of the perpetrator states. In the earlier case it is important to consider the Ottoman violence against Assyrian Christians and Greek Orthodox subjects, and programmes of forced assimilation of non-Turkish Muslim groups, including many Muslims victimized by other states; in the later case, it is impossible to understand the development of the 'final solution of the Jewish question' without paying attention to Nazi policy against Slavic groups, the 'disabled' and Europe's Romany population. Both genocides, furthermore, need to be examined in the deeper contexts of the multi-causal violence resulting from the collapse of the eastern and southeastern European dynastic empires from the late nineteenth century, and from the establishment of new types of state in their aftermath.

Finally, the book explains why these two major genocides occupy very different places in our contemporary memorial culture. It argues that the memory politics of the Armenian genocide illustrate the very tight limits to what we can expect in the way of meaningful international concern for ongoing genocides. Meanwhile, the instrumentalization of the memory of the Holocaust can actually inhibit self-criticism on the parts of the western states that increasingly foreground Holocaust memorial days and museums in their civic education.

2008 288 pages 978 0 85303 720 0 cloth £50.00/$79.95

978 0 85303 721 7 paper £19.95/$32.95

Memory of the Holocaust in Australia

Tom Lawson, University of Winchester
and **James Jordan,** University of Southampton (Eds)

This collection of essays considers the development of Holocaust memory in Australia since 1945. Bringing together the work of younger and more established scholars, the volume examines Holocaust memory in a variety of local and national contexts from both inside and outside of Australia's Jewish communities. The articles presented here emanate from a variety of different disciplinary perspectives, from history through literary, cultural and museum studies. This collection considers both the general development of Holocaust memory, engaging historically with particular moments when the Shoah punctuated public perceptions of the recent past, as well as its representation and memorialisation in contemporary Australia. A detailed introduction discusses the relationship between the Australian case and the general development of Holocaust memory in the Western world, asking whether we need to revise the assumptions of what have become the rather staid narratives of the journey of the Shoah into public consciousness.

2008   256 pages   978 0 85303 794 1   cloth   £45.00/$74.95
                    978 0 85303 795 8   paper   £18.95/$29.95

Film and the Shoah in France and Italy

Giacomo Lichtner

Film and the Shoah in France and Italy is a uniquely comparative analysis of the role of cinema in the development of collective memories of the Shoah in these countries. The work follows a chronological structure of which three French documentaries – *Night and Fog, The Sorrow* and *The Pity and Shoah* – form the backbone. These three sections are linked by comparative case studies on famous and lesser-known fictional works, such as Roberto Benigni's *Life is Beautiful,* Louis Malle's *Lacombe Lucien,* Armand Gatti's *The Enclosure* and Radu Mihaileanu's *Train of Life*. The book tackles crucial themes, such as the politics of history and its representation, the 1970s obsession with collaboration and the ethical debate around cinema's ability adequately to represent the Shoah. The book adopts a parallel analysis of the text and its reception in order to demonstrate the historical relevance of film as a cultural artefact. In so doing, the book offers a highly innovative methodological approach to the controversial relationship between film and history.

The book fulfils three complementary purposes: to offer a detailed historical and textual analysis of key cinematic works on the Shoah; to firmly situate the popular and institutional reception of these works within the political and socio-cultural context of the time, so as to link cinema to society's attitudes towards the Shoah; and thirdly, to show how these attitudes have changed over time, in order to evince the role cinema has played in the transmission of history and memory. *Film and the Shoah in France and Italy* shows that cinema has both reflected and affected the dominant perceptions of history, contributing to the transition from recognition to representation of the Shoah. Yet the book also shows how this transition has been slow and uneven, and questions whether recognition and commemoration necessarily imply a deeper historical understanding.

2008 256 pages
978 0 85303 786 6   cloth   £45.00/$74.95

HOLOCAUST STUDIES
A Journal of Culture and History

Dr Tom Lawson, University of Winchester, UK
Dr James Jordan, University of Southampton, UK

Reviews Editor: **Dr K. Hannah Holtschneider,** University of Edinburgh, UK
Consulting Editors: **Professor David Cesarani,** Royal Holloway, University of
London, UK. **Professor Tony Kushner,** University of Southampton, UK.
Professor Mark Roseman, University of Indiana, USA

Holocaust Studies: A Journal of Culture and History is an innovative and
interdisciplinary journal bringing together the best of current research
into the Nazi persecution and mass murder of the Jews and other Nazi
genocides. The journal provides a forum for both younger and
established scholars engaged in research at the cutting edge of
contemporary Holocaust studies. The interests of the journal are broad
and include the investigation of Nazi genocides as historical and social
phenomena, their origins and their consequences. Further, the journal
explores the issues of representation and memorialisation through the
investigation of film, literature, testimony and public rituals. The
geographical and chronological focus of the journal is also extensive. The
journal looks forward to publishing work which considers the Nazi
politics of destruction in a global context, including their continuing and
wide-ranging legal, social, cultural and political repercussions.

ISSN 1359-1371 Volume 13 2007
Three issues per year: Summer, Autumn, Winter
Individuals £45/$75 Institutions £150/$260

JEWISH CULTURE AND HISTORY

Editor: **Nadia Valman** (University of Southampton)
Deputy Editor: **Tony Kushner** (University of Southampton)
Reviews Editor: **Nathan Abrams** (University of Wales, Bangor)

Jewish Culture and History is an inter-disciplinary refereed journal which brings together the best of current research in Jewish social history with innovative work in Jewish cultural studies. The journal includes cutting-edge research by younger scholars as well as the work of established specialists. Together with research articles and book reviews, it regularly reproduces selected primary materials from archives, private collections and lesser-known resources for the study of Jewish culture and history.

The journal explores previously neglected areas of the Jewish experience in different cultures and from a range of different perspectives. Its interests include: popular culture, film and visual culture, music, media, cultural representations of Jews, Jewish/non-Jewish relations, Jewish literature in all languages, intellectual, social, political and cultural histories, historiography, gendered histories of Jews, class, consumption and lifestyles, and cultural geographies.

ISSN 1462-169X   Volume 10   2008
Three Issues per year: Summer, Autumn, Winter
Individuals £45/$75   Institutions £150/$260